The
Architect's Guide
to the
U.S. National CAD Standard

The
Architect's Guide
to the
U.S. National CAD Standard

Dennis J. Hall, FAIA, FCSI

Charles Rick Green, AIA, FCSI

THE AMERICAN INSTITUTE OF ARCHITECTS

WILEY

JOHN WILEY & SONS, INC.

Library of Congress Cataloging-in-Publication Data:

Hall, Dennis J., 1954–
  Architect's guide to the U.S. National CAD Standard / by Dennis J. Hall and Charles Rick Green.
       p. cm.
  Includes bibliographical references and index.
  ISBN-13: 978-0-471-70378-5
  ISBN-10: 0-471-70378-8 (cloth)
  1. Architectural drawing—Data processing. 2. Computer-aided design—Standards—United States. I. Green, Charles Rick, 1952– II. Title.
  NA2728.H35 2006
  620'.0042' 0285—dc22
                                                                                      2005019106

10 9 8 7 6 5 4 3 2 1

Dedication

Often, we neglect to properly acknowledge the many folks who put in countless hours doing "paying" work at the office, buying the groceries, feeding the dog, and in general taking care of the many activities we workaholics take for granted as we travel around the country and stay late at the office trying to keep pace with this crazy profession of architecture. Therefore, I dedicate this book to my wife Janet, daughters Leslie and Taylor, and the employees of Hall Architects, who all do their best to keep me out of trouble.

—Dennis J. Hall, FAIA, FCSI, SCIP

I dedicate this book to my wife Coral, whose love and support have blessed my life; our children Zane and Jessie, who bring us laughter and joy; and grandparents Charley and Marian Green and Joe and Pam Florio, who have been such a great influence on us; and to brother Michael, whose life touched us all.

—Rick Green, AIA, FCSI, CCS, CCCA

Disclaimer

This book contains the authors' analysis and opinions of potential interpretations of the U.S. National CAD Standard (NCS). The illustrations and examples are general in nature and are not intended to apply to any specific project. The NCS was intentionally created as a flexible standard to enable users working on different project types, sizes, and complexity to meet the unique requirements of their projects and comply with the NCS requirements. For these reasons, there can be many solutions to specific drawing issues that are NCS-compliant.

As with any standard, the NCS is subject to interpretation for its application to a specific project. Designers should consult with their clients early in the design phase regarding the interpretations relative to their specific projects, as facility owners often impose additional drawing requirements or have specific applications of the NCS that they may require.

The authors do not represent that their interpretations, illustrations, or analyses are definitive or all-inclusive of every reasonable interpretation, and they are not intended to take the place of detailed NCS compliancy analyses for a specific project. While this publication is designed to provide accurate and authoritative information regarding the subject matter covered, it is sold with the understanding that neither the publisher nor the authors are rendering professional services to the purchaser.

The interpretations, illustrations, and analyses in this book are based upon version 3.1 of the U.S. National CAD Standard (NCS version 3.1), but because the NCS is occasionally updated and republished, readers are encouraged to verify the current NCS version in effect by visiting www.nationalcadstandard.org. If discrepancies or conflicts are identified, readers will need to resolve them by making their own analyses and interpretations.

Contents

About This Book

The primary purpose of this book is to demonstrate the options and techniques that design firms can use to implement various concepts of the U.S. National CAD Standard (NCS) into the workplace. It is designed to provide you with an understanding of how the NCS is likely to be interpreted, as well as to supply some of the options available to meet the requirements. This book is intended to complement the NCS, not be a substitute for it.

The components that make up the NCS may seem intimidating at first glance. The standard is a living document and, as such, is modified and updated from time to time. Many organizations and government agencies have adopted the NCS since publication of the first version in 1999. The design firms they hire are expected to comply with the NCS and stay current with any changes made to it. Whether in response to meet the needs of their clients' requirements or simply to help streamline their own work processes, design firms throughout North America are adopting the standard.

Drawings, as instruments of service of professional design firms, must respond to the variety of project types and sizes that firms large and small deal with. This book has been created with the demand for that flexibility in mind, and to provide information on how the NCS implementation process can be streamlined to fit the different types of workplaces and project types.

How This Book Is Organized

This book presumes that you have a copy of the NCS as a companion document. The Introduction provides the starting point, with an overview of the NCS and its components. Chapters 1 through 8 are numbered and arranged in the same order as Modules 01 through 08 of the Construction Specifications Institute's Uniform Drawing System (UDS). The remaining NCS components, the American Institute of Architect's CAD Layer Guidelines and the Tri-Service CADD/GIS Technology Center's Plotting Guidelines, are discussed in Chapters 9 and 10. Chapter 11 includes guidelines for implementing the NCS into the workplace. (Note: There is no correspondence between the Appendices in the book and the Appendix in the NCS.)

Even though the chapters in this book may reference each other for related information, each chapter can be read independently. If information on a specific topic is needed, the Index can be used to identify pages where the subject is discussed.

A list of frequently asked questions is located at the end of each chapter. The responses are based on our interpretation of the standard; and, in many cases, we provide information from personal use and experience with the NCS in our own workplaces. We hope you will find the discussions informative and useful.

Terminology

The terminology used in this book is the same as that in the NCS. Therefore, the definitions given in the Glossary, which includes more than 200 terms, have been coordinated with definitions in the NCS and other publications that are referenced by it, such as MasterFormat and the Project Resource Manual. Where appropriate, we have also included definitions from AIA documents, such as AIA Document A201-1997 General Conditions of the Contract.

The first time a defined term from the Glossary is used in the book, it appears in bold print.

WHO SHOULD USE THIS BOOK

Architects, Engineers, and Designers

Whether driven by client requirements or simply to obtain the benefits of using a comprehensive standard that is maintained by someone else, the effort spent on the NCS adoption process can be a crucial investment of company time and resources. This book can help reduce costs during the transition from current office standards to those in the NCS. The illustrations and concepts contained in each chapter can streamline the adoption process and help reduce the learning curve. The guidelines included in Chapter 11 are presented to help companies and organizations decide how to approach the NCS implementation process.

CAD Technicians

CAD technicians can use this book as a desktop reference during the preparation of their drawings. In order to help drafters understand the graphic and CAD requirements more clearly, we've provided illustrations to demonstrate the requirements for NCS compliance. The examples and recommendations provided will give drafters a better understanding of the NCS and will help them comprehend the requirements in less time. In addition, a thorough understanding of the standard will improve productivity and result in drawings that fully comply with the NCS.

Some of the frequently asked questions at the end of each chapter were generated directly from CAD technicians. We hope the information contained in the responses will provide a more clearly defined understanding of the NCS. The book will provide drafters with an effective resource to determine NCS compliance requirements, which can help facilitate more effective data exchange between coworkers, collaborating firms, contractors, facility managers, and owners.

Emerging Professionals and Students

The book is written in a nontechnical, easy-to-understand manner appropriate for students and emerging professionals. The Introduction summarizes the NCS, identifies the organizations that helped to develop it, and outlines how it is maintained and kept up to date. The illustrations and information in the succeeding chapters will help clarify the intent of specific requirements in the NCS so that those new to the design profession can better understand the drawing standards that will be in effect in the workplace.

This book can serve as a tool to enhance the learning process while encouraging professional growth during the development stage of the emerging professional's career. When used as a resource to supplement the NCS, the book will make it easier for emerging professionals and students to get up to speed within their organization, and require less training to do so.

Facility Managers and Owners

Most facility managers and owners easily comprehend the benefits of having all their design teams prepare drawings in accordance with one standard. However, few can afford the cost or time needed to fully understand the NCS requirements to the level of detail they would like. Therefore, it is often difficult to determine whether the architects and engineers they hire are actually providing them with NCS-compliant documents. The Index and examples included in this book will help alleviate this concern by furnishing an affordable resource that can be used to determine compliance requirements. Most of the explanations offered will provide owners and facility managers with easy-to-read explanations that do not require a comprehensive understanding of the NCS or CAD software.

Acknowledgments

The authors wish to thank the following for their input and support:

The American Institute of Architects
The Construction Specifications Institute, with special thanks to Aaron Titus, Technical
Project Coordinator
The National Institute of Building Sciences
Members of the FY05 Uniform Drawing System Program Task Team, with special
thanks to:

Gary W. LaRose, FCSI, CCS
Jack Vest, PE, FCSI, CCS
Joseph A. Stypka, AIA, FCSI, CCS

National CAD Standard Project Committee members
The CADD/GIS Technology Center
Members of the Albuquerque Chapter, CSI

Special thanks to the employees of Hall Architects, Inc. who contributed to this book:

Nina Giglio, CSI, CCS, SCIP, Assoc. AIA
George Homsi
Mark Lekavich, CDT
Mary Beth Ott, CDT

Thanks to the employees at Wilson & Company, Inc., Engineers & Architects, including Jim Gibbs,
President, and Scott Perkins, Vice President; and especially the staff in the Albuquerque Buildings and Facilities Department (cheerfully known as the BFD):

Howard M. Kaplan, AIA, LEED AP, Manager, Buildings and Facilities Department
Ted Green, AIA, CSI, CDT, Project Manager
Michael J. Wright, Intern Architect
Colleen F. Martinez, CSI, Project Manager

Special thanks to the following Wilson & Company BFD members who provided help with the
illustrations:

Steve Willems, Senior CAD Designer
Stan Mills, Senior CAD Designer
Beau Baker, CDT, CAD Designer
Viera Kascak-Lydick, CAD Technician

Special thanks to the following from the Albuquerque office of Wilson & Company, for their technical assistance:

Ted G. Ortiz, Senior CAD Designer
Jim Haddock, IT Coordinator
W. Dave Hotchkiss, Graphics

Finally, special thanks to Janice Borzendowski, our copy editor at Wiley & Sons, who corrected our mistakes and made us look a lot more intelligent than we really are.

Introduction

GENERAL

In the late 1980s, many firms bought one of those "CAD machines." The primary goal was not to use it for **construction documents** or even presentation drawings; most just wanted to be able to look prospective clients in the eye and say, honestly, "Yes, we have CAD." **Plans** and **schedules** were about the only drawing types actually produced on this machine, and usually took twice as long to produce electronically as by hand. When the pen plotter was working, it was the only thing in the office that was; and then everyone stood around and watched the five pens magically produce a drawing from whatever had been developed on the computer monitor. At the time, a simple plan drawing could take an hour or two to plot, and when firms finally began using this contraption for production of full **drawing sets,** plotting had to start a few days before the project was due. Any mistakes or omissions were generally corrected by hand, as there was rarely time to replot the sheets.

A lot has changed in the last 20 years, and today most firms don't know how they ever got by without these wonderful tools. Like the evolution in both computer hardware and CAD software, industry standards for producing our construction documents have also undergone major changes.

In the 1980s, CAD standards seemed to be a lot like the weather: everybody was talking about them but no one was actually doing anything with them. The **American Institute of Architects (AIA)** introduced the first voluntary CAD standard in 1990, when it produced its **CAD Layer Guidelines (CLG).** The **Construction Specifications Institute (CSI)** produced a technical document on standard reference symbols, which was also rereleased in 1990 under the name "CSI Standard CAD Symbols" and produced in an electronic version in 1991. Shortly thereafter, CSI, which had established national standards for organizing written construction documents in the 1960s, announced it was forming a committee to create national standards for graphic construction documents as well. The **Uniform Drawing System Program Task Team (UDSPTT),** originally chaired by Dennis Hall, led the efforts to produce the first edition of the **Uniform Drawing System (UDS).** The UDSPTT continues to update this document to meet the needs of users and changes in the industry.

By the mid-1990s, several organizations, including the federal government, AIA, CSI, and others, were working on national drawing standards. In 1997, many of these organizations signed an agreement, known as the **Memorandum of Understanding (MOU),** to work together toward the creation of the **U.S. National CAD Standard (NCS).**

This group of contributing organizations, under the guidance of the **National Institute of Building Sciences (NIBS) Facility Information Council (FIC),** published version 1.0 of the United States National CAD Standard in July 1999. Since that time, the document has been periodically updated with versions 2.0, 3.0, and, in January 2005, version 3.1.

WHY A NATIONAL CAD STANDARD

The demand for a national CAD standard comes from two sources. First, major facility owners such as the federal government were looking to establish a mechanism for organizing graphic facility information so that it could be easily stored and retrieved. Whereas most architects think about drawings only as construction documents, many facility owners perceive them as the basis of facility management documents. This information is used throughout the life cycle of a **facility** for operation, renovations, additions, and, finally, facility decommissioning and demolition. What has now come to be known as the **facility cycle** was a major impetus in the participation by the U.S. Department of Defense (DOD) in the creation of the NCS. Figure I-1 shows a diagram of the facility cycle of a building.

FYI: The early roots of the current U.S. National CAD Standard trace back to 1986, when CSI published TD-2-4 Abbreviations, which consisted of a list of abbreviations recommended for use in the construction industry.

The second major reason for the creation of the NCS was demand by design professionals to develop standards to allow sharing of information on a project and to minimize the need for each user group to create their own CAD standards, which required teams to adapt different CAD standards for each project, thus wasting time and money while achieving no benefit. The NCS was perceived as a method to provide uniformity from project to project and save time in production, thus allowing architects to spend more time on design. It was also viewed as a means to allow CAD software vendors to create tools around these standards that would make the production of the construction documents easier and faster.

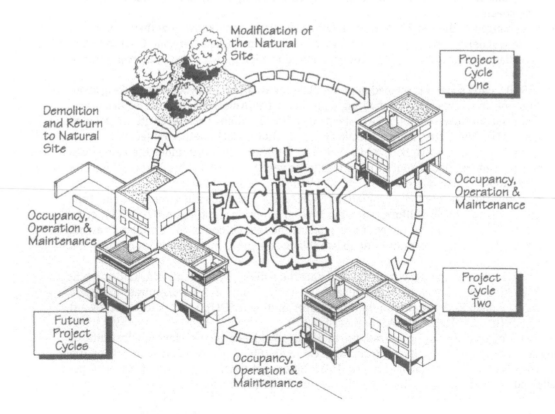

FIGURE I-1   Facility Cycle (Reprinted with permission from the Construction Specifications Institute.)

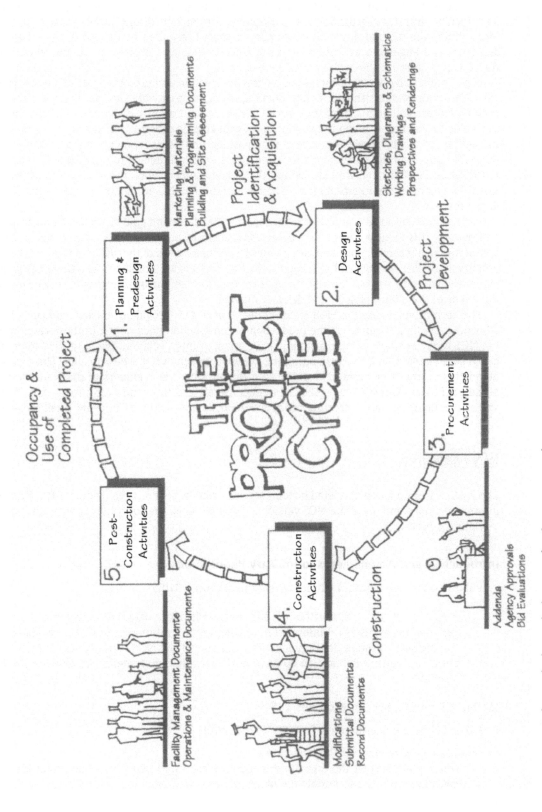

FIGURE I-2 Project Cycle (Revised and reprinted with permission from the Construction Specifications Institute.)

The benefits of a national standard should be clear to all design professionals, as it allows information to transfer throughout the **project cycle** from one design professional to another. Streamlining the manner in which information is shared results in better coordination between architects and engineers, as well as saving production time and improving the overall design of the project. Figure I-2 shows the typical project cycle.

There seem to be two philosophies regarding the creation and use of the NCS. The first is that the NCS is an *absolute* standard, hence violating any single part will cause the Earth to stop spinning on its axis and go flying off into space. The second philosophy is that the NCS was created as a guide to assist users in the preparation and use of graphic construction documents. And while the authors of this book take a middle ground position on this issue, one thing is perfectly clear: the NCS police will not show up on your doorstep should you decide not to follow the standard to the letter. Furthermore, we both believe that it is incumbent upon the architect to use professional judgment in the interpretation and execution of the NCS to fit the specific requirements of the **project.**

Furthermore, although the NCS provides specific standards and guidelines for the organization of drawings, it is flexible, rather than being constrained by arbitrary rules, so as to allow for the consideration of specific project requirements. The primary goals of the NCS are to make the documents more user friendly and to recognize that all projects are not alike. As trained design professionals, we must use our knowledge and expertise to craft our instruments of service to meet the needs of the client, project, and delivery method.

The current version of the NCS is not perfect, but it does provide users with guidance in establishing an office standard for the production of construction documents. In those cases where the NCS requires additional explanation, clarification, or interpretation, we have tried to provide our recommendations for incorporating the standard to achieve the best results. These recommendations come from years of working with the NCS both as members of the **National CAD Standard Project Committee (NCSPC),** frequently referred to as the NCS Project Committee, and as practicing architects creating construction documents for both large and small projects.

NCS COMPONENTS

The NCS is a compilation of related documents published by several organizations. The following information is a summary of the NCS version 3.1 components, the contributing organization, and a brief description.

Introduction and Amendments to Industry Publications

Published by the National Institute of Building Sciences (NIBS).

An overview of the NCS; much of the Introduction is out of date, but it does provide a general look at historical information relating to the evolution of the NCS, in addition to the process for future development. The contents of the NCS Introduction and Amendments to Industry Publication do not contain specific requirements or guidelines to the standard.

Uniform Drawing System Modules 1–8

Published by the Construction Specifications Institute.

Module 01—Drawing Set Organization

Provides guidelines for the organization of a drawing set, drawing set order, **sheet identification** system, and electronic file naming.

Module 02—Sheet Organization
Provides guidelines for the layout of the **drawing sheet,** location and numbering of drawings on the sheet, sheet sizes, **title block area,** and **supplemental drawing sheet** layout.

Module 03—Schedules
Provides guidelines for the layout of schedules and use of schedules, both on drawings and in the **project manual.**

Module 04—Drafting Conventions
Provides guidelines for the production of **construction drawings,** including line weights, dimensioning, orientation, **notations,** and other graphic drawing conventions.

Module 05—Terms and Abbreviations
Provides a searchable list of **preferred** and **nonpreferred terms,** as well as abbreviations used on drawings.

Module 06—Symbols
Provides standard **symbols** organized by **MasterFormat** 2004 **divisions** and symbol type classification structure.

Module 07—Notations
Provides guidelines for locating and using notations on drawings, including **general notes, general discipline notes, general sheet notes, reference keynotes,** and **sheet keynotes.**

Module 08—Code Conventions
Provides guidelines for presenting code-related information on drawings. This module establishes types of code-related information, preferred location, and format for display of the information.

> **FYI:** Prior to its decision to join with the other contributing organizations to the NCS, CSI originally planned to produce its own CAD Layering, Plotting, and Color modules, as a part of the UDS.

AIA CAD Layer Guidelines
Published by the American Institute of Architects.

Provides guidelines and organizational structure for creating CAD layer names for all **disciplines.**

Tri-Service Plotting Guidelines
Published by the **CADD/GIS Technology Center.**

Provides guidelines for pen color and pen width.

Appendices
Published by the National Institute of Building Sciences.

Appendix A—Statement of Substantial Conformance
Appendix B—Optional and Recommended NCS Items
Appendix C—Memorandum of Understanding
Appendix D—Members of the NCS Project Committees
Appendix E—NIBS Consensus Process
Appendix F—NCS Rules of Governance
Appendix G—Facility Information Council Board
Appendix H—Implementation of U.S. National CAD Standard

Administration of the NCS

In 2003, the NCS Project Committee established the **Rules of Governance (ROG)** for the NCSPC. The document, located in Appendix F of the NCS, explains the organizational structure and relationship of the contributing organizations and volunteers involved in the in the NCS development, revision, and administration process. The ROG are divided into three parts, discussing organizational structure, NCS development and revision process, and logistics of the revision/development process.

Organization

The primary group in the ongoing administration of the NCS is the NCS Project Committee. Membership on the NCS Project Committee is open to all members of the industry and may be completed online at www.nationalcadstandard.org. Figure I-3 illustrates the NCS organizational structure.

The administration of the NCS also involves several other groups, each performing a specific function. Below is a list of these groups and a brief description of their responsibilities.

FYI: There are no fees required to join the NCS Project Committee. The only requirements for membership are to possess a copy of the most recent version of the NCS. For membership to be renewed automatically, members must vote during an NCS revision cycle.

NCS Business Management Group: Comprised of one staff representative from each of the three contributing organizations with NCS ownership interest, which currently includes AIA, CSI, and NIBS. This group manages the NCS business affairs as determined by the terms of a **Memorandum of Agreement (MOA)** signed in 2003.

Consultative Council: Comprised of elected NIBS members, chairs of NIBS councils and committees, and a chair who is member of the NIBS Board of Directors. The Consultative Council is the group from which the NCS Project Committee derives its authority.

Steering Committee: Comprised of the NCS Project Committee officers and between five and nine other members appointed by the chair of the NCSPC, this committee is responsible for administering the balloting process and establishing NCSPC meetings. Generally, this committee serves as the governing body of the NCSPC.

Task teams: Established by the Steering Committee to address specific items during the revision process:
- **Standing task teams:** Provide oversight of revision issues, addressing existing NCS content, including CLG, UDS, and Plotting Guidelines.
- **Ad hoc task teams:** Provide oversight of issues, addressing items that may be outside the scope of the existing NCS. Examples of such items include addition or deletion of NCS components, marketing, implementation, and compliance.

NCS content can be divided into two categories: fundamental concepts and prescribed data. The ROG indicate that fundamental concepts are broader in scope than prescribed data, and typically address formats, conventions, and methodology;prescribed data relates more to individual items such as lists of discipline designators, list of terms and abbreviations, or graphic representation of symbols. Changes to fundamental concepts will typically require changes to prescribed data, but the opposite is not usually true.

FYI: In 1995, the CSI Drawing Subcommittee and the AIA CAD Layer Task Force met for the first time to discuss the activities of both groups. There was agreement on the term "discipline designator," to define the creator of the layer or drawing sheet.

NCS Development and Revision Process

The NCS is a living document that continues to be updated to meet the needs of the rapidly changing industry. At the heart of the ROG is the NCS development and revision process; and to maintain con-

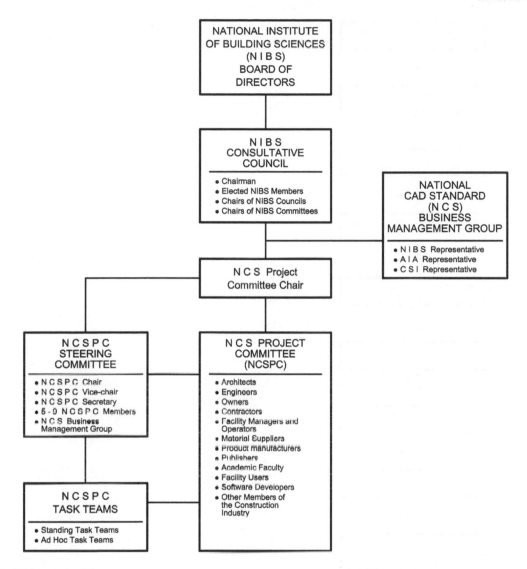

FIGURE I-3   NCS Organizational Chart

sistency throughout the revision cycle, a very specific submittal procedure needs to be followed. Changes to the NCS can only be made by members of the NCS Project Committee. Each modification that is proposed is submitted using a ballot item submittal form, which is then processed by the NCS Steering Committee and, eventually, voted on by members of the NCSPC during each NCS revision cycle. The revision cycle is anticipated to occur within a six-month period, but it is not expected that all issues can be addressed and resolved within that period of time. Figure I-4 illustrates a typical **revision cycle,** including the set time limitations for each period. Figure I-5 explains the steps a typical ballot item will follow during the Ballot Item Review Period. A ballot item can be submitted only by a member of the NCS Project Committee.

Logistics

The final part of the ROG dictates the requirements relating to the quorum requirements for meetings and balloting. Approval of a ballot item requires that two-thirds of the ballots cast must

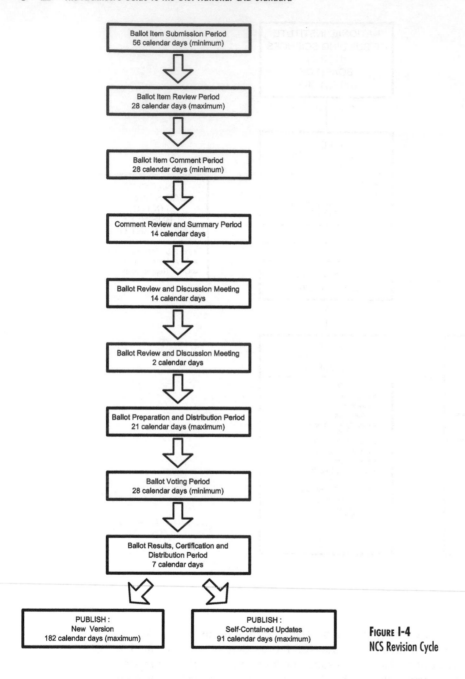

Figure I-4
NCS Revision Cycle

be in favor of adoption, and a minimum of two-thirds of eligible Project Committee members must cast ballots.

NCS History

The NCS began with competing organizations, each developing resource documents for specific drawing issues, and has evolved into a collaborative group working together to produce a well-coordinated document that addresses concerns of drawing users. The process has not always been

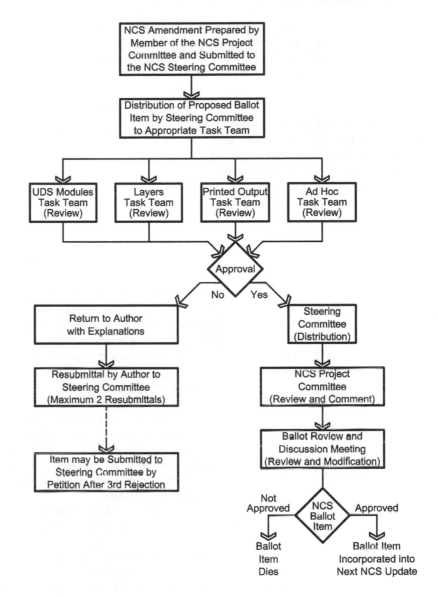

FIGURE 1-5
NCS Ballot Item Review Period

easy or smooth, and with no one group completely in charge, com-
promises have been required of all. In the early 1990s, several
joint meetings of organizations were held to discuss terminology
and other issues of mutual concern, but it was not until 1997, with
the signing of the Memorandum of Understanding, that these groups
formally banded together with a common purpose.

> **FYI:** The first national UDS seminar was pre-
> sented in November 1997 by Dennis Hall.
> The most frequently asked question: "Why
> isn't the UDS finished yet?"

The organization and administration of the NCS has undergone
many changes since 1997, but the primary goals have remained constant. Today, the NCS is seen
as a major success in uniting the entire design and construction industry in the creation of a common **facility model.** Graphic and written facility information must be integrated into a common
database, where drawings and specifications are only two of the many types of reports that can
be generated.

The NCS must be viewed not only from where it has been but where it is going. History is a glimpse into the future; and the future of this industry is one where collaboration is not just desirable, but required. Our history has taught us many lessons at the same time it has provided us with a model for future collaboration.

FYI: The NIBS CAD Council was renamed as the Facility Information Council to more accurately identify the group's focus on improving the performance of a facility throughout the various stages of the **facility cycle.**

NCS Timeline

The following dates represent NCS historical events:

1986:	CSI publishes the first of the Technical Documents (TD) series, titled TD-2-4 Abbreviations.
1990:	AIA publishes the first edition of the AIA CAD Layer Guidelines. (June): CSI publishes the TD-2-6 Standard Reference Symbols.
1991:	CSI creates the Drawing Subcommittee. (October): CSI publishes the Standard CAD Symbols, the electronic version of the TD-2-6 Standard Reference Symbols.
1992:	The Department of Defense establishes the Tri-Service CADD/GIS Technology Center.
1994:	NIBS forms the CAD Council (now called the Facility Information Council). CSI announces its intent to create the Uniform Drawing System.
1995:	The NIBS CAD Council proposes creation of the U.S. National CAD Standard.
1996:	CSI renames the Drawing Subcommittee the UDS Task Team (now known as the UDS Program Task Team).
1997:	AIA publishes the second edition of the CAD Layer Guidelines. (March): CSI publishes UDS modules 01, 02, and 03: "National CAD Standard Memorandum of Understanding," commonly known as the "Memorandum of Understanding," signed by AIA, CSI, NIBS, **Sheet Metal and Air Conditioning Contractors' National Association (SMACNA),** Tri-Services CADD/GIS Technology Center, the U.S. Coast Guard, and the **U.S. General Services Administration (GSA).**
1999:	Tri-Service CADD/GIS Technology Center produces the Plotting Guidelines. (June): CSI releases UDS Modules 04, 05, and 06, followed by the release of Modules 07 and 08. NCS version 1.0 is released; it includes AIA's CAD Layer Guidelines (second edition), Tri-Service Plotting Guidelines, CSI's UDS Modules 01–03, and the NIBS Introduction.
2000:	(August) NCS version 2.0 ballot is distributed.
2001:	(May) NCS version 2.0 is released; it includes AIA CAD Layer Guidelines, U.S. NCS version 2.0, Tri-Service Plotting Guidelines, CSI's UDS Modules 01–08, and the NIBS Introduction and Amendments to Industry Publications.
2002:	(January) NCS version 3.0 ballot is distributed.
2003:	(June) AIA, CSI, and NIBS sign the "Agreement for Publication and Distribution of the U.S. National CAD Standard," commonly known as the Memorandum of Agreement (MOA).
2004:	(July) NCS version 3.0 is released; it includes AIA CAD Layer Guidelines, U.S. NCS version 3, Tri-Service Plotting Guidelines, CSI's UDS Modules 01–08, and the NIBS Introduction and Amendments to Industry Publications. (December): The NCSPC Rules of Governance (ROG) is released (replacing the NIBS Consensus Process used for NCS versions 1.0, 2.0, and 3.0).
2005:	(January) NCS version 3.1 is released; it includes AIA CAD Layer Guidelines, U.S. NCS version 3, Tri-Service Plotting Guidelines, CSI's UDS Modules 01–08, and the NIBS Introduction and Amendments to Industry Publications;

it also marks the first time the NCS is provided in electronic format (searchable PDF). (July): The AIA, CSI, and NIBS issue a formal invitation to all software and CAD vendors, offering terms for a nonexclusive NCS license—with an emphasis on creative licensing terms. (September): Bentley Systems Inc., makers of MicroStation, announces the development of an NCS plug-in for its products and becomes the first CAD vendor to receive an NCS license for its products.

> *FYI:* Release of NCS version 3.0 was delayed 2-1/2 half years due to NCS licensing negotiations between the AIA, CSI, and NIBS. The negotiations resulted in the MOA, signed in 2003 by all three organizations.

REVIEW OF KEY CONCEPTS IN THE INTRODUCTION

1. The two key reasons for creation of the U.S. National CAD Standard were: (1) major facility owners needed to organize information for the life cycle of a facility, and (2) design professionals needed to organize information for the project cycle.
2. The original contributing organizations to the NCS were NIBS, CSI, AIA, SMACNA, GSA, USCG, and the Tri-Service CADD/GIS Technology Center.
3. The NCS Project Committee is the administering group for the NCS; membership is free and open to all drawing users.
4. The history, and future, of the NCS is one of collaboration among many industry groups.

FREQUENTLY ASKED QUESTIONS

Q: *The CDs that were available with NCS version 2.0 included CAD files for standard sheets, schedules, symbols, and a search engine for terms and abbreviations. Why were the CDs discontinued after version 2.0, and are they still available?*

A: The optional CDs were discontinued after version 2.0 because they were too costly to update. And because the NCS has changed since they were originally published, they are outdated and should not be used. That said, for those who have them, hang onto them! Who knows? Maybe someday they'll be as valuable as an original "Meet the Beatles" record!

Q: *What is the difference between NCS versions 3.0 and 3.1?*

A: When the AIA, CSI, and NIBS finalized their NCS licensing negotiations in 2004, they agreed to release NCS version 3.0 as "purple sheets," which simply listed each of the version 3.0 ballot items that had been approved by the NCS Project Committee. As part of the arrangement, it was also agreed to convert the hard copy of the NCS into an electronic PDF version, which was dubbed, NCS version 3.1. It took CSI, NIBS, and the AIA a few months to release version 3.1 because the agreement also mandated that the standard needed extensive updates to coordinate with the 2004 edition of MasterFormat.

Q: *Why has it taken so long for CAD vendors to include the NCS in their software?*

A: This is one of the most frustrating issues surrounding the NCS. After the release of NCS version 2.0, many of us hoped to see the NCS logo appear quickly on CAD software shrink-wrap. There are many reasons we are still waiting for an NCS toolbar to appear on our CAD display screens, including:

1. After the release of NCS version 2.0 in February 2001, NCS licensing negotiations between the AIA, CSI, and NIBS were deadlocked for over two years until they signed a new "Agreement for Publication and Distribution of the U.S. National CAD Standard (NCS)," in June 2003. The agreement resolved licensing and intellectual property issues and, in September 2005, Bentley Systems Inc., makers of MicroStation, became the first

NCS-licensed CAD vendor when it announced development of an NCS plug-in for its products. Hopefully, by the time this book is published, others will have felt compelled to follow Bentley's lead.

2. Some vendors claim that, since much of their sales are generated outside the United States, they are concerned there isn't a large enough market to include a U.S. standard such as the NCS in their software. Oddly enough, they haven't seemed to hesitate to include other U.S. based features such as outdated AIA CAD Layering Guidelines, Master-Format numbers, and components based on other American standards, such as those of the American Institute of Steel Construction (AISC), the Steel Joist Institute (SJI), the Steel Deck Institute, and the American Institute of Constructors (AIC). On a related note, it is also strange that specifications software manufacturers have yet to embrace the NCS. None of the manufacturers we know have coordinated the terms and abbreviations in their software with those in the NCS even though it would save substantial amounts of time for their customers, who currently must coordinate it manually.

Q: *Does the NCS include formats from* ConDoc?

A: Published by the AIA in 1990, *ConDoc* was one of many publications looked at by the authors of NCS version 1.0. However, none of the formats were included.

Q: *Can the NCS be used for three-dimensional CAD applications such as the* building information model (BIM)?

A: Not yet. The original intent of the NCS was to establish formats for two-dimensional graphics. However, it is anticipated that the building information model will be a very active topic during future NCS revision cycles.

Q: *If I join the NCS Project Committee, will I have to attend meetings?*

A: No. Communication between committee members is conducted via email and teleconferences. There have been only three, nonmandatory, face-to face meetings of NCS Project Committee members since the release of NCS version 1.0 in 1999.

Q: *Who is using the NCS?*

A: Many workplaces have adopted all, or portions of the NCS. The list, which is growing, includes:

- Federal agencies such as the GSA, the National Institutes of Health, the Architect of the Capitol, the National Gallery of Art, and the Veterans Administration
- The U.S. Coast Guard, Air Force, Navy, and Marines
- Schools and universities such as Albuquerque Public Schools, Indiana University, and the University of Kansas
- Sandia National Laboratory and Los Alamos National Laboratory
- Companies such as Ford Motor Company, Lockheed Martin Astronautics, Nextel, Intel, Pacific Gas and Electric, 3M Corporation, Einstein/Noah Bagel Corporation, Southern Steel Company, Idaho Power, and Duke Energy Corporation.
- Design firms such as HDR, Jacobs Engineering Group, CH2M Hill, Raytheon Engineers and Constructors, Richard Meier and Partners, RTKL Associates, Inc., Skidmore, Owings and Merrill, Dean and Dean/Associates, Murphy/Jahn Architects, and, of course, Wilson & Company, Inc., Engineers & Architects, and Hall Architects, Inc.

A list of some of the workplaces where the NCS is used can be viewed at the NCS website, www.nationalcadstandard.org.

Drawing Set Organization

GENERAL

The responsibility for organizing the drawing set falls within the architect's project role. A standardized organizational structure for the drawing set allows users to assemble, locate, and retrieve information quickly and efficiently. A project drawing set typically serves two primary purposes: one, as a component of the procurement documents, it is used for competitive bidding or direct negotiation; and, two, as a component of the construction documents, it is used to build the facility. The construction drawing set may also include supplemental information, including addenda drawings, **modification drawings,** and clarification drawings.

SET CONTENT AND ORDER

It is useful to establish a basic understanding of terms used throughout this book. A **drawing** is a graphic representation of information in a two-dimensional format used to indicate the configuration, location, and size of project components and elements. One or more drawings may be assembled onto a **sheet,** which can be a piece of paper or an electronic file. Drawing sheets are assembled into **subsets,** generally by design discipline, sometimes called **discipline sets.** These discipline sets are organized in a specific order. The drawing set may also include a **cover sheet,** General sheets, and Resource sheets, which are explained later in this chapter. Figure 1-1 illustrates the major subsets and their order within the drawing set.

Subsets (Discipline Sets)

The subset is the heart of the organizational structure for the drawing set. The U.S. National CAD Standard (NCS) identifies standard drawing subsets and prescribes their order within the drawing set. If a cover sheet is used, this is the first sheet in the drawing set. It may or may not include sheet identification. (Refer to Chapter 2, "Sheet Organization," for information about the layout of a cover sheet and the related use of sheet identification.) The broad scope subsets, such as General, Architectural, Mechanical, and Electrical, may be broken down into narrow scope subsets, such as Architectural Demolition or Architectural Site. The NCS does not prescribe the order of subsets when broad and narrow scope subsets are used together. The focus of the subset should be used to determine the order.

While most subsets represent design disciplines, the General sheet information pertains to all disciplines and Resource sheet information represents information that are not be part of the contract documents.

General Sheets

General sheets, sometimes called "G-sheets," are the first subset within the drawing set. Information that appears on these sheets applies to all sheets in the drawing set. These sheets may

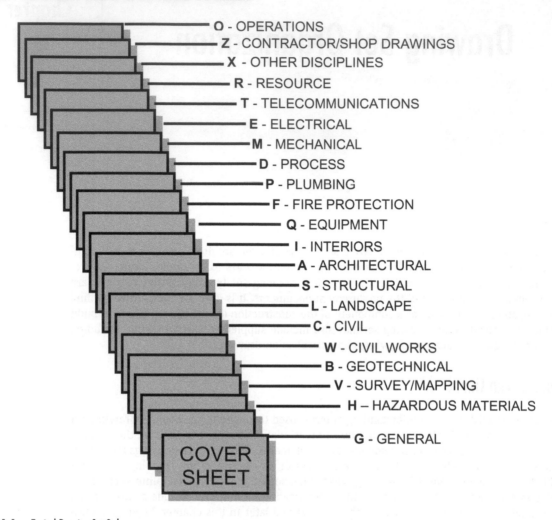

O - OPERATIONS
Z - CONTRACTOR/SHOP DRAWINGS
X - OTHER DISCIPLINES
R - RESOURCE
T - TELECOMMUNICATIONS
E - ELECTRICAL
M - MECHANICAL
D - PROCESS
P - PLUMBING
F - FIRE PROTECTION
Q - EQUIPMENT
I - INTERIORS
A - ARCHITECTURAL
S - STRUCTURAL
L - LANDSCAPE
C - CIVIL
W - CIVIL WORKS
B - GEOTECHNICAL
V - SURVEY/MAPPING
H – HAZARDOUS MATERIALS
G - GENERAL

COVER SHEET

Figure 1-1:   Typical Drawing Set Order

> **FYI:** The discipline designator was first called the "discipline code" by the AIA in its earlier versions of the CAD Layer Guidelines, but it was changed to the "discipline designator" to match CSI Uniform Drawing System terminology.

include code information, drawing sheet index, symbol legend, drawing sheet logic, general contract information, and other project information. Many jurisdictions are now requiring a list of "special inspections," as required by Chapter 17 of the International Building Code, to be included on a General sheet with the other code information for the project. Most firms produce a standard series of G-sheets and edit them for each project, saving time and ensuring that important information is always included in the drawing set. Figure 1-2 illustrates a typical G-sheet for a project.

Resource Sheets

Resource sheets are typically the last subset in a construction drawing set and may include information about existing conditions or new construction related to the work. Information contained on these sheets is typically important information to enable coordination but is not a part

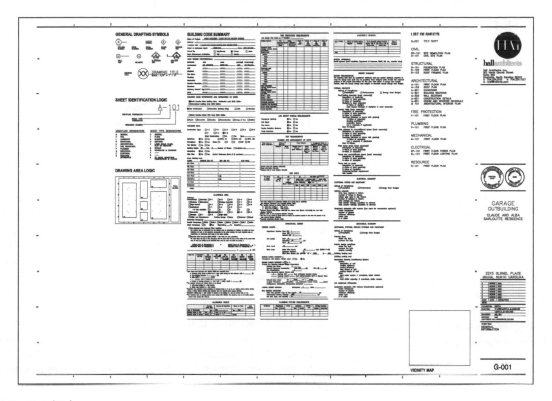

FIGURE 1-2:   Typical G-sheet

of the contract work. Resource sheets are the graphic equivalent to "Available Information" found within the project manual, and, as a result, these two documents should be coordinated. Some typical uses of these sheets may include kitchen equipment furnished by others; campus site information; drawings showing concealed conditions, such as existing footings or hazardous materials; and project information, such as technical subsurface boring locations, site conditions survey, or even photos of existing conditions.

SHEET IDENTIFICATION

Sheets are identified using a format that provides additional information about the contents of the sheet. The preferred format is the **standard sheet identification.** The standard sheet identification includes the **discipline designator, hyphen, sheet type designator,** and the **sheet sequence number.** However, on small projects, the architect may choose to use the **abbreviated sheet identification.** These two formats should not be mixed within a drawing set. The sheet identification includes a minimum of three sheet identification components. Both identification formats indicate the discipline set to which the sheet belongs, a hyphen, and a sheet sequence number, while the standard sheet identification also includes the sheet type designator. **User-defined** designators may also be included as a suffix to both the standard sheet identification and the abbreviated sheet identification formats.

Discipline Designator

The first component of the sheet identification is the discipline designator. The discipline designator is composed of one or two alphabetic characters. The Level 1 discipline designator includes

A A - N N N

A - 1 0 1   Level 1
A F - 1 0 1   Level 2

Discipline Designator

A = alphabetic character
N = numeric character

FIGURE 1-3
Two Formats of Discipline Designator

the **discipline character** indicating the sheet discipline. In a Level 2 discipline designator, a second alphabetic character is added, which acts as the **modifier character** to the discipline character. Both Level 1 and Level 2 discipline designators are followed by a hyphen (-). This is discussed in further detail in the FAQ at the end of this chapter. Figure 1-3 illustrates the two formats for discipline designators.

FYI: The use of a hyphen after the Level 2 discipline designator was added as a ballot item in NCS version 2. Prior to that, only Level 1 discipline designators were followed by a hyphen as a placeholder.

Appendices A and B include lists of sheets incorporating Level 1 and Level 2 discipline designators, respectively. Level 1 and Level 2 discipline designators may be used together within a drawing set or subset for each discipline. Appendix A of the UDS Drawing Set Organization Module includes the assigned modifier characters for each discipline character, some of which are shown in Figure 1-4 for Level 2.

Sheet Type Designator

The second component of the standard sheet identification is the sheet type designator, which is a single numeric character representing the predominant drawing view on the sheet. While recommended, using drawings of the same view (plan view, sectional view, etc.) on a single sheet is not always practical. The NCS allows placement of multiple drawing types on a sheet for greater efficiency. When this is done, the sheet type designation should be determined by the predominant drawing type, and the sheet title may include the name(s) of other drawing types that appear on the sheet, i.e., "ROOF PLAN AND DETAILS." Figure 1-5 illustrates the sheet type designators and the predominant information for each.

Designator	Description	Content
AS	Architectural Site	
AD	Architectural Demolition	Protection and Removal
AE	Architectural Elements	General Architectural
AI	Architectural Interior	
AF	Architectural Finishes	
AG	Architectural Graphics	

FIGURE 1-4
Level 2 Discipline Designators

	Sheet Type Designator	Description
A A - **N** N	0	General (symbols legend, notes, etc.)
	1	Plans (horizontal views)
Sheet Type Designator	2	Elevations (vertical views)
	3	Sections (sectional views, wall & stair sections)
	4	Large Scale Views (plans, elevations)
A = alphabetic character	5	Details
N = numeric character	6	Schedules and Diagrams
	7	User-defined (for types that do not fall in other categories)
	8	User-defined (for types that do not fall in other categories)
	9	3D Representations (isometrics, perspectives, photographs)

FIGURE 1-5
Sheet Type Designators

Sheet types 7 and 8 are indicated to be user-defined. There is no single purpose for these sheet designators, but there are several that are commonly used. For example, on small projects, when the architect wants to include the project specifications on the drawings, one of these user-defined sheet types may be used for this purpose. The user-defined sheet types may also be designated to indicate drawings representing potential project alternates. As an example of this use, an alternate architectural floor plan may be shown on sheet A-701 and the related electrical plan for the alternate may be shown on sheet E-701. In this case, "7" indicates an "alternate" sheet use, and "01" indicated it is the first sheet in this sequence. Depending on the specific project requirements, the architect may find other purposes for these user-defined sheet types.

Sheet Sequence Number

The final component used in the sheet identification is the sheet sequence number. This is a two-digit numeric character that represents the sequential sheet number in each of the sheet types within each discipline designator. The sequence number begins with 01 and can extend through 99. The NCS allows the user to identify the sheet sequence number in a nonconsecutive manner, thereby leaving room for sheets to be added in the future. Therefore, the architect could identify sheets in a sequence as A-110, A-120, A-130, and so on. Figure 1-6 illustrates the sheet sequence number.

User-Defined Designators

The NCS also allows for user-defined identifiers to be used in conjunction with both the standard sheet identification and the abbreviated sheet identification formats, as well as on supplemental

FYI: For most projects, the Level 1 sheet identification alone works just fine. This should be your starting place. Then you can add Level 2 sheet Identification and user-defined designators if needed for the more complex portions of the drawing set.

The architect can then work with his or her consultants to ensure that the drawing set sheet identification is consistent throughout the set. If you chose to use user-defined designators, this will require additional coordination.

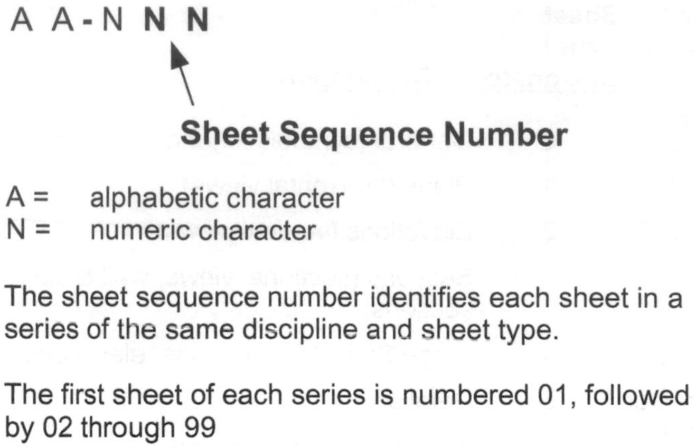

A A - N **N N**

Sheet Sequence Number

A = alphabetic character
N = numeric character

The sheet sequence number identifies each sheet in a
series of the same discipline and sheet type.

The first sheet of each series is numbered 01, followed
by 02 through 99

FIGURE **1-6**
Sheet Sequence Number

drawing sheets. These designators are considered a suffix to the base sheet identification and appear as the last component of the sheet identification. When selecting the order of the drawing sheets in the discipline set, the user-defined designator may dictate ordering. For example, the architect may wish to order the sheets by project phase. Thus, sheets with a user-defined designator of "P1" for "Phase 1" may be grouped together, while a modification to a drawing may have a user-defined designator of "R1" for "Revision 1" and may simply be included after the original drawing.

Note that the NCS does not specifically state when user-defined designators should be separated from the sheet sequence number by a hyphen. Some guidance is provided in Appendix C of the UDS Drawing Module, which includes examples of sheet identification with user-defined designators. Some of the examples, such as addenda drawings, are indicated to be provided with a hyphen (such as sheet A-101-AD). Other examples, such as sheets in projects with different buildings, are indicated without the dash (such as sheet A-1011 or A-101A). Other examples in Appendix C appear to conflict with the format explanation given earlier in the module (an example in the module indicates a revised drawing should be identified as A-101-R1; Appendix C indicates it should be identified as A-101R1). It appears that further clarification will be needed in future NCS updates. Until then, we recommend using a dash after the sheet sequence number whenever the user-defined designator begins with a numeral (this will help to differentiate it from the numerals in the sheet sequence number). Figure 1-7 shows a few examples of user-defined designators.

Standard Sheet Identification

The standard sheet identification includes all four sheet identification components and may also use Level 1 or Level 2 discipline designators or even a combination of both. Figure 1-8 gives a sample sheet index for these two levels.

Abbreviated Sheet Identification

The abbreviated sheet identification includes only the Level 1 discipline designator, hyphen, and the sheet sequence number. This form of sheet identification is suggested only for small projects; hence, it may be found on projects such as small single-family residential projects. The use of the abbreviated sheet identification on commercial projects of any scale is strongly discouraged.

User-defined Designator

	Sheet	Sheet Title
	G-001	Title Sheet
	C-101	Civil Site Plan
Sample Drawings	S-101-A	Foundation Plan
User-defined	S-102-A	Floor Framing Plan Phase A
Designators	S-102-B	Floor Framing Plan Phase B
(Phases)	S-103-A	Roof Framing Plan Phase A
	S-103-B	Roof Framing Plan Phase B
	A-101-A	Floor Plan Phase A
	A-101-B	Floor Plan Phase B
	A-102-A	Roof Plan Phase A
	A-102-B	Roof Plan Phase B
	A-201-A	Elevations Phase A
	A-201-B	Elevations Phase B
	A-301-A	Building Sections Phase A
	A-301-B	Building Sections Phase B
	P-101-A	Plumbing Plan Phase A
	P-101-B	Plumbing Plan Phase B
	EP-101-A	Power Plan Phase A
	EP-101-B	Power Plan Phase B
	EL-101-A	Lighting Plan Phase A
	EL-101-B	Lighting Plan Phase B

	Sheet	Sheet Title
	A-101-NE	Floor Plan North East Quadrant
	A-101-NW	Floor Plan North West Quadrant
Sample Drawings	A-101-SE	Floor Plan South East Quadrant
User-defined	A-101-SW	Floor Plan South West Quadrant
Designators	A-102-NE	Roof Plan North East Quadrant
(Quadrants)	A-102-NW	Roof Plan North West Quadrant
	A-102-SE	Roof Plan South East Quadrant
	A-102-SW	Roof Plan South West Quadrant

	Sheet	Sheet Title
	A-101-A	Building A – First Floor Plan
	A-201-A	Building A – Exterior Elevations
Sample Drawings	A-301-A	Building A – Building Sections
User-defined	A-401-A	Building A – Wall Sections
Designators		
(Buildings)	A-101-B	Building B – First Floor Plan
	A-201-B	Building B – Exterior Elevations
	A-301-B	Building B – Building Sections
	A-401-B	Building B – Wall Sections
	A-501-B	Building B – Construction Details

FIGURE 1-7
User-Defined Designators

FILE NAMING

The NCS identifies two broad categories of files, **library files** and **project files.** Library files are those containing information that may be incorporated into multiple projects, such as standard details, and then modified for the specific requirements of the project. Project files are project-specific and are organized by file types. These file types can include model, detail, sheet, schedule, text, database, symbols, border, and title block.

Sample Sheet Index Level 1 and 2 Discipline Designators Combined

Sheet	Sheet Title
G-001	General Information
CD-101	Site Demolition Plan
C-101	Civil Site Plan
S-101	Foundation Plan
S-102	First Floor Framing Plan
S-103	Second Floor Framing Plan
S-104	Roof Framing Plan
A-101	First Floor Plan
A-102	Second Floor Plan
A-103	Roof Plan
A-201	Elevations
A-301	Building Sections
A-302	Wall Sections
A-501	Construction Details
A-601	Doors and Windows Schedule
AI-101	Architectural Interior Plan
F-101	First Floor Fire Protection Plan
F-102	Second Floor Fire Protection Plan
P-101	First Floor Plumbing Plan
P-102	Second Floor Plumbing Plan
M-101	First Floor HVAC Plan
M-102	Second Floor HVAC Plan
EP-101	First Floor Power Plan
EP-102	Second Floor Power Plan
EL-101	First Floor Lighting Plan
EL-102	Second Floor Lighting Plan
E-601	Electrical Schedules

FIGURE 1-8
Level 1 and Level 2 Sample Sheet Index

Most library files are organized by work results (MasterFormat 2004) or by construction elements (**UniFormat**). However, because UniFormat is currently undergoing a major update, and we anticipate significant changes in the organizational structure to reflect all construction in the next several years, it is recommended that most firms consider organizing their library files by MasterFormat 2004 at this time. The naming convention uses the six- or eight-digit MasterFormat number with a three-character user identifier. The user-defined identifiers may be an alphanumeric series of characters that match the firm's reference keynoting system, or a simple sequence number. Below are a few examples of typical library file names:

081113-01: Hollow Metal Frame—Head
081113-01A: Hollow Metal Frame—Head
081113-02: Hollow Metal Frame—Jamb
081113-03: Hollow Metal Frame—Sill

The naming convention for project files varies depending on the file type. However, most firms that use project files use the file name to indicate location of drawings on project drawing sheets.

Therefore, a file name of A-502-C2.dwg would represent a drawing (AutoCAD file) located at drawing area coordinate C2 on sheet A-502.

IMPLEMENTATION ISSUES

We recommend the NCS format requirements included in the UDS Drawing Set Organization Module be the first portion of the standard to be adopted during the NCS implementation process for most firms. This is because most of the requirements can be adopted very easily, with little impact on current drawing office procedures. In addition, the time needed to incorporate the formats into drawing sets will usually result in minimal disruption and downtime for the workplace.

Organizing the disciplines in the drawing set according to the hierarchy in the UDS Drawing Set Organization Module should be the first step taken during the NCS implementation process. It is a good place to start because the hierarchy was originally based upon an order common and familiar to many workplaces. Thus, most offices will require only very minor adjustments to the drawing set order currently in use. A benefit to adopting this component early is that other than incorporating the same alphabetic characters used for discipline designators, only a few other changes need to be made to the sheets themselves.

Once proper organization of the set into subsets has been adopted, the next component to implement is sheet identification. We recommend using only the standard sheet identification format, no matter what size the project. This will require incorporating sheet type designators into the workplace, which will usually take a little more effort than the previous step, because some offices are either not familiar with them or are using a different sheet type designator system. However, the time and cost associated with the learning curve to adopt the sheet type designators is minimal, and most workplaces should be able to make the adjustment without much more discomfort than the effort needed to overcome the psychological hurdle associated with the change. Moreover, sheet type designators provide many benefits, and the positive impact they make on the organization of drawing sets is well worth the investment.

The next component to adopt is among the simplest of all: the sheet sequence number. Again, this is quite easy, as most offices only need refrain from identifying sheets with "00" numbers such as A-100, A-200, A-300, and so on.

The UDS Drawing Set Organization Module includes the entire electronic file-naming requirements in the NCS. Adopting this component from the module will probably be the most difficult step for most offices, because many workplaces are using systems they have grown very accustomed to, or that are formatted very differently from those in the module. If this issue is a concern, it will probably be better to delay this step until a little later in the implementation process. (For more information about incorporating the NCS into the workplace, refer to Chapter 11, "Implementation.")

REVIEW OF KEY CONCEPTS IN THIS CHAPTER

1. The UDS Drawing Set Module provides a standard for the ordering of the discipline sets within a drawing set.
2. The standard sheet identification format uses a four-component structure to identify the sheet.
3. User-defined designators may be used with standard sheet identification for project phase, building quadrants, and many other purposes.
4. The use of a discipline designator is common to sheet identification, file naming, and CAD layer naming.
5. Formats in the UDS Drawing Set Organization Module should be among the very first to adopt during the NCS implementation process.

FREQUENTLY ASKED QUESTIONS

Q: *Is it okay to mix Level 1 and Level 2 discipline designators in the drawing set?*

A: Yes, sheets in the drawing set can be identified with both Level 1 and Level 2 discipline designators (a sample sheet index is shown in Figure 1-8 and Appendices A and B).

Q: *Because of sheet size limitations, some of our designs for facilities with large footprints need to be separated into different parts per floor. What is the best way to identify the sheets for projects like this?*

A: Large buildings with multiple floors are similar to projects with multiple buildings, so you can break the drawing set into subsets with user-defined designators. An example of a sheet identification system worth considering for these types of projects is as follows:

A-101:	First Floor Plan (This overall plan and overall plans of the other floors could be drawn at 1/16″ or 1/32″ = 1′–0″.)
A-101A:	First Floor Plan—Part A (This plan and the other "parts" could be drawn at 1/8″, or 1/4″ = 1′–0″.)
A-101B:	First Floor Plan—Part B
A-101C:	First Floor Plan—Part C
A-102:	Second Floor Plan (overall plan of the second floor)
A-102A:	Second Floor Plan—Part A
A-102B:	Second Floor Plan—Part B
A-102C:	Second Floor Plan—Part C

Please note: When user-defined designators are used, we strongly recommend separating them from the sheet sequence number with a hyphen if the first character in the user-defined designator is a numeral (use A-101-1 instead of A-1011). This will help to avoid confusing it with the sheet sequence number.

Q: *When should an abbreviated sheet identification format be used to identify sheets?*

A: The NCS allows the use of two formats for sheet identification: standard sheet identification and abbreviated sheet identification. Standard sheet identification includes the Level 1 or Level 2 discipline designators, the hyphen, the sheet type designator, and the sheet sequence number. Abbreviated sheet identification only uses the Level 1 discipline designator and a sheet sequence number. That said, we see no good reason to use the abbreviated sheet identification format, except on very small residential projects, and discourage workplaces from using it.

The main problem with two sheet identification formats is that the NCS doesn't provide clear directions for using one system or the other. The UDS Drawing Set Organization Module does hint at using standard format for large, complex projects, and abbreviated format for small projects. However, the NCS doesn't say that drawing sets can't have both formats; neither does it define what is small and what is large. What about medium-sized projects? How are users supposed to know when to use a specific format? Using only the standard sheet identification format will eliminate this confusion and ensure that each drawing is formatted the same no matter what size the project is. This will result in more consistent drawing sets and a drawing standard that will be easier to enforce.

The standard sheet identification format will work very well on one-sheet projects. For example, when an architectural project that includes a plan can be drawn entirely on a single sheet, it can be identified as sheet A-101. This methodology works for all the other disciplines, also. We hope to see the abbreviated sheet format removed from future versions of the NCS.

Q: *The configuration of the floor plan of a building we are designing is so large that we need to locate Parts A, B, and C of the floor plan on separate sheets. Are the drawings of Parts A, B, and C considered large-scale views that need to be located on a sheet type designator 4-series (Enlarged Plans, Elevations, or Sections that are not details)?*

A: According to the UDS Drawing Set Organization Module, the intent of large-scale views is to provide more detailed information than can be accommodated at smaller scales. Somewhat surprisingly, one of the best places to find an answer for a question like this is in the UDS Drafting Conventions Module, which states that the intent of large-scale plans is to provide more detailed information for spaces such as auditoriums, kitchens, laboratories, stairwells, toilets, toilet rooms, elevator shafts, and mechanical and electrical rooms. When it becomes necessary to break a plan into larger-scale plans in order to better identify the overall layout of rooms, doors, windows, detail references, dimensions, and so on, it is okay to locate these types of drawings on a sheet type designator 1-series sheet (Plans). The UDS Drafting Conventions Module also mandates that the division between the different areas on the plans needs to be delineated with **match lines** and a **key plan.**

Q: *Now that NCS version 3.1 requires the use of a hyphen between the Level 2 discipline designator and the sheet type designator, we cannot fit 3/32" text of the sheet identifiers in the bottom half of reference symbols, such as detail indicators, elevation indicators, and section indicators. This is especially a problem when our sheets need to be identified with user-defined designators. What do you suggest?*

A: Unfortunately, when the Level 2 "hyphen amendment" was incorporated into the NCS, results like this were ignored by the NCS Project Committee (our concerns about this very issue fell on deaf ears). There are several options to resolve this, including:

1. Compress the horizontal proportion of the 3/32" text height (will have a very negative affect on readability; compressed text will often not fit in the symbol either).
2. Increase the diameter of the reference symbol to accommodate the additional character (will require more room in drawing blocks and will not be consistent with size of other reference symbols; also does not comply with the NCS).
3. Reduce text height to less than 3/32" (will have a very negative affect on readability, especially if text-wrapping is used; also does not comply with the NCS).

Our recommendation is to break the circle (bubble) to allow the characters to extend outside the symbol. (This does not comply with the NCS, either, but it is a better option than the others.)

Q: *The Level 1 discipline designator and the Level 2 discipline designator can both be used to name sheet files—but can they both be used to name model files?*

A: According to the UDS Drawing Set Organization Module, the first character of a model file name is the single-letter discipline designator, and the second character is the hyphen, which acts as a placeholder. This implies that Level 2 discipline designators are not allowed. However, since the model file-naming format also allows user-defined prefixes, we see no reason why Level 2 discipline designators shouldn't be used.

Q: *Where do we locate partition drawings? Are they sections, large-scale views, or details?*

A: There are two good options for partition drawings:

OPTION 1
1. Reference the partitions on the plans with wall type indicators, as indicated in the sheet type designator 6-series sheets (Schedules and Diagrams) portion of the UDS Drafting Conventions Module.
2. Include a partition schedule in the sheet type designator 6-series sheets (Schedules and Diagrams). An example of a partition schedule is not included in the NCS, but it won't take much imagination to create one using the UDS Symbols Module for guidance. A typical partition schedule will need a **heading** ("Partition Schedule") and will often contain columns for a Mark, Detail, Fire Rating Label, and Notes. The Detail column should include a detail reference for each partition type, similar to the way head, jamb, and sill details are referenced in a door and frame schedule.

3. Partition details are typically viewed as partial horizontal sections or full-height vertical sections. If there is room in the drawing area of the same sheet the partition schedule is on, you can locate the details there (different drawing types on the same sheet are allowed). If you need to locate the details on another sheet, use sheet type designator 5-series sheets (Details) for partial sections and sheet type designator 3-series sheets (Sections) for full-height vertical sections.

OPTION 2

1. Reference each partition on the plan with either a section indicator symbol or, if space in the **drawing area** is limited, with the detail indicator for small conditions symbol (refer to the UDS Symbols Module).
2. Detail each partition as a full-height vertical section on a sheet type designator 3-series sheet (Sections); or, if room in the drawing area is available, the sections could be included on the same sheet with the floor plan.

Q: *What are the Civil Works and Operations disciplines used for?*

A: Each of these disciplines was incorporated into version 2.0 of the NCS. According to the discussion by members of the NCSPC at the time, the intent for Civil Works discipline (W-series sheets) was for large scale civil work or existing conditions outside project limits; or for civil projects "that could be seen from an airplane at 30,000 feet." This was quite controversial because no other discipline is subdivided according to size or existing conditions. Another way to analyze the content of the Civil Works discipline is for use on larger civil projects within a public right-of-way such as highways and street utilities. These explanations are not in the UDS Drawing Set Organization Module. We still disagree with the NCSPC about the decision to include Civil Works as a separate discipline from the Civil discipline in the NCS because there is no clear definition when to use the C-discipline, and when to use the W-discipline.

The argument for including the Operations discipline (0-series sheets) in version 2.0 of the NCS was that it was needed for data for facility management and operation purposes. There is no explanation about the use of this discipline in the UDS Drawing Set Module either.

Sheet Organization

GENERAL

Perhaps one of the most important issues to many architects is the design of their drawing sheet, especially the title block area. Since this is an outward reflection of their creative skills, many firms go to great lengths to ensure that their drawing sheets reflect their "personality" as designers, while others are only concerned that the sheet design contains the information necessary for the project requirements. The basic requirements for sheet formats are located in the Construction Specification Institute's (CSI) Uniform Drawing System (UDS) Sheet Organization Module, and they provide the flexibility to suit the needs of most firms for both creative expression and organization of necessary information.

This module was one of three UDS modules to be included in the first version of the NCS, released in 1999. Since being incorporated into the NCS, very few changes have been made to the module by the National CAD Standard Project Committee (NCSPC), and those changes have made it somewhat more flexible to use.

The UDS Sheet Organization Module provides assistance in designing and understanding the graphic layout of the cover sheet, sheets (drawing sheets), and supplemental drawing sheets. The standardization of sheet organization allows users to find information quickly and reduces time needed for the preparation of construction documents.

Most firms design their sheets in various standard sizes based on project requirements. Common project information such as project name and location, project numbers, consultants, and sheet title are incorporated into the sheet title block area. This sheet, commonly referred to as the title block sheet template, is then distributed to all members of the design team and becomes the template for all project drawing sheets. The template also includes layer names and their associated pen widths. This process helps ensure uniformity and consistency in the graphic display of the construction documents.

Corporate and governmental clients often establish standard drawing sheet designs. In many cases, these organizations may try to follow the spirit of the standard, albeit with some unique requirements that result in minor deviations from NCS compliance. Ironically, since 1999, many federal agencies have required the use of the NCS yet have imposed their own specific sheet design requirements that deviate from the standard. These clients should be applauded for their efforts but be encouraged to modify their standardized drawing sheets so as to fully comply with the NCS.

One of the primary goals of the NCS is to create flexible standards and guidelines, to enable users to meet the needs of a variety of project types and sizes. With a little creativity, the architect can create sheet layouts that reflect the uniqueness of the design firm while still following an industry standard for the presentation of construction information. To address that topic, the next section examines the sheet organization issues that need to be considered during the development of office or organization standard sheet templates and in working with clients' specific sheet requirements.

SHEET SIZES

Precut sheets can be purchased in three commonly available sizes, including **American National Standards Institute (ANSI)**, **International Organization for Standardization (ISO)**, and Architectural sizes. Sheets can also be cut from a roll, based on standard sheet sizes chosen from CAD or plotter software. Roll widths vary and are usually determined based upon client requirements or the most common sheet sizes typically used in the workplace. Figure 2-1 shows Architectural sheet sizes and typical uses.

Most architectural firms use a combination of ANSI and Architectural size sheets based on typical uses and printer/plotter output requirements.

> *FYI:* The UDS Task Team originally attempted to establish a single, universal sheet size, but quickly came to the conclusion that no single size could fit all needs.

ANSI Sheets

The two most commonly used ANSI size sheets used by architects are A (8–1/2″ × 11″) and B (11″ × 17″), which are both typically used for **supplemental drawings, mock-up sheets,** and detail libraries. The reason for their popularity is that they can easily be printed on most desktop printers and can be bound into project manuals, detail books, proposals, and other documents commonly formatted in these document sizes.

MARK	SIZE in (mm)	TYPICAL USES
A	9 x 12 (229 x 305)	Project book Supplemental drawings Mock-up sheets
B	12 x 18 (305 x 457)	Supplemental drawings Mock-up sheets Reduced drawings from "D" and "A1"
C	18 x 24 (457 x 610)	Small projects in Preferred plan scale
D	24 x 36 (610 x 914)	Projects in preferred plan scale Government projects
E	36 x 48 (914 x 1219)	Large projects in preferred plan scale Mapping and GIS
F	30 x 42 (762 x 1067)	Alternate size for projects in preferred plan scale.

FIGURE 2-1
Architectural Sheet Sizes

Architectural Sheets

The most commonly used Architectural size sheets are C (18″ × 24″), D (24″ × 36″), E (36″ × 48″), and F × (30″ × 42″). Many small projects and residential projects work fine using C and D size sheets, while larger projects can be more easily accommodated on E or F size sheets.

SHEET LAYOUT

Cover Sheet

The first sheet in a **drawing set** is typically the cover sheet. Some cover sheets are intended to be more decorative in nature and may only include the name of the project, a rendering, or the client's name and logo. Other cover sheets are intended to convey useful project information that may include building code information, location maps, or a list of sheets (the sheet index). The only NCS requirement for cover sheets containing project information is the inclusion of sheet identification, as described in Chapter 1, "Drawing Set Organization." Therefore, the cover sheet would use the sheet identification G-001, and all subsequent General (G-series) sheets would use sequential numbers (G-002, G-003, etc.). Cover sheets without project information do not require sheet identification. Figure 2-2 illustrates examples of both cover sheets with and without project information.

While the use of sheet identification is the only hard-and-fast requirement for cover sheets with project information, we have found the use of the other principles of sheet organization very helpful in designing the project cover sheet. In general, the cover sheet will include a drawing area and a title block area. The drawing area may contain graphic information such as a rendering of the project, project name, list of drawing sheets, and building data. The title block area may include designer identification, project identification, sheet title, sheet identification, and set number. This information should be displayed such that when the drawing set is rolled up, the project name and set number are visible.

The cover sheet follows the same minimum margin requirements as the drawing sheets, but the title block area requirements may not apply. The use of professional and corporate seals on cover sheets may vary with each jurisdiction. The architect should verify this requirement with the local board of architecture.

Drawing Sheets

The drawing sheet is the media for the location for graphic information within the drawing set. Each drawing sheet is divided into three areas: the **drawing area,** the **title block area,** and the **production data area.** Each of these areas of a drawing sheet provides a location for specific types of information and will be discussed later in this chapter. An assembly of drawing sheets within the same discipline form the discipline set, and an assembly of one or more discipline sets form the drawing set. The drawing sheet is the smallest physical document in a drawing set. Figure 2-3 shows a typical drawing sheet and illustrates the three main areas. (See Chapter 1 for the organization of the drawing set.)

According to the AIA Document A201-1997 General Conditions of the Contract for Construction, the architect often considers the drawing sheet as the primary component of the graphic construction documents known as "Drawings." The sheet identification, sheet titles, and date issued are typically incorporated as part of the completed Owner-Contractor agreement to designate the graphic construction documents that help form the **contract documents.**

Specific sheet margins are not an absolute requirement of the NCS and may vary depending on plotter capabilities and sheet design. Most firms use 1/2″ or 3/4″ top, bottom, and right side margins, and a 1–1/2″ margin on the left, or binding side, of the drawing sheet. These margin

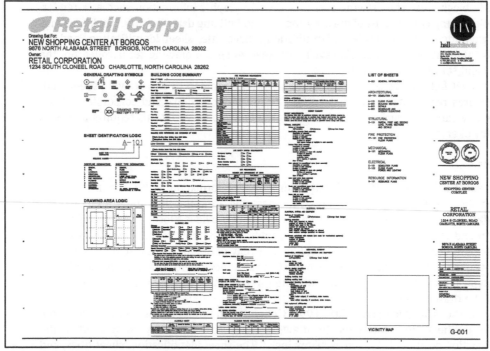

FIGURE 2-2 Examples of Cover Sheets

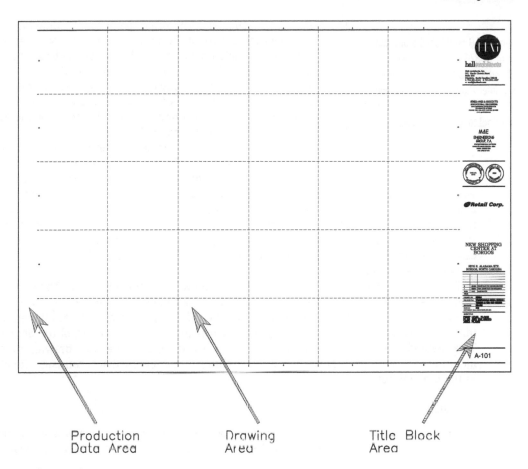

Production   Drawing   Title Block
Data Area   Area   Area

Figure 2-3   Typical Drawing Sheet

sizes have been found to be the most practical for the various sheet sizes, and aid in providing an efficient layout of the space. Borders, tic marks, or other graphic devices may be used to define the sheet margins.

Drawing Area

The drawing area is the portion of the drawing sheet where one or more drawings are located. Drawings may include plans, details, sections, elevations, schedules, diagrams, **three-dimensional (3D) views,** or other graphic information. Drawings are placed in the drawing area of the drawing sheet using a **drawing area coordinate system.**

Drawing Area Coordinate System

The drawing area coordinate system is an organizational structure for subdividing the drawing area into cells or **drawing modules,** using a coordinate system similar to that used on street maps or a spreadsheet. The columns are identified using numbers, and the rows are identified using

FYI: NCS version 1.0 established a drawing module size of 5–3/4" × 6" because it worked well with D and E size sheets; however, this was later changed to user-defined sizes to allow smaller (or larger) modules that could be beneficial to more disciplines.

alphabetic characters. The origin point for the drawing area is in the lower left corner of the drawing area. The NCS recommends the row and column identifiers be located outside the drawing area, if practical. The NCS requires **row identifiers** to be located on the right side of the drawing area, and **column identifiers** on either the top or bottom of the drawing area; however, all four sides are preferred. Each drawing module should be identified using a tic mark or other graphic device.

The size of the drawing modules is user-defined and should be established to suit the sheet size and design, and user needs. Whichever size is used, it must be used consistently on all sheets within the drawing set. We recommend the architect establish the sheet design for the project and provide an electronic template to all members of the project team to ensure all drawing sheets in the set will have a consistent layout. Many firms establish a standard drawing module size and develop typical details, notes, and other drawings based on this office standard. These can then be stored as library files to be used on future projects. Figure 2-4 illustrates the typical drawing area coordinate system.

Drawings may comprise one or more modules known as a **drawing block.** The drawing block is identified by the coordinate location of the lowest left module of the drawing block according to its row identifier and then the column identifier. If a single drawing utilizes the entire drawing area, it is identified as "A1," being the origin point (lower left corner) of the drawing area. This method provides a pattern for identifying drawings and ensures that drawing numbers or identifiers are not repeated on a sheet, thus resulting in numbering that is consistent for all sheets in the drawing set.

Note Block

The **note block,** when used on a sheet is the portion of the drawing area where general notes, reference keynotes, sheet keynotes, and key plans are located. The note block is always located

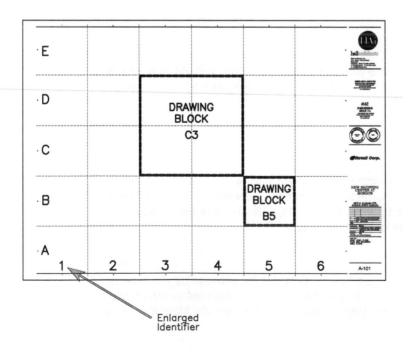

Enlarged
Identifier

FIGURE 2-4
Drawing Area Coordinate System

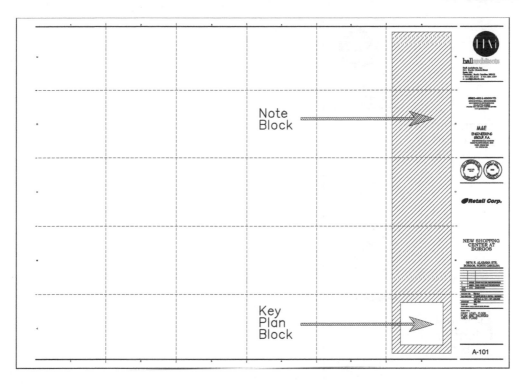

FIGURE 2-5   Note Block Location

on the right side of the drawing area, next to the title block area. Some sheets may not require the use of a note block, in which case this area is used for drawing blocks. The note block may be one or more drawing modules in either dimension, depending on the size of the sheet design and the amount of information required. Note blocks begin at the top of the sheet even if the entire column is not used. The use of note blocks is optional and is generally not required on all sheets. Key plans should always be located in the lowest module of the note block. Figure 2-5 shows the location of the note block within the drawing area.

The note block may include one or more data blocks, including **general notations**, reference keynotes, and sheet keynotes. Chapter 7, "Notations," will discuss the organization and use of the note block in greater detail.

Title Block Area

The title block area is that portion of the drawing sheet where project and sheet information is located. The title block area is subdivided into six data blocks. These are the **designer identification block, project identification block, issue block, management block, sheet title block,** and the **sheet identification block.** The data blocks are organized in that order within the title block area starting at the top of the sheet. Each of the data blocks will be discussed in detail later in this chapter. The data blocks should be separated using borders, space, tic marks, or other graphic devices. Figure 2-6 illustrates a typical horizontal text title block area and its components.

Formats for Title Block Area

There are two standard formats for the title block area, **horizontal text format** and **vertical text format.** These formats indicate the direction of the text in the data blocks in relation to the bottom of the drawing sheet. In the horizontal text format, the text in all the data blocks is oriented

Designer Identification Block

Project Identification Block

Issue Block

Management Block

Sheet Title Block

Sheet Identification Block

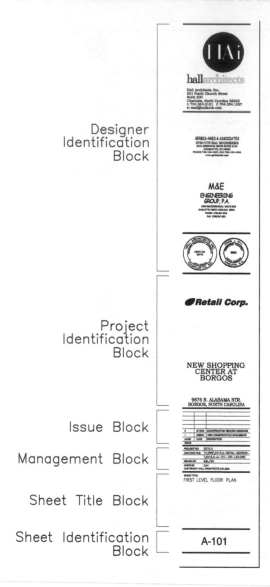

FIGURE 2-6
Horizontal Text Title Block Area

parallel with the bottom of the sheet. In the vertical text format, the sheet identification block, the sheet title block, and the management block are horizontal; and the issue block, the project identification block, and the designer block are vertical. The purpose of this orientation is to allow the sheet numbers, sheet titles, and management block to be easily read when stored in either rolls or flat files.

Architects attempting to comply with NCS title block requirements for the first time have much greater design flexibility than they probably realize. The guidelines allow creativity to personalize the appearance of the title block to fit the desires of most organizations. Once a title block design has been created, firms will likely create a template for each sheet size commonly used in the office and then modify the template for each specific project.

FYI: According to a survey of the members of the UDS Program Task Team at the time, the horizontal text format is the most commonly used title block format used by architectural firms and it was selected as the NCS preferred title block format.

In determining the most appropriate **compliant** title block design for the workplace, there are important factors to consider. Even though NCS format requirements should be followed, some of them are flexible enough to allow a substantial amount of personalization. Following is a list of some of the key issues to consider when designing the title block:

- Title blocks must extend vertically along the entire right-hand margin of the sheet.
- There are no minimum or maximum width requirements for the title block.
- The order, or sequence, of the data blocks cannot be altered.
- The orientation of the data blocks cannot be altered.
- There are no minimum or maximum size requirements for the data blocks.

Many architects will have predetermined the style they want to use (horizontal text format or vertical text format) before they begin the title block design process. This may not be the best approach, however, because each style has unique features worth considering. In addition to project and client requirements, some of the key influences on the title block design will include the following:

- Most frequently used sheet size(s)
- Module size
- Margin size
- Note block size
- Drawing area size

Even though the NCS does not impose minimum or maximum width requirements, we have found the following widths to be the most practical.

- Vertical text format: 2–1/2″ maximum width
- Horizontal text format: 4″ maximum width

Once a style has been selected, the sizes of the data blocks can be adjusted to accommodate the individual requirements of each workplace. Figures 2-7 and 2-8 show examples of both formats for the title block area. Each figure shows an example of a title block area defined by a borderline and a title block area defined by an implied border.

Designer Identification Block

The designer identification block is always located at the top of the title block area. Its purpose is to identify the designer or preparer of the sheet. Each jurisdiction and licensing board for every discipline may have requirements for the designer identification that must appear on each sheet. Examples of the requirements include the firm's legal name, address, and telephone number.

The designer identification may include only the designer identification for the preparing firm or that of the entire project team. If the entire project team is included, the architect should coordinate with the other team members to ensure that all legally required identification information by other licensing boards of each discipline are included in the designer identification block.

The designer identification block is also where professional seals are located, specifically at the bottom of the designer identification block. Some jurisdictions may require a corporate seal for professional corporations in addition to the individual professional seal. The designer identification block should take into consideration this requirement, depending on the region of practice of the firm. When the preparer of the sheet is not required to be a licensed design professional, the professional seal portion of the designer identification area should be omitted or left blank.

Other information is often included in the designer identification block, such as firm logos, e-mail addresses, website addresses, and fax numbers. Figure 2-9 provides an example of the designer identification block.

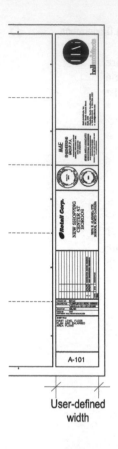

understanding the most appropriate coordinate to likely desire... here are important things to consider. ... such as NCS panel setups serve us all for a general work or down to more smooth headings... complete alignment if the properties of the subsystems to conform when designing... the entity plan.

- You all may must extend... ... ...
- You also to undertake the... ... if it turns to...
- The other to complete all the... each have to be equal...

User-defined width

User-defined width

FIGURE 2-7
Examples of Vertical Text Format

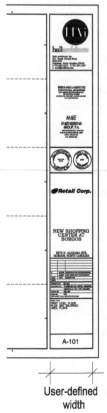

User-defined width

User-defined width

FIGURE 2-8
Examples of Horizontal Text Format

34

Match width of title block

User-defined

Location:	Must appear at the top of the title block.
Orientation:	Horizontal or vertical (match orientation of project identification and issue blocks).

Figure 2-9
Designer Identification Block

Project Identification Block

The project identification block is the portion of the title block area allocated for the identification of the project, owner, and client. The requirements for information in this data block are project- or client-dependent and may include project and owner logos. Many architectural firms tend to provide additional space in the title block area for this data block. Figure 2-10 is an example of the project identification block.

Issue Block

The issue block is the portion of the title block area allocated to tracking the history of the sheet from the issuance date through construction. The hierarchy of information within the issue block is inverted with the initial issue of the sheet on the bottom, with subsequent issues located from

Match width of title block

◢ Retail Corp.

User-defined

NEW SHOPPING
CENTER AT
BORGOS

9876 N. ALABAMA STR.
BORGOS, NORTH CAROLINA

Location: Must appear at the top of the title block.

Orientation: Horizontal or vertical (match orientation
              of project identification and issue blocks).

Figure 2-10
Project Identification Block

bottom to top, and the last or current issue at the top of the list. The issue block consists of three columns with headings entitled, "Mark," "Date," and "Description." "Mark" is a sequential numbering of the issue; "Date" is the date of the issue; and "Description" is the description or reason for the issuing or reissuing of the sheet. An example of an issue block is provided in Figure 2-11.

Management Block

The management block is the portion of the title block area allocated to the architect for placement of sheet management information. This information may include the architect's project number, CAD file, copyright, "drawn by," and so on. Owners sometimes require information be placed in each title block that should be located in the management block; this may include an owner project number and owner approvals. Figure 2-12 illustrates a typical management block.

Sheet Title Block

The sheet title block is the portion of the title block area allocated for the identification of the sheet title. Often, the title of the sheet is based on the drawing view such as "First-Floor Plan" or "Exterior Elevations." The UDS Drawing Set Organization Module indicates that all drawing types are to be clearly identified in the sheet title block. In conflict to this, the UDS Sheet Orga-

ISSUE		
MARK	DATE	DESCRIPTION
1	9/29/04	100% CONSTRUCTION DOCUMENTS
2	3/10/05	CONSTRUCTION RECORD DRAWINGS

User-defined

FIGURE 2-11
Issue Block

Location: Must appear beneath the project identification block.

Orientation: Horizontal or vertical (match orientation of designer identification and project identification blocks).

nization Module indicates that sheet title block may include only the major type of information shown on the sheet, or may indicate the multiple type of information. We anticipate this error being corrected in the next NCS update; until then, our recommendation is that when a sheet contains multiple drawing types, it is better to title the sheet after the most prominent drawing, rather than list each type. Remember, this is the title that will also appear in the Owner-Contractor Agreement, and long titles may not be advantageous. Figure 2-13 provides an example of the sheet title block.

Sheet Identification Block

The sheet identification block is that portion of the title block area allocated for the location of the sheet identifier, which is more commonly known as the sheet number. Standard sheet identification is discussed in Chapter 1. Figure 2-14 shows two typical sheet identification blocks, one with the title block defined by a borderline and the other with the title block area defined by an implied border.

Some firms include a sheet count in their sheet identification block so that each sheet is provided with a unique, sequential number, similar to pages in a book. This can be a useful tool to help reprographics companies and other drawing users keep the sheets in the proper order. It can also help to ensure team members are, literally, "on the same page" during telephone conferences. However, including sheet counts requires additional time and coordination, and frequently results in last-minute, CAD or handwritten changes prior to issuance. Another option is to base

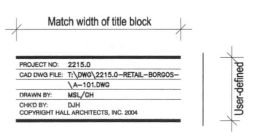

Match width of title block

PROJECT NO:	2215.0
CAD DWG FILE:	T:\DWG\2215.0—RETAIL—BORGOS—\A—101.DWG
DRAWN BY:	MSL/GH
CHK'D BY:	DJH
COPYRIGHT HALL ARCHITECTS, INC. 2004	

User-defined

FIGURE 2-12
Management Block

Location: Must appear beneath issue block.

Orientation: Always horizontal

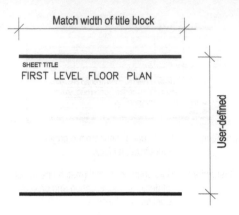

Location: Must appear beneath management block

Orientation: Always horizontal

Figure 2-13
Sheet Title Block

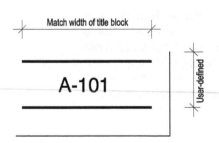

Location: Must appear beneath management block

Orientation: Always horizontal

Figure 2-14
Sheet Identification Block

sheet count by discipline, rather than on the entire drawing set, though this typically does not assist in providing a benchmark in an entire set. An example of sheet count is "X of Y," where X is the sequential sheet count and Y is the total number of sheets in the discipline set.

Given the potential problems associated with including a sheet count with the sheet identification data block, we recommend that firms evaluate the need for this information in your practice. We believe most firms will find that the disadvantages outweigh the advantages and will choose to only include the sheet identification in this data block.

Production Data Area

The production data area is an optional area on the drawing sheet where the architect can locate information about the production of the sheet. The production data area is located in the binding margin. Most commonly, this area is used to identify the sheet plot date and time. This information can be very useful when reviewing hard copy sheets. Other information that may be included in the production data area includes the file path, pen settings, production hours, graphic scanning scale, and so on. If you chose to use the production data area, our recommendation is, keep it simple. An electronic file path and plotting date/time is usually very helpful; after that, the "less is more" adage applies.

SUPPLEMENTAL DRAWING SHEETS

Supplemental drawing sheets, sometimes called "bulletin drawings," are small-format sheets most often used to present graphic information as a part of a detail book, addendum, clarification, or modification. The most common sizes for supplemental drawing sheets are 8–1/2″ × 11″ and 11″ × 17″, as previously discussed in this chapter.

Supplemental drawing sheets have a minimum practical margin of 1/2″ on three sides, with 3/4″ on the binding side. The title block area must contain all six data blocks in the hierarchy as used on standard sheets; however, the design of the sheet is generally left up to the architect.

We recommend that the supplemental drawing sheet use the vertical text format and include only one drawing in the drawing area. Vertical text format will typically conserve space on supplemental drawing sheets, allowing the most efficient use of the space. By incorporating more than one drawing onto a supplemental drawing sheet, readability may be compromised and require additional clarification. Figure 2-15 is an example of two supplemental drawing sheets, one with the drawing area and title block area defined with a borderline and the other with the drawing area and title block defined with implied borders.

MOCK-UP SHEETS

To help organize cover sheets, General sheets, and the architectural discipline set, architects often use a mock-up set, also known as a "mini-set" or "cartoon set." Our survey shows that mock-up sets are rarely used by engineers, but are frequently created by architects in the Design Development Phase or early stages of the Construction Documents Phase of a project. To assist in the preparation of the mock-up set, many firms use scaled versions of their drawing sheets to create mock-up sheet templates on ANSI A size (8–1/2″ × 11″) and B size (11″ × 17″) sheets. It is also popular to use 1/2 size sheets for mock-up sheets because they are easier to scale. Therefore, a 24″ × 36″ sheet would be mocked-up on a 12″ × 18″ sheet (Architectural B size sheet) or a 30″ × 42″ sheet would be mocked-up on a 15″ × 21″ sheet. Note that the 15″ × 21″ sheet is a custom size; and therefore we recommend placing the image on an Architectural C size sheet (18″ × 24″) if it is more practical. When creating mock-up sheet templates, we also recommend including the column and row identifiers of the drawing area coordinate system. Include the drawing modules with light or dashed lines. This will provide a fast and accurate means to

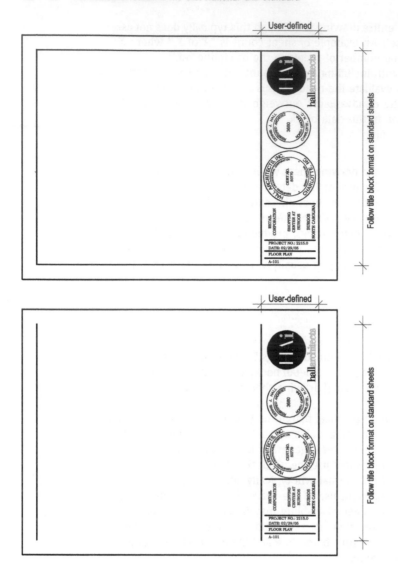

FIGURE 2-15
Examples of Supplemental Drawing Sheet

determine the space needed for standard details, note blocks, and other drawings, as well as a means to identify drawing blocks.

The NCS provides a scaling factor to convert the final drawing scale to a scale appropriate to the mock-up sheet. The architect hand-sketches the drawings on the mock-up sheets and assigns sheet titles and sheet identification. This process makes it easier for more than one person to work on the sheets within a single discipline set; and by indicating which drawings will be the responsibility of each person assigned a drawing sheet, this also encourages coordination. As new drawings or sheets are determined to be necessary for the project, these may be included in the mock-up set to assist in sheet and set organization and keep track of the completion of the final drawing sheets. Once an architect is familiar with this process, the mock-up set is also a valuable tool in estimating production hours, determining progress, and identifying possible scope creep. Figure 2-16 shows an example of two standard mock-up sheets, one with the drawing area and title block area defined by a borderline and the other with the drawing area and title block area defined by implied borders.

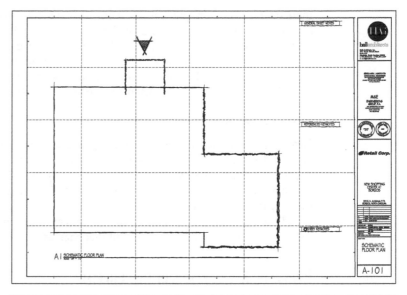

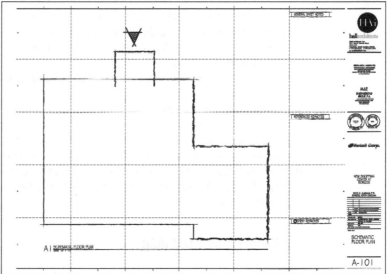

FIGURE 2-16
Mock-up Sheet

IMPLEMENTATION ISSUES

The UDS Sheet Organization Module needs to be one of the earliest NCS components to be adopted by a firm, because it will serve as the foundation from which to incorporate many of the other components later in the NCS adoption process. We recommend incorporating it after establishing format requirements for other NCS components such as those in the UDS Drawing Set Organization Module, the AIA CAD Layer Guidelines, and the Tri-Service Plotting Guidelines. (For more on the implementation process, see Chapter 11, "Implementation.")

In most cases, the biggest challenge will be determining which of the two formats for compliant title blocks (horizontal or vertical text formats) is most appropriate to adopt. Many organizations designed their title block years ago, and consider it to be one of the key elements giving their documents a unique identity. Thus, it is understandable that adopting one of the required formats that "everyone else is using" may be a hard pill to swallow; however, once it is understood that company names, logos, and other elements can still provide a unique appearance, the transition process should be a little easier. It has been our experience that once adopted and established as the standard, most firms will look back at the title block adoption process and wonder why so much time was wasted in resisting the change.

Layers and Pen Widths

Layers and pen widths used to create sheet components such as title blocks, note blocks, margins, and the sheet coordinate system should be established in accordance with the AIA CAD Layer Guidelines, U.S. National CAD Standard version 3.0, and the UDS Drafting Conventions Module. The examples in Appendix E can be treated as guidelines for CAD layer names used for these types of sheet components.

Additional information related to the implementation process is located in the Frequently Asked Questions section at the end of this chapter, as well as Chapter 11.

REVIEW OF KEY CONCEPTS IN THIS CHAPTER

1. The rules for sheet organization are flexible enough to allow the creation of personalized title blocks that will be unique to each workplace.
2. Format requirements for cover sheets are unique and dependent upon the project information included on them.
3. Determining the most appropriate NCS-compliant title block is dependent upon the unique requirements of each workplace.
4. There are no size requirements for title blocks; however, their optimum size will usually be determined by the sheet size, margins, and drawing module sizes.
5. Data blocks in the title block area must appear in the required order. However, their size can be adjusted as needed, though they must remain consistent throughout the drawing set.
6. The UDS Sheet Organization Module should be one of the earliest components to adopt during the implementation process because it will help streamline adoption of other NCS components.

FREQUENTLY ASKED QUESTIONS

Q: *Which of the two title block formats is better, vertical text format or horizontal text format?*

A: The UDS Sheet Organization Module states that horizontal text format is the most commonly used. It also states it is the *preferred* format. However, in some instances it may not be the *best* format. Even though horizontal format makes it easy to read drawing titles in rolled-up sets, the format typically requires more drawing space than the vertical format. The drawing area in smaller sheets is precious, and the extra width usually required for the horizontal style will have an impact on the space needed for the drawing area. If maximizing the drawing area is a concern, the vertical text format may be a better choice. Firms may wish to have sheets with both formats and select the most appropriate format for each project. However, do not combine formats within the drawing set.

Q: *Are the alphabetic characters used to identify rows of the drawing area coordinate system along the right-hand side of the drawing area required? Won't they just clutter up the drawing blocks or otherwise get confused with notation text?*

A: The UDS Sheet Organization Module requires the row and column identifiers be placed on the right-hand side and the top or bottom of the drawing area (it is preferred to have them appear on all four sides of the drawing area). The preferred locations for the coordinate characters are *outside* the drawing area—except they must be placed within the drawing area on the right-hand side if the sheet design causes a conflict with the title block area.

To minimize conflicts, use a text height of at least 1/4" and a pen width of 0.50 mm for the characters. This will differentiate them from other text in the drawing area, most of which is created with smaller fonts and thinner pens. In addition, as users become more familiar with the sheet format throughout the set, the row identifiers on the right-hand side of the sheet will become less of a problem. That said, if the row identifiers on the right side of the drawing area conflict too much with text and graphics in the drawing area, we recommend removing them, and only including row identifiers on the left side of the sheet. Don't forget: drawings used for schematic design do not need to be provided with coordinates.

Q: *Which drawing module size works best?*

A: Since the release of NCS version 2.0, sizes for drawing modules can be user-defined, as long as the size is the same on all the sheets in the drawing set. In determining the best size to use, consider the following:

1. Which is the most frequently used sheet size in the workplace?
2. Which size is needed for the most frequently used drawings in the workplace's standard detail library?
3. How much space is required for the sheet's title block?
4. How much space is required for the sheet's note block?

In many workplaces, the majority of the projects are designed based on one or two sheet sizes. The best module size will be the one that can accommodate the most frequently used details on each of the most frequently used sheet sizes. For example, if the two most commonly used sheets are D size (24" × 36") and F size (30" × 42"), look at a module size that will work for both. In this situation, if the layout of the sheets meets the following criteria, a similar module size will work for both:

D Size Sheets (24" × 36")
Left margin: 1.5"
Top, bottom, and right margins: 0.5"
Title block width (vertical text format): 2.0"
Note block width: Match module width
Module size: 6.4" wide × 5.75" high

F Size Sheets (30" × 42")
Left margin: 1.5"
Top, bottom, and right margins: 0.5"
Title block width (vertical text format): 2.0"
Note block width: Match module width
Module size: 6.33" wide × 5.8" high

In this example, the margins and/or the title block dimensions of one of the sheet sizes can be adjusted slightly so the modules are exactly the same for both sheet sizes. However, this is usually not necessary because the modules for both sheet sizes are so similar the majority of standard details used in the workplace will not need to be modified to accommodate either sheet.

Q: *Is the drawing block title symbol required for a drawing block that takes up the entire drawing area?*

A: The drawing block for views such as site plans and floor plans are often large enough to consume all of the modules within a sheet's drawing area. Even though there may be only one drawing block on the sheet, the UDS requires drawing blocks to be identified using the drawing coordinate system. These drawing blocks are identified as A1 since their lower left-hand corner is located in the lower left-hand module of the drawing area.

Q: *The title block in our workplace does not comply with the NCS. Are there any exceptions to the format requirements for vertical or horizontal text title blocks?*

A: Even though there is quite a bit of room for creativity in either of the two styles, adopting one of the title block formats can be a huge stumbling block for many firms adopting the NCS. There are no exceptions in the standard: one of the two formats must be used to be compliant. Including company logos and similar features will provide most firms with an acceptable compromise.

Q: *Since the most frequently used drawing block is located at the* lower right-hand side *of the drawing area, why is A1, the origin point of the drawing area coordinate system, located at the* lower left-hand side *of the sheet?*

A: During the development of the UDS Sheet Organization Module, pros and cons of potential origin points were investigated. The lower left-hand corner had at least two good arguments: (1) It is consistent with the 0,0 origin point used in CAD software; and (2) a drawing block taking up the entire sheet, such as a site plan, is identified as A1. However, when weighed against arguments for some of the other locations, it is probably fair to say the decision to locate the origin point at the lower left-hand corner was arbitrary.

Q: *Is it okay to locate legends in the note block?*

A: No. According to the UDS Sheet Organization Module, the only other information allowed in a note block is a key plan block, which must be located at the bottom of the note block. When space is available and the width of the legend does not need to exceed the width of the note block, we recommend locating legends *below* the note block, within their own border. Like schedules, legends should also be laid out to coordinate with the size of the sheet's module size. These strategies will result in more useful space in the sheet's drawing area (See Chapter 3, "Schedules," for examples of these types of legends).

Q: *Where do I put a key plan if the sheet doesn't have a note block?*

A: Key plan blocks, when used, must be located in the lowest module of the note block. Note blocks, when used, must be located at the right-hand side of the drawing area. If the sheet doesn't have a note block, pretend it does, and locate it in the lowest right-hand module in the drawing area.

Q: *Can the "Mark" column in the issue block of the title block area be left blank for the first issuance of the drawing set? If not, what gets put there?*

A: The NCS does not require anything to be put in the "Mark" column the first time the drawing set is issued—the space can either be left blank or sometimes is provided with the initials "NA" for "not applicable." However, the date and description blocks must always be identified.

Q: *What is the difference between a cover sheet and a title sheet?*

A: Cover sheet is the correct name as used in the UDS Sheet Organization Module for the first sheet in the drawing set though it is frequently called the title sheet, which is the slang term.

Schedules

GENERAL

Schedules are often a common method of communicating construction information used by architects in both the graphic and written construction documents. As such, the architect has the responsibility to identify the types of schedules that need to be used in each type of construction document, their content, as well as their appearance, and the location of the construction information within the construction documents. The coordination of this information falls within the responsibility of the architect's role. The U.S. National CAD Standard assists in providing a format for this information whether located in the drawings or the specifications.

The U.S. National CAD Standard (NCS) format requirements for schedules used in construction documents are located in the Schedules Module of the Construction Specification Institute's (CSI) Uniform Drawing System (UDS). This module was one of three UDS modules to be included in the first version of the NCS, released in 1999. Since its debut, the module has been subjected to only a few revisions, resulting from NCS updates, and, overall, the current standard is very similar to the original. The UDS Schedules Module also provides guidelines for locating schedules in construction documents and includes **legends, keys,** and **indexes,** which are close relatives of schedules.

GENERAL FORMAT REQUIREMENTS FOR SCHEDULES

The UDS Schedules Module establishes format requirements for schedules located in both drawings and specifications. The most notable revisions that have been made to the module since its release in 1999 are the results of the publication of two standards that occurred after it was originally issued:

- UDS Terms and Abbreviations Module
- MasterFormat 2004

> **FYI:** NCS version 2.0 included a CD-ROM containing ready-to-use schedules, in both CAD and word processing formats. However, the CD-ROM was discontinued after NCS version 2.0 because of the costs associated with updating it for future NCS versions.

The changes these two documents caused are significant, but like many of the other requirements in the UDS Schedules Module, they are straightforward and not overwhelming. The specific impact they had on NCS-compliancy issues will be discussed later in this chapter.

To comply with NCS requirements, schedules must contain all four of the following components:

- **Heading** (subject title)
- **Mark** (column identifying an item)

THE MARK COLUMN
LISTS EACH ITEM WITH
AN ALPHANUMERIC OR
GRAPHIC RELATED TO
THE ITEM (REQUIRED)

THE HEADING DESCRIBES THE
MAIN SUBJECT OR TITLE OF A
SCHEDULE (REQUIRED)

THE DISTINGUISHING FEATURE
COLUMN IDENTIFIES
CHARACTERISTICS
ABOUT THE ITEM (REQUIRED)

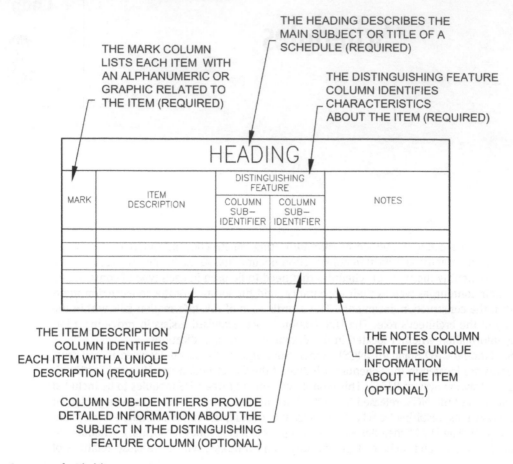

THE ITEM DESCRIPTION
COLUMN IDENTIFIES
EACH ITEM WITH A UNIQUE
DESCRIPTION (REQUIRED)

COLUMN SUB-IDENTIFIERS PROVIDE
DETAILED INFORMATION ABOUT THE
SUBJECT IN THE DISTINGUISHING
FEATURE COLUMN (OPTIONAL)

THE NOTES COLUMN
IDENTIFIES UNIQUE
INFORMATION
ABOUT THE ITEM
(OPTIONAL)

FIGURE 3-1   Components of a Schedule

- **Item description** (column describing the item)
- **Distinguishing feature(s)** (column identifying notable characteristics)

Most schedules also include a fifth feature, the **notes column.** Refer to Figure 3-1 for an illustration that demonstrates the location of each component of a schedule.

Most schedules will be more complex than the example in Figure 3-1, in that they will contain more columns to identify distinguishing features; and, often, they are expanded even further by dividing a single column into a single tier of subcolumns, known as **column subidentifiers.** In more complex schedules, column subidentifiers can be further subdivided into a third tier of column subidentifiers. Figure 3-2 illustrates an example of more complex schedules, with second- and third-tier column subidentifiers.

The graphic requirements for different types of schedules are illustrated in Appendix B of the UDS Schedules Module, which presents a few examples of how different types of schedules might appear. The examples, however, represent a limited number of disciplines because the intent is only to demonstrate general format techniques and organizational principles. Thus, each of the examples should be considered a template for *all* the disciplines, which can then be modified to meet the user's needs.

FYI: Formerly, the preferred location for schedules that include information from multiple specification sections within the same division was on the drawings. But once MasterFormat 2004 was incorporated into NCS version 3.1, these types of schedules could be located in appropriate locations in the project manual.

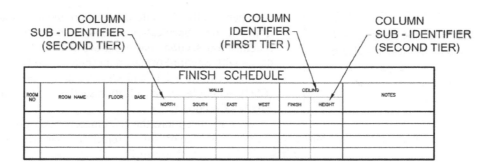

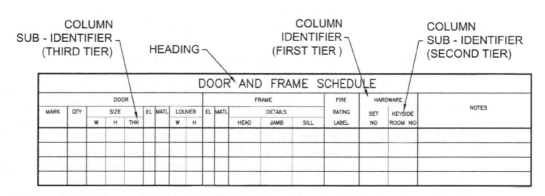

FIGURE 3-2 Examples of More Complex Schedules

LOCATING SCHEDULES IN THE CONSTRUCTION DOCUMENTS

The NCS provides requirements for schedules located in the drawings and in the specifications. Deciding on where to locate them will depend on the needs of the project, but in many cases it is simply a matter of personal preference (user-defined). To help determine if one location may be more advantageous than another, the following criteria should be considered:

- *Use:* Which location will be better suited for those creating the schedules and for those using them? Creating and editing schedules containing detail references or other drawing-related information will usually be easier to coordinate if located on the drawings, rather than the specifications.
- *Cost:* Which location requires the fewest man-hours to create and edit (CAD-related man-hours versus word processing-related man-hours)? Word processing costs will usually be less than costs associated with CAD.
- *Product type:* Will information on products or materials from more than one specification division be included in the schedule? If so, they should be located on the drawings. Even though we recommend locating schedules with products from more than one specification section (within the same division) on the drawings, they can be included in the project manual in accordance with MasterFormat 2004, if desired.
- *Available space:* Can the layout of the schedule be situated within the page size of the project manual without affecting legibility? Many schedules need to be located on the drawings simply because they will not fit on letter-size pages (8–1/2″ × 11″).

> **FYI:** The original UDS Schedules Module that was incorporated into NCS version 1.0 included noncompliant abbreviations, because the UDS Terms and Abbreviations Module had not been written yet. They were later corrected when the module was updated and republished in NCS version 3.1.

> **FYI:** The MasterFormat 2004 Level 2 number, 06, which is used to determine locations for schedules in the project manual, is based upon the UDS sheet type designator, 6, for Schedules and Diagrams.

Schedules that include information about products or materials from only one specification section can be located at the end of the specification section that describes the work involved. In accordance with **SectionFormat,** published by the Construction Specifications Institute (CSI) and **Construction Specifications Canada (CSC),** schedules in specification sections are located at the end of Part 3—Execution.

Since its inception, the NCS incorporated principles from MasterFormat, the numbering system that is used to organize project manuals. The original NCS components were based upon the 1995 edition of MasterFormat. In 2004, CSI/CSC released an updated version of the document, which contained some significant changes. When NCS version 3.1 was released in 2004, the update included revisions that were a result of changes between the MasterFormat 1995 and MasterFormat 2004. The UDS Schedules Module was impacted in some very positive and significant ways by the revised format requirements. To understand how MasterFormat 2004 affected schedules-related implementation issues, a general understanding of MasterFormat 2004 format requirements is necessary.

MasterFormat 2004 established a six-digit or eight-digit numbering structure for organizing the project manual. The numbers are grouped in pairs, with each pair representing one level of classification. The first two digits represent the Level 1 division number, the second two digits represent the Level 2 number, and the third two digits represent the Level 3 number. When an additional level of detail is required, a Level 4 number is also available, which features an additional pair of digits, preceded by a "dot." Figure 3-3 illustrates the organizational principles of the format.

MasterFormat 2004 now includes specific locations for schedules containing products or materials from multiple specification sections within the same division. For example, 06 in Level 2, or the second pair of numbers, provides the location for any schedules within that division. Therefore, schedules for concrete materials would be located in specification section 03 06 00. As locations for more specific types of concrete are needed, Level 3 and Level 4 numbers can be used. When schedules containing information from multiple specification sections have to be located in the specifications, MasterFormat 2004 must be used as a resource to determine the proper location. Some typical examples of locations for schedules in the project manual are provided in Figure 3-4. (For more on the numbering structure and the required specification section numbers for the location of schedules, refer to MasterFormat 2004.)

Even the simplest schedule requires adequate layout space. The cells formed by the columns and rows need to be large enough so that all the text located in them is legible. Quite often, the area needed to accommodate the schedule exceeds that which is available on a standard 8–1/2″ × 11″ specification page. Reducing the scale of many types of schedules to fit the page size often results in poor readability. Therefore, when the size of the schedule requires a greater area than can be made available on the project manual page, locate it on the drawings, in the appropriate discipline set, on the sheet type designator 6-series (Schedules and Diagrams) sheets.

MASTERFORMAT NUMBERS			MASTERFORMAT TITLES
LEVEL 1	08 00 00		OPENINGS
LEVEL 2	08 11 00		METAL DOORS AND FRAMES
LEVEL 3	08 11 13		HOLLOW METAL DOORS AND FRAMES
LEVEL 4	08 11 13.16		CUSTOM HOLLOW METAL DOORS AND FRAMES

FIGURE 3-3
MasterFormat Numbering Structure

	SPECIFICATION
SECTION NUMBER	SCHEDULE NAME
09 06 00.13	ROOM FINISH SCHEDULE
11 06 50	LAB EQUIPMENT SCHEDULE
12 06 30.13	CASEWORK SCHEDULE
22 06 40.13	PLUMBING FIXTURE SCHEDULE
26 06 50.16	LIGHTING FIXTURE SCHEDULE
32 06 90.13	PLANTING SCHEDULE

MASTERFORMAT
NUMBER

FIGURE 3-4
Examples of Locations for Schedules
in the Specifications

Locating Schedules in the Drawing Set

Schedules can appear in just about any discipline within the drawing set. In order to determine the best location within the discipline, the following issues must be analyzed:

- What types of schedules are needed?
- What size will be required for each schedule?
- Will all schedules be located on sheet type designator 6-series (Schedules and Diagrams) sheets?
- Where on the sheet will the schedule be located?

The types of schedules needed are determined by the discipline and project type. Most firms can identify each type quite easily, based upon past experience with projects of similar nature. Templates from the standard detail library are the best resource for determining schedule size (width × height). Usually, the width of the template will remain constant from project to project because the items and features in them do not change. The height is determined simply by identifying the number of rows needed. Once the general sizes of the schedules are known, the **mock-up drawing set** can be used to determine the most appropriate locations for them in the discipline set. (For more information about the mock-up drawing set, see Chapter 4, "Drafting Conventions.") Requirements for locating schedules in the drawing set are quite flexible. In general, they are usually located on Schedules and Diagrams (6-series) sheets. In accordance with the UDS Drawing Set Organization Module, these could include sheets such as:

- S-601 (Structural schedules and diagrams)
- A-601 (Architectural schedules and diagrams)
- E-601 (Electrical schedules and diagrams)

Locating schedules and **diagrams** on sheets other than the Schedules and Diagrams (6-series) sheets is also allowed. Combining them with other drawing types is often very beneficial, especially on smaller projects because it can help reduce the number of sheets in the drawing set. (For more information about combining different drawing types on the same sheet, see Chapter 1, "Drawing Set Organization.")

Use of a mock-up drawing set will streamline the decision-making process for locating schedules in the discipline set and will help to identify their locations within each sheet's drawing area. This effort will determine how many sheet type designator 6-series (Schedules and Diagrams) sheets will be needed for all the schedules. More importantly, this process would determine whether one or more sheets could be deleted from the set if the schedules were combined on the same sheet with other drawings (views).

Determining the best locations for schedules in the drawing set will depend on a variety of factors. Some of these include:

- Is there a compelling reason to locate all schedules within the set on sheet type designator 6-series (Schedules and Diagrams) sheets only? Is it important to the client or other drawing users?
- Which is more important, locating all schedules on sheet type designator 6-series (Schedules and Diagrams) sheets or minimizing the quantity of sheets in the drawing set?
- Would combining a schedule with other drawing types make the drawing set easier or more difficult to use?

If locating a schedule on a sheet other than the Schedules and Diagrams (6-series) sheets is desired, the first priority must be to locate it on a sheet in the same discipline set. The second priority is to include it on a sheet that contains information related to the schedule, if possible. The following are some typical examples of locating schedules on sheets other than the sheet type designator 6-series (Schedules and Diagrams) sheets:

- Footing pad schedule: Locate on sheet S-101 with the foundation plan.
- Room finish schedule: Locate on sheet A-101 with the floor plan.
- Lighting fixture schedule: Locate on sheet E-102 with the lighting plan.

Sometimes, combining a schedule with other drawings on the same sheet is desired in order to reduce the sheet count of a particular discipline set. If the schedule cannot be located on a sheet containing related information, it can be placed on any sheet, as long as it is located on a sheet from the same discipline. For example, a plumbing fixture schedule could be located on a Plumbing discipline (P-series) sheet such as P-001 or P-501. Combining schedules on sheets with unrelated drawing types is not the ideal scenario, but it can often help conserve resources and keep the quantity of sheets in the drawing set to a minimum.

Whenever a schedule is included on the same sheet with other drawing types, the UDS Drawing Set Organization Module requires the names of the different drawings to be included in the sheet title block. The following are some examples of how the titles of these types of sheets could appear:

- S-101: Foundation Plan and Footing Pad Schedule
- A-101: Floor Plan and Room Finish Schedule
- E-102: Lighting Plan and Lighting Fixture Schedule

Please note, however, that the UDS Sheet Organization Module indicates the sheet title block may include only the major type of information shown on the sheet. For more information on this conflict, see Chapter 2, "Sheet Organization." For an example of combining schedules on the same sheet with other drawings, refer to Figure 3-5.

Another strategy that will help reduce the number of sheets in the drawing set is to include other types of drawings on the Schedules and Diagrams (6-series) sheets, such as S-601, A-602, M-601, and so on. When considering this option, the first priority should be to combine drawings and schedules that are related to each other. For example, door and frame details can be combined on the same sheet with a door and frame schedule (such as sheet A-601). In addition to helping save space, this approach often enables users to locate a detail referenced from the schedule a little faster. For an example of combining other drawings on a sheet type designator 6-series (Schedules and Diagrams) sheet, refer to Figure 3-6. The NCS also includes more infor-

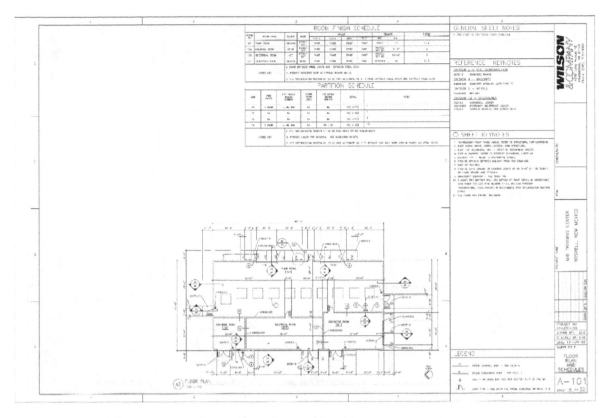

FIGURE 3-5   Combining Schedules on Sheets with Other Types of Drawings

mation on this topic in the "Sheet Type 6—Schedules and Diagrams" article near the end of the UDS Drafting Conventions Module.

Locating Schedules in the Drawing Area

Once a sheet has been identified for a schedule location, during the creation of the mock-up drawing set, a decision must be made with regard to its location on the sheet. To determine where to locate a schedule in the sheet's drawing area, the most important factors to consider are:

- What is the most important drawing on the sheet?
- How many drawing modules will the schedule require?
- Will the location allow for expansion if additional rows need to be added later?

Once a general location for a schedule has been determined within the drawing set, follow these guidelines to locate the schedule within the sheet's drawing area, in accordance with NCS requirements:

- Size schedules to fill the entire drawing module(s). Stretch or enlarge the schedule as needed to avoid using only a part of the module(s).
- When border(s) of a schedule will be located adjacent to one of the borders of the sheet, abut the edge of the schedule tight against the border. Do not allow any space to occur between the border of the sheet and the border of the schedule.

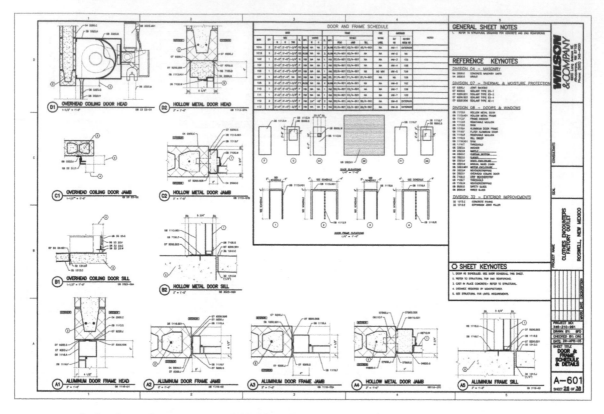

FIGURE 3-6 Example of Combining Other Drawing Types with Schedules and Diagrams (6-Series) Sheets

- When border(s) of a schedule will be located adjacent to a border of another schedule, abut the borders of the schedules tight against each other. Do not allow any space to occur between the borders.

Figure 3-7 provides an example of how schedules should be located within the drawing area.

Determining Drawing Hierarchy for Schedules

In accordance with the UDS Drafting Conventions Module, the most frequently referenced drawing is to be located in the drawing area at the lowest drawing module adjacent to the title block area or note block. Other drawings are then added to the drawing area from bottom to top and from right to left. This concept is based on the premise that unused space in the drawing area should be located on the left side of the sheet and at the top of the sheet so that drawings are easier to view in bound sets. That said, this concept doesn't always work quite as easily when it comes to schedules.

According to the NCS, if a sheet contains a schedule, its location in the drawing area should be prioritized the same as other types of drawings. That is, the most frequently referenced schedule (if there is one) should be placed in the lowest right-hand drawing module; additional schedules would be placed above the first one, working from bottom to top and from right to left. The problem with this approach is that schedules are unique, and there are good reasons to begin locating them at the highest right-hand drawing module instead. One of the best arguments is that, as the drawing set evolves, rows are often added to schedules and space beneath them is needed

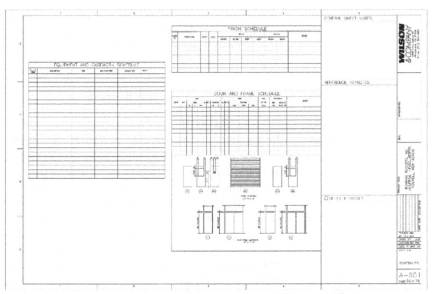

SCHEDULES NOT ABUTTING MODULES OR EACH OTHER

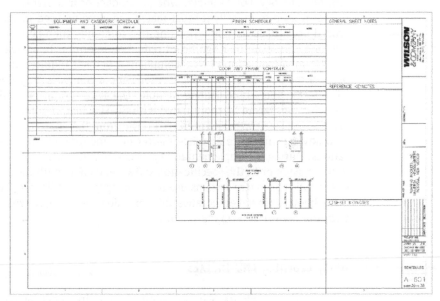

FIGURE 3-7
Locating Schedules in the
Drawing Area

PROPER LAYOUT OF SCHEDULES

for expansion. Another is that additional diagrams such as door and frame elevations (commonly located beneath schedules) may be added. Sometimes a notes legend is located at the bottom of the schedule and it may need to expand to accommodate more notes. If these issues are a concern, we recommend locating the schedules at the top of the sheet so that the space beneath them can be used for expansion later, if needed.

Another situation regarding drawing hierarchy occurs when a schedule is included on a sheet with other drawing types. However, in this situation, the most frequently referenced drawing may not be the schedule. For example, if a schedule is combined on a sheet with a floor plan, the floor plan will usually be referenced more frequently, and therefore it should be located in the bottom right-hand corner of the sheet. The room finish schedule can then be located either above the plan or to the left of it, depending on the available space. For an example of drawing hierarchy on a sheet with combined drawing types, refer back to Figure 3-5.

COORDINATING SCHEDULES WITH SPECIFICATIONS

In accordance with AIA A201-1997 General Conditions of the Contract for Construction, the construction documents are complementary. That is, they are to be considered as one. Therefore, in situations where conflicting information occurs between the drawings and the specifications, neither one prevails over the other. A conflict between the drawings and the specifications is no different from a conflict between one drawing and another or between two different specification sections. In these situations, the architect is required to make an interpretation and issue it to the contractor. To help avoid these situations, the specifier must work closely with the design team and come to agreement on the wording, or terms, to be used throughout the set of documents. This includes the terms that will be used in the schedules. To meet the requirements of the NCS, terms in schedules must comply with the UDS Terms and Abbreviations Module. The NCS refers to noncompliant terms as nonpreferred terms; compliant terms are referred to as preferred terms.

To avoid conflicts, a properly coordinated set of construction documents will contain consistent terminology. For example, when a product or material is being referenced in the drawings, the term used to identify it must match the wording used in the specifications. This concept is crucial because consistent terms improve communication between the various users of the drawings and will result in a significant reduction in errors. To ensure consistency between the documents, implementation of NCS-compliant schedules requires an examination of the terms being used in the schedules and specifications and a comparison of them to their counterparts in the UDS Terms and Abbreviations Module. Updating the terms in the specifications with those in the schedules has to be coordinated with the specifier. If nonpreferred terms are discovered, they must be replaced with the preferred terms from the NCS.

Many specifiers use an office master or some form of specification software to create specifications. During the implementation process, it is very common to discover that some of the terms in the master, or in the specification software, conflict with those in the NCS. For example, some specification software systems use the term "gypsum wallboard," which is often included in a Finish Schedule. However, because this term does not comply with the NCS, it should be replaced with the preferred term, "gypsum board."

KEYS, LEGENDS, AND INDEXES

As illustrated in Figure 3-1, the minimum requirements for NCS schedules include a heading (subject title), and three columns for the mark (column identifying an item), item description (column describing the item), and distinguishing feature (column identifying notable characteristics).

A schedule containing a list of items containing fewer than these four components is not a schedule. Instead, it is a legend, a key, or an index. Typical examples of these close cousins of schedules include the following:

- List of sheets
- Symbols legend
- Keyed notes (reference keynotes and sheet keynotes)

Locations for these types of lists can vary, depending on the information they contain and the discipline or drawing sheets to which they apply. It is important to coordinate the lists to avoid

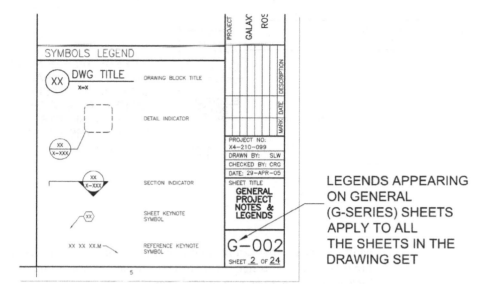

FIGURE 3-8
Example of a Legend That Applies
to All Sheets in the Drawing Set

conflicts. For example, a symbols legend located on a General discipline (G-series) sheet such as G-002 is applicable to the entire drawing set. However, a symbols legend on a General (0-series) sheet such as E-001 would only pertain to the sheets in the Electrical discipline (Sheets E-101, E-301, etc.). When two or more legends featuring the same items, such as abbreviations legends, are included within the same drawing set, they must be coordinated in order to avoid conflicts. They must also be located in accordance with the sheets to which they apply. Figures 3-8, 3-9, and 3-10 illustrate typical examples of legends in a drawing set and the hierarchy for the sheets to which they apply.

Keys and Notes Legends in Schedules

The horizontal rows and vertical columns in the schedules form a grid made up of cells. One of the problems associated with schedules is that the amount of data that needs to be placed in the cells often exceeds the space available. Sometimes, increasing the row height will provide

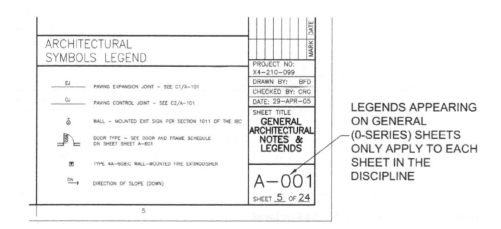

FIGURE: 3-9
Example of a Legend That
Applies Only to the Sheets in
a Single Discipline

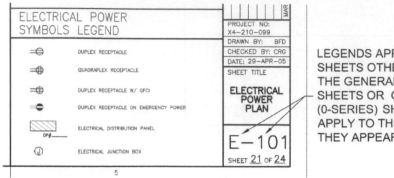

LEGENDS APPEARING ON
SHEETS OTHER THAN
THE GENERAL (G-SERIES)
SHEETS OR GENERAL
(0-SERIES) SHEETS, ONLY
APPLY TO THE SHEET
THEY APPEAR ON

Figure 3-10
Example of a Legend That
Applies Only to the Sheet on
Which It Appears

additional space that can be used to wrap, or add, more lines of text in the cell. The use of abbreviations can also help fit more text into less space. Another option, which is often overlooked, is to use a key or a **notes legend.**

Many schedules contain columns for notes that are used to provide unique information about an item. When space is limited, or if more efficient use of space in the drawing area is desired, a notes legend should be used. The principle is similar to notations that are keyed on the drawings: each note is assigned to a numeral or letter of the alphabet. The notes are placed at the bottom of the schedule in a separate note box, which is user-defined. An example of a schedule with a notes legend is included in Figure 3-11.

When columns need to be expanded to include additional column subidentifiers, the resulting cells can sometimes accommodate only a few characters of text. In this case, keys should be used. The keys can be used to describe materials, colors, finishes, installation information, and other

EQUIPMENT SCHEDULE

ITEM	DESCRIPTION	SIZE	MANUFACTURER	CATALOG#	NOTES
EQ-1	AUTOCLAVE	21" x 18" x 14 1/2"	STEAMRITE	S6AA5335	1,3
EQ-2	DRAIN RACK	22" x 24 "x 7 "	DRIP-DRI, INC.	J1893-A0078	5
EQ-3	GLASSWARE WASHER	24"L x 26"D x 36"H	CRYSTAL CLEAR MFG, INC.	Z40-03-01	2,8
EQ-4	DRYING OVEN	21 1/2" x 24" x 28"	D-HIDRATE CO.	ILO-VE-CO-RAL	2
EQ-5	MUFFLE FURNACE	16" x 10" x 16"	TOUCHOT COMPANY	430-1-410J	2, 4
EQ-6	REFRIGERATOR	28" x 31" x 62"	BREWSKI, INC.	L4-15BBMR-WW3	7
EQ-7	INCUBATOR	32" x 29 1/2" x 73 1/2"	WARMINHERE COMPANY	IV-22837	
EQ-8	WATER PURIFICATION	31" x 7 3/4" x 29"	WATER-CLEAN	H20-88	
EQ-9	VACUUM PUMP	10 1/2" x 4" x 5 1/2"	SUCKITIN PUMP CO.	ZA-NES-N0-1	6
EQ-10	TUB SINK	28"L x 18"W x 15 1/2"D	SANITARY SINKS, INC.	J-ES-SIES-NO12	

EQUIPMENT SCHEDULE NOTES LEGEND

1. PROVIDE XW-344 INSTRUMENT POUCH AND XY-333 SPORE TEST KIT
2. PROVIDE WITH POWER CONVERSION KIT. CONCEAL TRANSFORMER - VERIFY LOCATION WITH ARCHITECT.
3. PROVIDE COPPER PIPING FOR VENT. VERIFY SIZE WITH MANUFACTURER.
4. LOCATE CENTER OF UNIT BELOW EXHAUST HOOD. ALIGN WITH DOOR 4" BEHIND FACE OF HOOD.
5. PROVIDE WITH DRAIN TUBING. DIRECT TUBING TO DISCHARGE INTO SINK. DO NOT ANCHOR TUBING TO COUNTERTOP.
6. PROVIDE 6" X 6" OPENING IN BACK OF BASE CABINET TO PROVIDE ACCESS TO ELECTRICAL OUTLET.
7. PROVIDE WITH X34-00-2 ICEMAKER AND WA-345 WATER FILTER. CONCEAL FILTER BEHIND REFRIGERATOR.
8. PROVIDE B00 GLASSWARE RACK AND XYZ-23 IN-LINE WATER FILTER. CONCEAL FILTER BENEATH UNIT.

Figure 3-11 Example of a Schedule with a Notes Legend

FINISH SCHEDULE

ROOM NO	ROOM NAME	FLOOR	BASE	NORTH			SOUTH			EAST			WEST			CEILING FINISH			HEIGHT	NOTES
				MTL	FIN	CLR	MTL	FIN	CLR	MTL	FIN	CLR	MTL	FIN	CLR	MTL	FIN	CLR		
101	LOBBY	M-3 C-1	M-3 C-1	M-2	F-1	C-1	M-2	F-1	C-1	M-2	F-4	C-3	M-2	F-1	C-1	M-7	NA	NA	10'-0'	
102	CONFERENCE	M-6 C-4	M-8 F-3	M-2	F-1	C-2	M-9	F-3	C-2	M-2	F-4	C-2	M-9	F-5	NA	M-7	NA	NA	9'-0'	
103	TOILET	M-10 C-6	M-1 C-8	M-1	NA	C-7	M-1	NA	C-8	M-1	NA	C-7	M-1	NA	C-7	M-2	F-2	C-9	9'-0'	
104	JANITOR	M-4 C-10	M-5 C-5	M-2	F-2	C-9	M-2	F-2	C-9	M-2	F-2	C-9	M-2	F-2	C-9	M-2	F-2	C-9	8'-0'	

ROOM FINISH KEY

MATERIAL KEY			FINISH KEY		COLOR KEY			
M-1	GLAZED TILE	M-6	CARPET	F-1	FLAT PAINT	C-1	NATURAL QUARRY RUSTIC BROWN	C-6	MOUNTAIN GREEN MOSAIC #2
M-2	GYPSUM BOARD	M-7	SUSPENDED ACOUSTICAL TILE	F-2	SEMI-GLOSS PAINT	C-2	CREAMY TAN	C-7	GLAZED GREEN
M-3	QUARRY TILE	M-8	RED OAK	F-3	MATTE VARNISH	C-3	STRAW WEAVE PATTERN 3	C-8	NATURAL GREEN GLAZE
M-4	VINYL COMPOSITION TILE	M-9	RED OAK PANELING	F-4	VINYL WALL COVERING	C-4	TUFTED TURQUOISE	C-9	LOOKS KINDA WHITE #3007-AH
M-5	RUBBER	M-10	CERAMIC MOSAIC TILE	F-5	GLOSS VARNISH	C-5	MATTE BROWN	C-10	NATURAL COFFEE SWIRLS 4-98A

FIGURE 3-12   Keys in a Schedule

characteristics about the material or product. Keys are similar to notes legends and are placed at the bottom of the schedule. See Figure 3-12 for an example of keys used in schedules.

The use of keys and legends will help reduce the width needed to create schedules. They will also help reduce errors and streamline the process of inserting notations in the schedules. Therefore, we highly recommend using them.

IMPLEMENTATION ISSUES

Organizations considering implementation of the schedules formats may be relieved to know that when members of the construction industry got together to create the UDS Schedules Module, they did not reinvent the wheel with regard to the requirements. Instead, the same rows, columns, and tabular appearance of schedules, already familiar to design professionals, were adopted. However, though at first glance, it might appear that the UDS Schedules Module might be one of the easiest components in the NCS to comply with, because the layout requirements for the columns and rows are very similar to what most firms are currently using, the amount of effort that will be needed to adopt all of the formatting requirements is more than first meets the eye. That is why this portion of the NCS should be scheduled after many of the other NCS components have already been adopted.

To ensure that schedules are adopted in a manner that will preclude the necessity to make additional changes later, it will be beneficial if NCS components such as the AIA CAD Layer Guidelines and Tri-Service Plotting Guidelines are adopted *before* the concepts in the Schedules Module. This will allow the schedules to be created on the proper layers, and with the proper pens. It will also be helpful if file naming from the UDS Drawing Set Organization Module is being used, so that the schedules can be given the proper file names. One of the most important components to adopt ahead of the UDS Schedules Module is the UDS Terms and Abbreviations Module, because for schedules to comply with the NCS, the terms and abbreviations used in them must also comply. See Chapter 11, "Implementation" for more specific information.

Adopting the Graphic Organization of Columns and Rows

The graphic criteria for establishing how a schedule must be organized are very flexible. The requirements will pose very few implementation problems because the tabular arrangement of the rows, columns, and headings is very similar to those that have been in use for many years by architects, engineers, and other design professionals in the construction industry.

One of the features that make this portion of the UDS Schedules Module so flexible and easy to adopt is the user-defined spacing for the row heights and column widths. These can be modified as needed for each type of schedule and for each type of project. This allows most workplaces to use the same organizational layout as the schedules already in place.

The issues that will take the most effort to adopt are those that occur once the graphic organization of the columns and rows has been adopted. After that has been accomplished, the amount of effort to complete the remaining format requirements is notable. These include:

- Proper use of line widths and text height
- File naming
- CAD layer naming
- Updating terms and abbreviations used in schedules to coordinate with those in the UDS Terms and Abbreviations Module and those in the project manual

Lines Widths Used in Schedules

The Tri-Service Plotting Guidelines provides eight pen widths that can be used on NCS drawings. However, not all eight can be used to create schedules. The UDS Drafting Conventions Module includes a table that identifies the proper use of line widths for the borders, rows, and columns for schedules. The table specifies three pen widths: 0.25 mm, 0.35 mm, and 0.70 mm. Each of the pens is assigned to a specific component of the schedule, as indicated in Figure 3-13.

Text Used in Schedules

According to the UDS Drafting Conventions Module, the minimum size of text used on CAD drawings is 3/32″ high, which also applies to text used in schedules. Since it is customary, al-

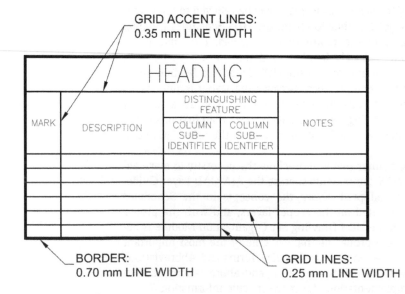

Figure 3-13
Line Width Requirements for Schedules

though not required, to use larger text in the heading of a schedule, we recommend matching the 1/4″ text height used in the heading bars in the note blocks; this is also in accordance with the text size indicated in the example schedules included in Appendix B of the UDS Schedules Module.

CAD Layer Names for Schedules

The layer-naming requirements for schedules in each discipline are established in accordance with the layer-naming formats in the AIA CAD Layer Guidelines. There are three fields for layer names associated with schedules: the discipline designator(s), followed by the major group, ANNO, followed by the minor group, SCHD. A second minor group is usually needed to differentiate one schedule from another. Examples of layer names that could be assigned to each of the schedules that appear in Appendix B of the UDS Schedules Module are as follows:

Concrete Beam Reinforcing Schedule: S-ANNO-SCHD-BMRB
Concrete Slab Reinforcing Schedule: S-ANNO-SCHD-SLRB
Door and Frame Schedule: A-ANNO-SCHD-DOOR
Window Schedule: A-ANNO-SCHD-GLAZ
Room Finish Schedule: A-ANNO-SCHD-ROOM
Exterior Signage Schedule: A-ANNO-SCHD-ESGN
Interior Signage Schedule: I-ANNO-SCHD-ISGN
Plumbing Pump Schedule: P-ANNO-SCHD-PUMP
Water Heater Schedule: P-ANNO-SCHD-WHTR
Plumbing Fixture Schedule (Expanded): P-ANNO-SCHD-FIXT
Plumbing Fixture Schedule (Simple): P-ANNO-SCHD-FIXT
Variable/Constant Volume Air Terminal Unit Schedule: M-ANNO-SCHD-VAVT
HVAC (Exhaust) Fan Schedule: M-ANNO-SCHD-EXHF
Fan Schedule: M-ANNO-SCHD-FANS
Diffuser, Register, and Grille Schedule (Expanded): M-ANNO-SCHD-DIFF
Diffuser, Register, and Grille Schedule (Simple): M-ANNO-SCHD-DIFF
HVAC Air Cleaning Device Schedule (Air Filter Schedule): M-ANNO-SCHD-CLNG
Water Cooled Reciprocating Chiller Schedule: M-ANNO-SCHD-CHLL
Distribution Panelboard Schedule: E-ANNO-SCHD-DIST
Electrical Panel Schedule (Expanded): E-ANNO-SCHD-PANL
Electrical Panel Schedule (Simple): E-ANNO-SCHD-PANL
Electrical Circuit Schedule: E-ANNO-SCHD-CIRC
Lighting Fixture Schedule (Expanded): E-ANNO-SCHD-LITE
Lighting Fixture Schedule (Simple): E-ANNO-SCHD-FIXT

File Names Used for Schedules

Once a schedule has been formatted to comply with the UDS Schedules Module, it can be saved as a template in a library for future projects. Each template should be stored electronically, using NCS-compliant library file names included in the UDS Drawing Set Organization Module. The file names are formatted according to MasterFormat 2004 or UniFormat 1998. Although either format is acceptable, we recommend naming library files in accordance with MasterFormat 2004 because many users are more familiar with the system; and, if desired, the same number MasterFormat assigns for a schedule location in the project manual can be used for the schedule's file name. See Figure 3-14 for examples of schedule file names. (Note: Those of you who are considering using UniFormat for library file names need to be aware that CSI is in the process of updating the document, so it will probably be worthwhile to wait until more about the changes is known. For more information about UniFormat, visit CSI's website at www.csinet.org.)

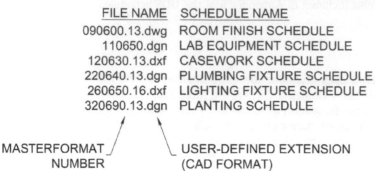

EXAMPLES OF
SCHEDULE FILE NAMES USING MASTERFORMAT

FILE NAME	SCHEDULE NAME
090600.13.dwg	ROOM FINISH SCHEDULE
110650.dgn	LAB EQUIPMENT SCHEDULE
120630.13.dxf	CASEWORK SCHEDULE
220640.13.dgn	PLUMBING FIXTURE SCHEDULE
260650.16.dxf	LIGHTING FIXTURE SCHEDULE
320690.13.dgn	PLANTING SCHEDULE

MASTERFORMAT
NUMBER

USER-DEFINED EXTENSION
(CAD FORMAT)

EXAMPLES OF
SCHEDULE FILE NAMES USIING UNIFORMAT

FILE NAME	SCHEDULE NAME
C30.dwg	ROOM FINISH SCHEDULE
E1020.dgn	LAB EQUIPMENT SCHEDULE
E2010.dxf	CASEWORK SCHEDULE
D2010.dgn	PLUMBING FIXTURE SCHEDULE
D5020.dxf	LIGHTING FIXTURE SCHEDULE
G2050.dgn	PLANTING SCHEDULE

UNIFORMAT
NUMBER

USER-DEFINED EXTENSION
(CAD FORMAT)

FIGURE 3-14
Library File-Naming Formats for Schedules

Terms and Abbreviations Used in Schedules

The biggest hurdle to overcome in adopting the requirements of the UDS Schedules Module will most likely be that of adopting something that isn't even in the module: the requirements for terms and abbreviations used in schedules. Abbreviations are commonly required because the names for many terms are often too long for the space, or cell, to write them in. The dilemma most users will need to address is that even though the cell layout in their current schedules may already meet NCS requirements, quite often the terms and abbreviations used in them do not. However, with a little effort, this can be corrected.

To determine whether the terms and abbreviations being used in the workplace are NCS-compliant, they must be compared with those in the UDS Terms and Abbreviations Module. If a noncompliant term or abbreviation is discovered, it can be replaced fairly quickly because a simple text change is all that is necessary. Figure 3-15 illustrates some of the types of changes a firm might need to make to a schedule in order to update it to comply with the NCS.

Depending on the time and manpower available, a workplace can make the terms and abbreviations conversions in a single effort; or they can be updated one at a time, as needed for each project. Once the corrections are made, the NCS-compliant schedule can then become the template for the workplace to use on future projects.

ROOM FINISH SCHEDULE

ROOM NO.	ROOM NAME	FLOOR	BASE	WALLS				CEILING	
				NORTH	SOUTH	EAST	WEST	MAT.	HGT.
101	LOBBY	QUAR. TILE	QUAR. TILE	GYP. PLAST.	GYP. PLAST.	WD. PNLBD.	GYP. PLAST.	GYP. PLAST.	18'-0"
102	RECEPT.	VINYL TILE	VNL	WALL PAPER	N/A	WALL PAPER	STUCCO	CLG. TILE	10'-0"
103	ADMIN.	CRPT.	CRPT.	FABRIC WALLCVG.	PAINTED DRYWALL	PAINTED DRYWALL	PAINTED DRYWALL	SUSPEND. CLG.	9'-0"
104	TOIL.	PORCEL TILE	PORCEL TILE	GLAZED WT.	GLAZED WT.	GLAZED WT.	GLAZED WT.	PAINTED DRYWALL	9'-0"

NON-PREFERRED (NON-COMPLIANT) TERMS AND ABBREVIATIONS

ROOM FINISH SCHEDULE

ROOM NO	ROOM NAME	FLOOR	BASE	WALLS				CEILING	
				NORTH	SOUTH	EAST	WEST	MAT	HGT
101	LOBBY	QT	QT	GYP PLAS	GYP PLAS	WOOD PB	GYP PLAS	GYP PLAS	18'-0"
102	RCPTN	RESIL TILE	VINYL	WC	NA	WC	CEM PLAS	ACT	10'-0"
103	ADMIN	CPT	CPT	FWC	PAINTED GYP BD	PAINTED GYP BD	PAINTED GYP BD	SUSP CLG	9'-0"
104	TOILET	PORC TILE	PORC TILE	GWT	GWT	GWT	GWT	PAINTED GYP BD	9'-0"

PREFERRED (COMPLIANT) TERMS AND ABBREVIATIONS

FIGURE 3-15   Updating a Schedule with Terms and Abbreviations That Comply with the NCS

REVIEW OF KEY CONCEPTS IN THIS CHAPTER

1. MasterFormat 2004 had significant impact on the UDS Schedules Module, including file naming and the provision for identifying specific section numbers in the project manual for schedule locations.
2. Combining schedules with other drawing types can help reduce the amount of sheets in the drawing set.
3. The use of notes legends and keys can help to further identify specific characteristics about the items in a schedule and can help to reduce the space needed for schedules in the drawing area.
4. One of the biggest hurdles during the implementation process is coordinating terms and abbreviations used in the schedules with those in the UDS Terms and Abbreviations Module and those in the project manual.
5. Specifiers will usually need to be involved with the implementation of the UDS Schedules Module in order to coordinate the use of NCS-compliant terms in the schedules with the terms used in the specifications.

6. Scheduling the implementation of the UDS Schedules Module after components such as the CAD Layer Guidelines, Plotting Guidelines, File Naming (from the UDS Drawing Set Organization Module), and the UDS Terms and Abbreviations Module have been adopted will help to avoid having to reformat schedules later.

FREQUENTLY ASKED QUESTIONS

Q: *The Door Schedule in our office doesn't look exactly like the one in the UDS Schedules Module. Do we have to change it in order to comply with the NCS?*

A: Not if your schedule contains each of the following four components: a heading, columns for a mark, item description, and distinguishing feature. Minimum text height is 3/32"; however, there is no format requirement for row height or column width. The names of column identifiers and the terms used in the cells of the schedule are also user-defined, as long as they comply with the UDS Terms and Abbreviations Module. Line widths used to create schedules must comply with the line use table in the UDS Drafting Conventions Module.

The schedules included in Appendix B of the UDS Schedules Module are examples and are meant only to represent how some schedules could appear. It is quite possible that yours will be different, depending on the unique needs of your workplace or client.

Q: *If I locate my schedule at the top the drawing area of a sheet type designator 6-series (Schedules and Diagrams) sheet, does it conflict with the NCS requirement to locate the most frequently used referenced drawing at the bottom of the sheet?*

A: Schedules are unique. They are not drawing views such as plans, details, or sections. As the drawing set evolves, the space beneath schedules is often needed for expansion to accommodate additional rows to the schedule, for more diagrams, or for additional notes that may need to be added to the notes legend. Locating schedules at the top of the sheet will usually make it easier to incorporate these types of changes later on. The NCS police shouldn't have any problems with this exception.

Q: *What is the difference between a legend, a key, and an index?*

A: They are the same thing. Each is a list of paired items. Whatever one chooses to call them is simply a matter of personal preference.

Drafting Conventions

General

Many architectural firms have established drafting standards based upon decades of hand-drafting experience and have attempted to apply these conventions to CAD. As a national standard for CAD, the format requirements for the production of CAD drawings are located in the UDS Drafting Conventions Module of the Construction Specification Institute's (CSI) Uniform Drawing System (UDS). The UDS Drafting Conventions Module was one of five UDS Modules to be included in version 2 of the NCS, released in 2001. Since its debut, the UDS Drafting Conventions Module has been subjected to several revisions resulting from updates to the NCS, but overall the current standard is very similar to the original.

The UDS Drafting Convention Module covers numerous subjects related to the creation and production of construction documents. This chapter is not intended to repeat this material, but to supplement the UDS Drafting Conventions Module by providing additional information and commentary.

North Arrows

Three types of north arrows are used on construction drawings: **plan north, true north,** and **magnetic north.** While the NCS prescribes many standards and guidelines, there is no official NCS north arrow. Many firms have customized north arrows that combine the types of north arrows into a single graphic; other firms may elect to include multiple north arrows on sheets with plan views. Figure 4-1 illustrates three north arrow options. The NCS does state that all sheets with plan views should have a north arrow. We recommend that if you choose to include only one north arrow on a plan, it should be the plan north, because this will provide for consistent identification of objects, such as the north wall.

> **FYI:** During the development of the UDS Drafting Conventions Module, a decision was made to use the term, "line width" because it more accurately described the two-dimensional characteristic of a line; whereas "line weight" and "line thickness" imply three-dimensional characteristics of mass and volume.

Lines

Definitions for the use of NCS line widths are established in the UDS Drafting Conventions Module. There are eight designated line widths and each of them matches those used in the Tri-Services Plotting Guidelines. The line widths and guidelines for their use are as follows:

- 0.18 mm: Material indications, hatch lines, surface marks, and patterns
- 0.25 mm: 3/32″ to 3/8″ text; **dimension lines, leaders, extension lines, break lines,** hidden objects, dotted lines, dashed lines, setback lines, **centerlines, grid lines,** and schedule grid lines

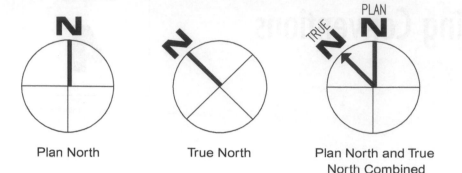

Plan North   True North   Plan North and True
North Combined

FIGURE 4-1
North Arrows

- 0.35 mm: 5/32″ to 3/8″ text; object lines, **property lines,** text, lettering, **terminator** marks, door and window elevations, schedule grid accent lines
- 0.50 mm: 7/32″ to 3/8″ text; titles, edges of interior and exterior **elevations,** profiling, cut lines, property lines, **section** cutting plane lines, drawing block borders
- 0.70 mm: 1/2″ to 1″ text; match lines, large titles, building footprints, title block borders, sheet borders, schedule outlines
- 1.00 mm: Major title underlining and separating portions of designs
- 1.40 mm: Border sheet outlines and cover sheet line work
- 2.00 mm: Border sheet outlines and cover sheet line work

NOTATIONS

The NCS identifies five types of notations: general notes, general discipline notes, general sheet notes, reference keynotes, and sheet keynotes. Each of the notations has specific use and formatting requirements, as described in the UDS Notations Module. For example, reference keynotes can be used for notations that describe products, materials, components, and assemblies that are included in the project manual. Their format includes an alphanumeric symbol that includes the specification section number where more specific information on the item is located. Terminology of the reference keynote should be coordinated to match the terminology used in the specification section. An example of reference keynotes is shown in Figure 4-2, where the

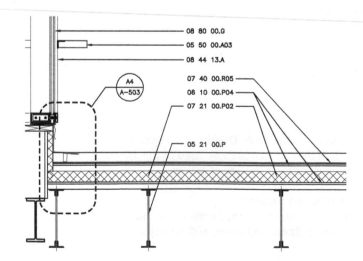

FIGURE 4-2
Reference Keynotes

REFERENCE KEYNOTES

DIVISION 05 — METALS
05 21 00.J   STRUCTURAL STEEL JOIST
05 31 00.M   METAL FORM DECK
05 50 00.A03   ALUMINUM TUBE
DIVISION 06 — WOODS, PLASTICS, AND COMPOSITES
06 10 00.P04   PLYWOOD
06 41 00.A01   ADJUSTABLE SHELVES
DIVISION 07 — THERMAL AND MOISTURE PROTECTION
07 11 13.B   BITUMINOUS DAMP PROOFING
07 21 00.P02   POLYISOCYANURATE BOARD INSUL.
07 40 00.F02   FLASHING
07 40 00.R05   ROOF PANEL
07 40 00.S   SOFFIT PANEL
07 71 23.G   GUTTER
DIVISION 08 — OPENINGS
08 11 13.S   STEEL DOOR
08 11 13.S01   STEEL FRAME
08 44 13.A   ALUMINUM CURTAINWALL
08 80 00.G   GLAZING

FIGURE 4-3
Note Block

reference designations occur in the drawing block; and Figure 4-3 shows the associated note block, indicating materials and products. For more information on reference keynotes, see Chapter 7, "Notations," which provides a detailed explanation of each of the types of notations used on construction drawings.

CROSS-REFERENCING

Reference symbols are used to refer the reader from one part of a drawing to another part of the documentation, either on the same sheet or on another sheet. Symbol size must be large enough to contain the sheet identification. This can be an issue when Level 2 sheet identification or a user-defined designator is added as a suffix to the standard sheet identification. In these cases, we recommend that the symbol be broken to allow the full sheet identification to be shown.

The three-part reference symbol (sometimes referred to as the "split-bottom bubble") once commonly used on military projects is not included in the NCS, and its use is strongly discouraged. Due to the duplication of information used in the three-part reference, thereby increasing the opportunity for mistakes, the use of this symbol can increase liability for architects and owners; moreover, it is nearly impossible to include all the sheet identifications.

FYI: As a result of discussion regarding problems associated with the use of the three-part reference symbol (sometimes referred to as the "split-bottom bubble"), the Tri-Service CADD/GIS Technology Center removed the requirement for its use as a part of its A/E/C CADD Standard.

SHEET TYPES

Sheet Type Designator 0-Series (General) Sheets

Sheet type designator 0-series (General) sheets are the preferred location for information that pertains to all drawings in the set or a specific subset. However, sometimes this information is insufficient in quantity to require the use of an entire sheet. In this case, consider combining the cover sheet with the general drawing set information, such as the list of sheets or code summary. In the case of general discipline notes, these must be placed on the first sheet of the discipline set even if it is not a sheet type designator 0-series (General) sheet. Be sure to identify them to the discipline they apply to, such as "General Architectural Notes," so that it is clear to the user that they apply to all sheets in the architectural subset. These notes should be located at the top of the note block, above general sheet notes and below any general notes.

Sheet Type Designator 1-Series (Plans) Sheets

> **FYI:** While the UDS Task Team felt that standardization of all symbols was important, the north arrow was the one symbol that was unanimously voted to be flexible, to allow individual creativity in the design of the symbol.

The architect often prepares multiple types of plan sheets as a part of a set of construction drawings. Although the NCS does not provide a standard for the order of architectural plan sheets within the subset, a typical arrangement would be floor plans, reflected ceiling plans, roof plans, and interior plans.

Drafting conventions that need to be addressed on plan sheets include establishing the floor and room naming and numbering. The NCS provides guidance in all these areas. Additionally, correct dimensioning of plans is addressed in the UDS Drafting Conventions Module. Dimensioning starts at the exterior face of the building and may be dimensioned to the face of structure, centerline of wall or column line, or the face of finish. Depending on the type of construction and type of plan sheet being used, the architect should choose the location of dimensioning that is most appropriate. Only dimension to one side of each wall, as over a long string of dimensions, the "rounding" factor for most nominal dimensions will generate errors.

Sheet Type Designator 2-Series (Elevations) Sheets

Elevation sheets are ordered with the exterior elevations followed by the interior elevations. If a key plan is used to assist in identification of the elevations, it should be located in the lower portion of the note block or the lower right module of the drawing area. Remember to include a north arrow on all plan views, including key plans.

Naming conventions for elevations is based on the direction the elevation faces, not the direction from which the elevation is being viewed. For example, the "North Elevation" is the elevation that faces plan north. When dimensioning elevations and sections, an elevation mark (sometimes called a target) should be used only once per drawing.

Depending on the size of the project, the architect should determine whether reference symbols for window types, building sections, and wall sections are going to be indicated on the plans or the elevations. In larger commercial projects, the elevation sheets may be the more appropriate location for this information, whereas smaller projects and residential projects typically include these reference symbols on the plans.

Sheet Type Designator 3-Series (Sections) Sheets

The ordering of sectional views begins with building sections and then wall sections. A naming convention for sections is based on the direction of the section. Therefore, a title might be "Building Section Looking North" or "Wall Section Looking East."

Sheet Type Designator 4-Series (Large-Scale Views) Sheets

A **large-scale view** is a portion of a plan, section, or elevation that is shown at a larger scale, yet not large enough to be considered a detail. Common uses for large-scale views include enlarged floor plans, toilet rooms, stair sections, elevator shafts, and equipment rooms. Generally, large-scale views show complete spaces, but may also show partial elevations.

Sheet Type Designator 5-Series (Details) Sheets

Details may be horizontal, vertical, or three-dimensional (3D) views of a product or assembly. We recommend that these be grouped according to similar location. Therefore, exterior wall details should be located together, roof details should be located together, cabinet details together, and so on. We also recommend that details should be ordered, whenever possible, with exterior details, followed by interior details.

Sheet Type Designator 6-Series (Schedules and Diagrams) Sheets

Many firms prepare standard schedule and diagram sheets, depending on their typical work. These sheets may include door and frame schedule, window schedule, room finish schedule, door and frame diagrams, partition type diagrams, threshold diagrams, and fixture mounting height diagram. These standard sheets are then modified to relate to specific project requirements. This practice saves time, money, and helps to ensure quality. Like the use of any standard detail, the architect must be sure to edit the standard diagrams for the specific project requirements. Figure 4-4 illustrates a schedules and diagram sheet.

Sheet Type Designators 7-Series and 8-Series (User-Defined) Sheets

The NCS provides two user-defined sheet type designator series, giving the architect the option to assign them for a specific uses. Some of the typical uses for these sheet types include alternates and specifications. This was explored in greater detail in Chapter 2, "Sheet Organization."

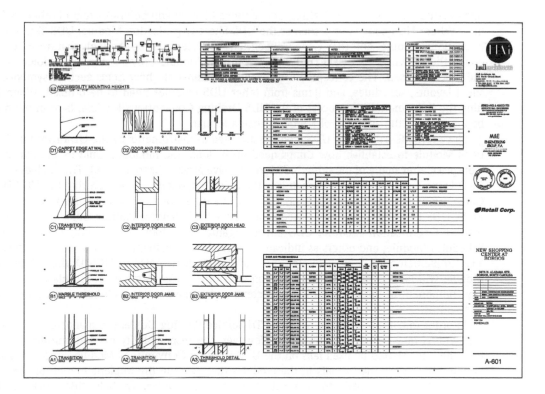

FIGURE 4-4 Standard Diagram and Schedules Sheet

Sheet Type Designator 9-Series (3D Representations) Sheets

Three-dimensional representations such as **axonometric drawing, perspectives,** photographs, and wire-frame drawings are not used frequently in most new, ground-up construction projects, whereas their use in renovation projects or very complex design work is more common.

MOCK-UP DRAWING SET

The NCS explains the use and procedures for creating a mock-up drawing set. A mock-up drawing set is an often-underutilized tool for the planning of the drawing set. Many firms that use this tool experience greater efficiency in the overall production of the construction documents. Our surveys indicate that the use of mock-up drawing sets is primarily limited to architectural firms. We have no explanation for its lack of use by engineers or other design professionals, and we believe that all design professionals would benefit from proper planning of their work.

The mock-up drawing set, sometimes called a "cartoon set," is a hand-sketched version of the final construction documents. Each sheet in the mock-up set represents a final sheet in the completed drawing set, drawn to scale. The development of a mock-up set is essential to efficient sheet layout and man-hour planning. It also will allow more than one person to work on the sheets within a single discipline set, as well as allowing the entire project team to see how all the drawings relate to the final product. Mock-up drawing sets were discussed in further detail in Chapter 2, "Sheet Organization."

IMPLEMENTATION ISSUES

Implementation of the UDS Drafting Conventions Module will be unlike that of other NCS modules. Where NCS components such as the UDS Sheet Organization Module, UDS Terms and Abbreviations Module, and UDS Code Conventions Modules provide the tools that must be used to create the drawings, the UDS Drafting Conventions Module provides the methodology for how the tools are used. The concepts in the module demonstrate how items such as symbols, lines, sheet layouts, schedules, and items from other UDS modules need to be utilized. When beginning the implementation process of the UDS Drafting Conventions Module, bear in mind it will be more about the adoption of a process than a format.

Since formats from other UDS modules are used as instruments by the UDS Drafting Conventions Module to establish how things need to be done, the module should be brought into the workplace after many of the other NCS formats have already been adopted. This includes the AIA CAD Layer Guidelines, even though it is the only component in the NCS that the UDS Drafting Conventions Module doesn't address. Some of the other formats we recommend adopting prior to the UDS Drafting Conventions Module are those in Tri-Service Plotting Guidelines, UDS Drawing Set Organization Module, UDS Sheet Organization Module, UDS Symbols Module, UDS Schedules Module, and others as indicated in the NCS implementation plan included in Chapter 11, "Implementation." Even though most of the methodologies in UDS Drafting Conventions Module will be less problematic to take on after other NCS elements are in place, there is one key component of the module that we recommend implementing well before the others: use of line widths.

In order to comply with the NCS, the Tri-Service Plotting Guidelines mandate that only eight line widths may be used on drawings. However, the responsibility for determining where and how the lines should be used falls on the UDS Drafting Conventions Module. Since lines are the building blocks for the formats in the modules that precede the implementation of this component, using them properly to create items such as schedules, symbols, title blocks, and note blocks will be a critical time-saver.

Adapting to the module's requirements for the use of line widths is going to be a difficult obstacle for some firms to get past, primarily because many workplaces either use more than the eight NCS line widths on their drawings and/or the line widths they are using do not comply. Another aspect of the problem may be that the lines are not being used in accordance with the module. Trying to adjust to both proper line width and line use at the same time multiplies the degree of difficulty for the process and can cause much frustration. Therefore, we recommend prioritizing proper line width first, because even though it might aggravate drafters who are accustomed to using something else, once the line widths are in place, everyone will be better able to focus on how they should be utilized. This approach will also help to minimize downtime.

When it is time to incorporate the rest of the information from the UDS Drafting Conventions Module into the workplace, this process should be approached like other NCS modules—that is, it should be scheduled in segments. The process will take less time if the easiest steps are taken first. These include drawing orientation and use of the north arrow, drawing block formatting, formatting of the reference grid system, and methodology for use of **cross-referencing,** material indication, match lines, mock-up sets, and scale.

Once the first group of procedures is in use, it will be easier to include those that might take a little more effort, such as methodology for dimensioning, the identification of spaces and objects, and guidelines for sheet types.

REVIEW OF KEY CONCEPTS OF THIS CHAPTER

1. The UDS Drafting Conventions Module provides examples and commentary on many of the NCS formats.
2. The UDS Drafting Conventions Module identifies the use for each of the eight NCS line widths that are included in the Tri-Services Plotting Guidelines.
3. The UDS Drafting Conventions Module establishes drafting conventions for each drawing type.
4. The development of a mock-up drawing set is essential to efficient drawing production.
5. Even though most of the methodologies in the UDS Drafting Conventions Module should be scheduled later in the NCS implementation process, the procedures for use of line widths will be needed much sooner and will make implementation of other modules more efficient.

FREQUENTLY ASKED QUESTIONS

Q: *Can more than one type of drawing or view be included on the same sheet?*
A: It is perfectly acceptable to combine different drawing types (drawings that would normally appear on their own sheet type designators) on the same sheet. This is especially useful on smaller projects or when needed to help to reduce the number of sheets in the drawing set. This decision should be made during the creation of the mock-up drawing set, and it should only include drawings from the same discipline.

When it is practical, we recommend combining drawings that are also related to each other. For example, a room finish schedule normally appearing on a Schedules and Diagrams (6-series) sheet and a floor plan can be combined on a Plans (1-series) sheet such as A-101; a coping detail that would normally appear on a sheet type designator 5-series (Details) sheet and the wall section it is referenced from could both be combined on a sheet type designator 3-series (Sections) sheet such as A-301.

Q: *What is the difference between a large-scale view and a detail?*
A: The NCS defines large-scale views as plans, elevations, and sections that are not details. The scale of the drawing will determine whether it is a large-scale view or a detail. Details are usually views that are drawn at a minimum scale of $1-1/2'' = 1'-0''$.

Q: *What is the minimum text size allowed by the NCS?*

A: The minimum text height is 1/8″ for hand-drafting and 3/32″ for CAD. Smaller sizes are not allowed because their legibility diminishes when sheets are reduced.

Q: *Does the NCS identify the proper line types that should be used to represent demolition, new, existing, hidden, and future objects?*

A: The UDS Drafting Conventions Module establishes the following types of lines for each of these conditions, as follows:

>   Hidden objects: Thin (0.25 mm) dashed lines
>   Objects to be demolished or removed: Medium (0.35 mm) dashed lines
>   Existing objects: Medium (0.35 mm) lines
>   New objects: Medium (0.35 mm) lines
>   Future objects: Medium (0.35 mm) dashed lines
>   If further delineation is needed between the objects, these line types can be screened

or indicated with halftone.

Q: *We've noticed that the illustrations in the UDS Drafting Conventions Module all seem to use slashes for dimension line terminators. Can arrowheads or other terminators be used?*

A: Terminators define the intersection between a dimension line and an extension line. In order to ensure consistency for a critical concept such as dimensioning, the UDS Drafting Conventions Module requires slashes to be used for terminators. The module also includes procedures for their use.

Terms and Abbreviations

GENERAL

At the heart of any communication is a "common language," whether it is a graphic, oral, or written communication. The construction industry has developed its own language, and the selection and understanding of the correct terms, abbreviations, and other conventions that communicate the desired intent are critical to all users of the documents. As architects, our instruments of service must convey our design intent in both graphic and written documents. We must ensure the coordination of these terms and abbreviations used throughout all the construction documents, including documentation with our consultants.

The format requirements for terms and abbreviations are located in the UDS Terms and Abbreviations Module of the Construction Specification Institute's (CSI) Uniform Drawing System (UDS). This module became part of the U.S. National CAD Standard (NCS) when it was adopted into NCS version 2.0 in 2001. Since its publication, very few revisions have resulted from NCS updates and, overall, the current standard is almost identical to the original.

> **FYI:** A database of more than 6,000 terms was reviewed for consideration to be included in the UDS Terms and Abbreviations Module. The list was eventually reduced to include approximately 2,500 terms that appear in the module today.

The UDS Terms and Abbreviations Module establishes format requirements for the use of terms and abbreviations, including spelling, format, and use. The primary focus of the requirements is aimed at establishing consistent terminology in the construction industry. This includes establishing the correct term, spelling, and abbreviation throughout the construction drawings. However, since consistency throughout the entire set of construction documents needs to be maintained, use of correct terms also applies to the project manual.

One of the few revisions that have been made to the UDS Terms and Abbreviations Module occurred in NCS version 3.1, when all the UDS modules were updated to coordinate with MasterFormat 2004. Until then, the terms and their abbreviations in the module were assigned numbers from documents and specification sections in the project manual that most closely represented the documents or sections where the terms would be located. However, when MasterFormat 2004 expanded the number of divisions from 16 to 50, it resulted in many terms being related to multiple documents and sections, instead of just one, to reflect that specifications are organized by work results rather than products and that similar products can be incorporated into multiple work result sections. In response to this issue, the section numbers were deleted and the module was published without them.

TERMS AND ABBREVIATIONS USED IN DRAWINGS

Terms and abbreviations on drawings are primarily used in notations and schedules. Terms are the words used on drawings to identify things such as: materials, products, components, measurements, locations, names, and properties. Some typical examples of terms include:

FYI: The terms in the first version of the UDS Terms and Abbreviations Module were associated with the 16-division MasterFormat 1995 numbers. This feature was discontinued when the module was updated to coordinate with the 50 divisions in MasterFormat 2004, because too many terms were shared by multiple numbers.

- Aluminum
- Locker
- Intake fan
- Pounds per square foot
- Three-ply
- International Building Code
- Diagonal

Consistent use of the correct terms, and the correct abbreviations for the terms, will improve communication among all **drawing users** and will help to save time and reduce errors throughout the various stages of the project cycle and the facility cycle. Establishing a standard for consistent format requirements for terms and abbreviations will help **CAD** software vendors to improve their software by including conveniences such as a spell-checking feature that could automatically notify users when they were using terms, abbreviations, or spellings that did not comply with the NCS. Standard abbreviations also give CAD vendors the opportunity to provide features such as an abbreviations legend that would automatically get updated each time an abbreviation was used.

The UDS Terms and Abbreviations Module includes more than 2,500 terms. These are commonly referred to as preferred terms. Terms that do not comply with the NCS, hence are to be avoided, are referred to as nonpreferred terms. This classification is necessary to help prevent the use of different terms to identify the same item. When one term is used on the drawings and another in the specifications, it results in confusion that often leads to wasted time and errors. For example, the following terms are used to describe the same material:

gypsum wallboard
gypsum wall board
gypsum board
gypsum panel
sheet rock
drywall

In this list, the NCS identifies gypsum board as the preferred term. The other terms are nonpreferred and should not be used. In some cases, the decision by the module's authors to label a term preferred over its nonpreferred counterparts was somewhat arbitrary. But in most cases, there were valid reasons not to use certain terms. As a case in point, in the above example, sheet rock and drywall are nonpreferred terms because they are trademarked, proprietary names, which should not be used on drawings. Gypsum wall board (or gypsum wallboard) implies the material is for use on walls only. Of the terms remaining, gypsum board was selected as the preferred term over gypsum panel because it was more commonly used by the manufacturers and other members of the industry. Other examples of nonpreferred terms include the following (the preferred term is in parentheses after each nonpreferred term):

apply (install)
block (concrete masonry unit)
gauge (gage)
sand (porous fill)
wire glass (wired glass)

In addition to the confusion that results when multiple terms are used for the same item, these problems are complicated even further when inconsistent abbreviations are used. For example, the following are just some examples of how the term "hardware" could be abbreviated on a drawing:

HDW
HDW.
hdwr
hw.
Hdwr.
hdw.

This example is typical of many construction terms, and demonstrates that in order to ensure clear communication, a single, consistent abbreviation must be used throughout the drawing set. When all the abbreviations used on the drawings comply with those in the NCS, it will help to avoid conflicts and will result in better transfer of information among all the drawing users. (Note that in the example above, HDW is the preferred abbreviation—an explanation for the reason follows.)

The requirements for use of abbreviations included in the UDS Terms and Abbreviations Module were based, primarily, upon the following three criteria:

1. Avoid abbreviating words of five letters or fewer.
2. Do not use lowercase text.
3. Do not use periods.

It should be noted, however, that the NCS does make a few exceptions to some of these abbreviation rules. For example, lowercase text abbreviations are used for a few words, such as millimeter (mm) and kilometer (km), because this is the way they appear internationally. The module also includes more than 100 abbreviations for words of five letters or fewer, such as foot (FT), north (N), and room (RM), because they have been commonly used for many years throughout the industry.

> *FYI:* Even though the abbreviations in the Terms and Abbreviations Module were developed under the guideline of avoiding use of abbreviations for terms of five letters or fewer, the module actually includes more than 100 abbreviations for terms of this type.

Terms and Abbreviations Used in Drawing Notations

Most terms used on drawings occur within a sheet's drawing area, either as general notations, reference keynotes, or sheet keynotes. (For more information on types of notations, refer to Chapter 7, "Notations.") Using abbreviations in the note block should be avoided because there is usually enough room to spell out the entire term. However, when space is limited, such as in **reference keynote modifiers,** abbreviations should be used to avoid cluttering up the drawing with lengthy amounts of text. For an example of abbreviations used in reference keynote modifiers, see Figure 5-1.

In accordance with the UDS Notations Module, terms used in notations should be concise and generic. It is also essential that the notation terminology match terms in the project manual because, in accordance with AIA A201-1997 General Conditions of the Contract for Construction, the construction documents are complementary. This concept is also consistent with recommendations in CSI's **Project Resource Manual (PRM).** Therefore, when notations are created, the terms they contain must also be coordinated with the specifier to ensure consistent terminology is used throughout the construction documents.

Terms and Abbreviations Used in Schedules

Terms and abbreviations are used in schedules in text format to describe an item's characteristics, such as finishes, locations, manufacturers, and ratings. The schedule's grid, which is made

03 20 00.R
(#5 @ 12" OC EW)

05 50 00.B
(5/8 DIA X 12"
SST EXP BT)

07 62 00.S
(20 GA GALV)

01 23 00.A02
(ALT NO 2)

FIGURE 5-1
Examples of Abbreviations Used in Reference Keynote Modifiers

up of the headings, rows, and columns, is comprised of cells, many of which have very limited area. The use of abbreviations allows more text to be used in the cells, which allows the overall schedule size to be minimized, resulting in more efficient use of space in the drawing area. The UDS Schedules Module requires terms and abbreviations used in schedules to be in accordance with those in the UDS Terms and Abbreviations Module.

Since the drawings and specifications are complementary, terms used in schedules need to be coordinated with the specifier to ensure consistency between the drawings and the specifications. This concept is crucial and is in accordance with AIA A201-1997 General Conditions of the Contract for Construction. (For more on the use of terms and abbreviations used in schedules, see Chapter 3, "Schedules.") For an example of terms and abbreviations used in a schedule, see Figure 5-2.

Use of Abbreviations Legends

Abbreviations legends are often included in the drawing set to inform users of the meaning of abbreviations used in the notations and schedules. To avoid confusion, they should contain only the abbreviations actually used in the drawing set. Unfortunately, many workplaces often include their own unedited master abbreviations legend on the drawings. This practice can result in questions from consultants, clients, contractors, and material suppliers regarding products appearing in the legend but not used in the drawing set. Inconsistent or undefined abbreviations also result in confusion, and so must also be avoided. Therefore, abbreviations legends, when used, must comply with the abbreviations and terms in the NCS, and they must also represent only those abbreviations used in the drawing set.

When abbreviations legends are included in the drawing set, they need to be located in accordance with the UDS Drawing Set Organization Module. When the abbreviations apply to all the disciplines throughout the drawing set, the legend should be located

> **FYI:** The Terms and Abbreviations Module includes a list of more than 100 terms that should be avoided; these are referred to as "nonpreferred terms."

FINISH SCHEDULE

ROOM NO	ROOM NAME	FLOOR	BASE	WALLS				CEILING		NOTES
				NORTH	SOUTH	EAST	WEST	FINISH	HEIGHT	
101	LIBRARY	CPT	CPT	FACED CMU	PAINTED GYP BD	FWC	PAINTED GYP BD	SUSP ACOUS PANL	12'-0"	SEE SHT A-106 FOR CPT PAT SEE SHT A-203 FOR FACED CMU PAT
102	CONFERENCE	HDWD T & G	HDWD WB	NA	VWC	VWC	FAB TK BD	ACT	9'-0"	SEE SHT A-201 FOR FAB TK BD ELEV N WALL IS GL BLK — NO FIN REQD
103	OFFICE	CPT	RESIL	PAINTED GYP BD	PAINTED GYP BD	PAINTED GYP BD	VWF	SUSP ACOUS PANL	9'-0"	COORD VWF INSTL W/ OF/OI CSKW & OF/OI FF & E
104	TOILET	CT	CB	GWT	GWT	GWT	GWT	PAINTED GYP BD	9'-0"	SEE SHT A-201 FOR GWT ELEVATIONS SEE SHT A-403 FOR CT PAT

ABBREVIATION LEGEND

ACOUS PNL	ACOUSTICAL PANEL	N	NORTH
ACT	ACOUSTIC CEILING TILE	NA	NOT APPLICABLE
CB	CERAMIC BASE	OF/OI	OWNER FURNISHED/OWNER INSTALLED
CMU	CONCRETE MASONRY UNIT	PAT	PATTERN
COORD	COORDINATE	REQD	REQUIRED
CPT	CARPET	RESIL	RESILIENT
CSWK	CASEWORK	RM	ROOM
CT	CERAMIC TILE	SHT	SHEET
ELEV	ELEVATION	SUSP	SUSPENDED
FAB	FABRIC	SUSP CLG	SUSPENDED CEILING
FF&E	FURNITURE, FIXTURE, & EQUIPMENT	T&G	TONGUE AND GROOVE
FIN	FINISH	TK	TACKBOARD
FWC	FABRIC WALLCOVERING	VWC	VINYL WALL COVERING
GL BLK	GLASS BLOCK	VWF	VINYL WALL FABRIC
GWT	GLAZED WALL TILE	WB	WOOD BASE
GYP BD	GYPSUM BOARD	WD	WOOD
HDWD	HARDWOOD	W/	WITH
INSTL	INSTALL		

FIGURE 5-2 Examples of Terms and Abbreviations Used in Schedules

within the General discipline (G-series) sheets, on a General (0-series) sheet, such as G-002. For an example of an abbreviations legend that is applicable to all of the sheets in the drawing set, see Figure 5-3.

In some instances, abbreviations are only applicable to a specific discipline. This is quite common when a consultant's drawings include an abbreviations legend. In these situations, the legend needs to be located on a General (0-series) sheet within the specific discipline to which the abbreviations apply. Usually, this will be the first sheet in the discipline set, such as sheet M-001. On smaller projects where General (0-series) sheets are not used, the legend can be located on the first sheet in the discipline set. For an example of an abbreviations legend that is only applicable to the sheets in a discipline, see Figure 5-4.

When an abbreviations legend is only applicable to the sheet on which it appears, it can be located on any sheet other than the General discipline (G-series) or General (0-series) sheets. Sometimes this strategy is used to make it easier for users to locate any abbreviations being used on the sheet. For an example of an abbreviations legend that only applies to the sheet on which it is located, see Figure 5-5.

Once a sheet is identified for the location of an abbreviations legend, a location on the sheet has to be determined. If the legend will fit, locate it in the lowest module beneath the note block, with a **heading bar** above it similar to that used to identify general notations, reference keynotes, and sheet keynotes. The heading bar for an abbreviations legend appearing on the General (G-series) sheets should include the wording "ABBREVIATIONS LEGEND," with each of the abbreviations listed in alphabetical order beneath it. If the abbreviations legend is too large to fit beneath the note block, locate it adjacent to the note block, with the same criteria used to locate schedules (see Chapter 3, for placement of schedules within the drawing area). Figures 5-3, 5-4, and 5-5 illustrate how heading bars can be used with abbreviations legends.

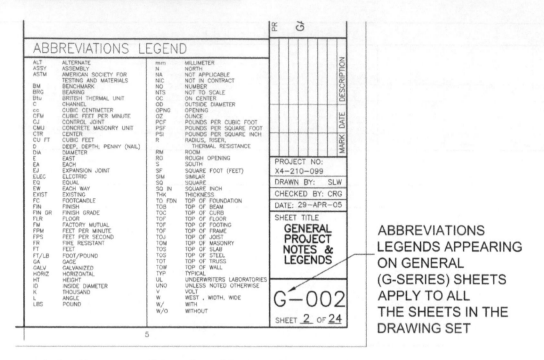

ABBREVIATIONS
LEGENDS APPEARING
ON GENERAL
(G-SERIES) SHEETS
APPLY TO ALL
THE SHEETS IN THE
DRAWING SET

FIGURE 5-3 Example of an Abbreviations Legend That Applies to All the Sheets in the Drawing Set

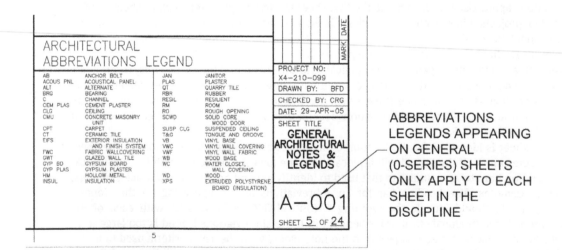

ABBREVIATIONS
LEGENDS APPEARING
ON GENERAL
(0-SERIES) SHEETS
ONLY APPLY TO EACH
SHEET IN THE
DISCIPLINE

FIGURE 5-4 Example of an Abbreviations Legend That Only Applies to the Sheets in a Single Discipline

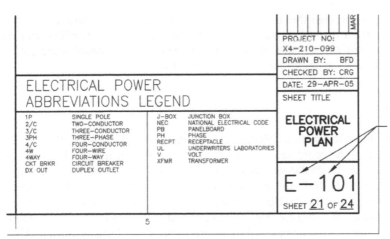

FIGURE 5-5   Example of an Abbreviations Legend That Only Applies to the Sheet on Which It Appears

COORDINATING TERMS AND ABBREVIATIONS WITH THE PROJECT MANUAL

In accordance with AIA A201-1997 General Conditions of the Contract for Construction, the construction documents are complementary; that is, they are to be considered as one. Therefore, in situations where conflicting information occurs between the drawings and the specifications, neither one prevails over the other. A conflict between the drawings and the specifications is no different from a conflict between one drawing and another or between two different specification sections. In these situations, the architect is required to make an interpretation and issue it to the contractor. To help avoid these situations, the specifier must work closely with the design team and come to agreement on the wording, or terms, to be used throughout the set of documents.

> **FYI:** The NCS format requirements for abbreviations are intended only for use on the drawings; they are not intended for use when writing specifications, because the abbreviations format would create conflicts with text and punctuation.

To avoid conflicts, a properly coordinated set of construction documents will contain consistent terminology. For example, when a product or material is being referenced in the drawings, the term used to identify it must match the wording used in the specifications. This is important because using the same terminology improves communication between the various drawing users and will significantly reduce time spent answering questions and will help reduce errors. To ensure NCS compliancy, the terms being used on the drawings and specifications must be compared with those in the UDS Terms and Abbreviations Module. When nonpreferred terms are discovered, they have to be replaced with preferred terms. Updating the specifications with preferred terms needs to be coordinated with the specifier.

Coordination with Specification Software and Masters

Many specifiers use an office master or some form of master guide specification software to create project specifications. During the implementation process, it is very common to discover that some of the terms in the office master specification or in the specification software conflict with those in the NCS. For example, some specification software systems use the term "batt insulation," but this term does not comply with the NCS and should be replaced with the preferred term, "blanket insulation."

Coordinating the terms between the drawings and the specifications will help to ensure consistency and NCS compliancy throughout the set of documents. In this effort, which will result in improved communications, the specifier plays a key role. (For more on coordinating the terms on the drawings with those in specifications, refer to Chapter 7.)

IMPLEMENTATION ISSUES

Before the UDS Terms and Abbreviations Module can be implemented properly, the list of preferred terms it includes must be coordinated to match the terms used in the specifications office master used in the workplace. Since this will usually require a moderate amount of time and manpower, this component of the NCS should be implemented after some of the easier components have been adopted, such as those in the UDS Drawing Set Organization Module and in the UDS Sheet Organization Module. And because one of the most common uses of terms and abbreviations is in schedules, we also recommend adopting the concepts in the UDS Terms and Abbreviations Module first, followed later by the concepts from the UDS Schedules Module.

In general, adopting the format requirements for terms and abbreviations will require an analysis of the following workplace issues:

- Terms and abbreviations used in notations
- Terms and abbreviations used in schedules
- Terms used in the project manual

Minimize the Use of Abbreviations

The table of terms in the UDS Terms and Abbreviations Module often includes more than one term for the same abbreviation. When this occurs, the abbreviations are identified as "shared" abbreviations. For example, FC is a shared abbreviation for both face of curb and face of concrete; FT is a shared abbreviation for feet, foot, fire treated, and fully tempered; RB is a shared abbreviation for rubber base and resilient base.

> **FYI:** The original UDS Terms and Abbreviations Module included a CD-ROM containing each of the terms and abbreviations and a search engine feature. The CD-ROM was discontinued after NCS version 2.0 because of the costs associated with updating it for future NCS versions.

The confusion that results from the use of inaccurate or shared abbreviations, coupled with the technology available from the computer, has led us to make the following recommendation for the use of abbreviations: Except for schedules and reference keynote modifiers, where there will be no doubt about their meaning, *do not use abbreviations.* This methodology is not difficult to adopt because terms no longer have to be hand-drawn with a drafting pencil. The keyboard, copy/paste technology, and notation toolbars in CAD software have dramatically reduced the effort needed to spell out all the letters in each term. More importantly, drawings with terms spelled out completely communicate better with all users, especially those such as owners and others who often do not have a thorough knowledge of construction terminology.

The effort needed to administrate and coordinate the abbreviations used throughout the drawing set, on all sheets in each discipline, and include them in abbreviations legends is costly and very time-consuming. Accuracy is difficult, regardless of the care taken to check each notation and schedule throughout the set. As indicated in the UDS Terms and Abbreviations Module, in many cases, the same abbreviation is shared and used to identify two or more items. These are all reasons to minimize their use, and why abbreviations should only be used in schedules and reference keynote modifiers. Due to the inaccuracies that occur, along with the labor needed to create them, we also recommend avoiding the use of abbreviations legends and replacing them with a simple general note on one of the General discipline (G-series) sheets, such as G-001, which states the following: "Abbreviations: Referenced from version 3.1 of the U.S. National CAD Standard."

This methodology is in accordance with the recommendations in the UDS Terms and Abbreviations Module and in the UDS Notations Module. Until CAD vendors can make the creation of accurate, NCS-compliant legends an automatic and transparent process, it is a recommendation we highly support.

Coordinating Terms on the Drawings with the Specifications

There are various approaches to streamlining the coordination of preferred terms in drawing notations with those in the specifications. Three tools are available that can help streamline the process. These include **reference keynote office masters, sheet keynote office masters,** and schedules and legends office masters.

Masters for schedules and legends can be created from scratch, using the requirements from the UDS Schedules Module for the organization of the headings, rows, and columns. Once the layout is configured, the columns can be identified with the preferred terms from the UDS Terms and Abbreviations Module. When abbreviations are needed, they should be used in accordance with those in the module. All of the terms and their abbreviations also need to be cross-referenced with those in the project manual to make sure they are coordinated.

Schedules and legends can also be created from those that reside in CAD software, some of which are "intelligent," in the sense that they are capable of updating themselves automatically, in response to changes on the drawings. An example of this type of schedule is a door and frame schedule that updates itself each time a door opening is added or removed from a wall. Most of the schedules that are included with CAD software will require a bit of manipulation to change the defaults to those that comply with the terms and abbreviations in the NCS. However, it will usually be well worth the effort, because once they are established, they can be used over and over again. Hopefully, this will become less of an issue once CAD vendors begin including schedules that are already set up and in compliance with those in the NCS. (For more discussion on the implementation of schedules, see Chapter 3.)

Reference keynote and sheet keynote office masters are used for the notations in the drawing area and in the note block. They consist of an electronic database of terms that comply with those in the UDS Terms and Abbreviations Module, as well as the project manual. This methodology is available as a keynoting feature in some CAD software; however, most of what is currently available will require a considerable effort to set up and maintain. Third-party, add-on notation software also is available from some manufacturers, and it can usually make the job of administrating and using these types of databases much easier. Hopefully, in the near future, CAD vendors will improve the methodology by which a notations database can be created, used, and maintained in their software, but until then, third-party software is probably the best option for creating notations that comply with the NCS. (For more information on notation office masters, refer to Chapter 7.)

Creating and maintaining office masters for schedules and notations is a very worthwhile investment of time because it will help to ensure that the use of terms and abbreviations used on the drawings is consistent with those in the project manual, as well as those in the UDS Terms and Abbreviations Module. Once these types of masters have been created, they can then be used as a template and modified as necessary for each project.

> **FYI:** When the same term is used to identify two or more items, it is referred to as a shared abbreviation. Approximately 700 of the 2,500 abbreviations in the Terms and Abbreviations Module are shared abbreviations.

REVIEW OF KEY CONCEPTS IN THIS CHAPTER

1. It is essential that terms used on the drawings match those used in the project manual.
2. Computer technology has simplified the effort needed to create notations. Therefore, to reduce errors and avoid confusion regarding their meaning, do not use abbreviations except when necessary to save space in schedules and reference keynote modifiers.

3. Since implementation of the UDS Terms and Abbreviations Module usually requires a moderate amount of time and manpower to adopt into the workplace, do so only after some of the easier NCS formats have been put into practice, such as those in the UDS Drawing Set Organization Module and the UDS Sheet Organization Module.

FREQUENTLY ASKED QUESTIONS

Q: *If an abbreviation does not exist for a term, can we create one for it if we comply with the capitalized text format requirements and don't use periods?*

A: Drawings that comply with the NCS can only use abbreviations listed in the Terms and Abbreviations Module. New terms and abbreviations must be submitted to the National CAD Standard Project Committee for approval before they can be added. (For more on amending the NCS, see the Introduction.)

Q: *The UDS Terms and Abbreviations Module indicates that the abbreviation for water is the letter W. Shouldn't the abbreviation be H2O or H_2O?*

A: According to the UDS Terms and Abbreviations Module, symbols that contain letters are not abbreviations. Since H_2O is a symbol for the water molecule, the letter W was used instead. One exception to this rule is where CO^2 is used for the carbon dioxide abbreviation to avoid confusion with the carbon monoxide abbreviation, CO.

Symbols

GENERAL

The architect often uses hundreds of graphic symbols in the creation of a construction drawing set to depict objects incorporated into the project. The Construction Specifications Institute's (CSI) Uniform Drawing System (UDS) Symbols Module establishes the standard for these graphic representations in the NCS. The UDS Symbols Module appeared in the second edition of the UDS, and the presentation of symbols was originally organized by symbol type. In NCS version 3.1, the UDS Symbols Module was reorganized to provide a hierarchy for the organization of symbols, first by MasterFormat 2004 Level 2 numbers, then by symbol classification type, and then alphabetically by symbol description. NCS version 3.1 also provides an index with an alphabetical listing of the symbols, as another method of locating them within the module.

UNDERSTANDING SYMBOLS

Graphic symbols used in construction documents are representations of objects, materials, or words. Symbols may be **scale-dependent, scale-independent,** or both.

Most of the symbols used in this module were originally provided by the U.S. Department of Defense: CADD/GIS Technology Center (formally known as Tri-Service CADD/GIS Technology Center). Only a portion of the symbols contained in the Tri-Service CAD Library were selected for inclusion in the UDS Symbols Module. Many of the symbols not included were military object symbols or deemed as not commonly used in construction documents. The symbols were included in both hard copy and electronic form, the latter on CD-ROM. The CD-ROM was included in versions 1.0 and 2.0 but discontinued in versions 3.0 and 3.1.

> **FYI:** The first two versions of the NCS included a CD-ROM containing more than 1,000 CAD symbols. The CD-ROM was discontinued after NCS version 2.0, because of the cost associated with updating it for future NCS revisions.

SYMBOLS CLASSIFICATION

The NCS provides for six classifications of symbols. The listing that follows gives the symbol types, description, and examples of each type.

Identity symbols: Symbols that indicate individual objects but are not representations of the object. Identity symbols are generally used to indicate object such as valves, fire alarms, light fixtures, and electrical outlets. Figure 6-1 shows several examples of identity symbols.

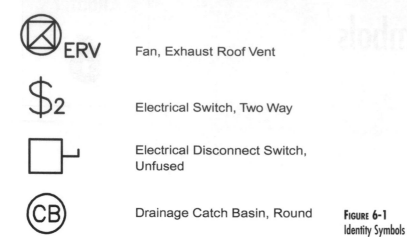

⊗ERV	Fan, Exhaust Roof Vent
$2	Electrical Switch, Two Way
⊐	Electrical Disconnect Switch, Unfused
CB	Drainage Catch Basin, Round

Figure 6-1
Identity Symbols

Line symbols: Symbols that indicate continuous objects and are drawn using either single or double lines. Line symbols are generally used to indicate objects such as walls, ductwork, and utility lines. Examples of line symbols are shown in Figure 6-2.

Material symbols: Symbols that graphically indicate construction materials or materials of existing conditions. Material symbols may be shown in elevation, section, or plan views, and are generally used to indicate objects such as brick, stone, earth, wood, concrete, and steel, as illustrated in Figure 6-3.

Object symbols: Symbols that graphically represent an item being depicted. Object symbols are generally used to indicate objects such as doors, windows, toilet fixtures, and furniture (see Figure 6-4 for examples).

FYI: Object symbols were originally called "template symbols," but the term was changed in NCS version 2.

Reference symbols: Symbols that refer the reader to information in another area of the set of drawings or that provide basic information regarding the drawings or data on the sheet. Reference symbols generally include elevation indicators, detail indicators, north arrow, graphic scale, section indicators, and revision

——◆——	1 Hour Fire Resistive Construction
— — CS — —	Pipe Line, Chemical Supply
— — SD — —	Storm Drain
— — LN — —	Liquid Nitrogen Line

Figure 6-2
Line Symbols

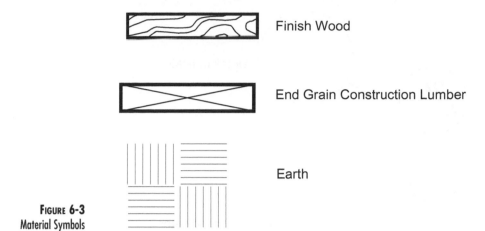

FIGURE 6-3
Material Symbols

Finish Wood

End Grain Construction Lumber

Earth

clouds. The use of abbreviations for "similar" or "opposite" in conjunction with section indicator symbols is not mentioned in the NCS; however, it is a common practice in architectural construction documents and, we believe, an acceptable practice. Several examples of reference symbols are given in Figure 6-5.

Text symbols: These symbols graphically depict a word or words and may appear in notations and on drawings. Text symbols are typically found on a computer keyboard; some examples of text symbols are shown in Figure 6-6.

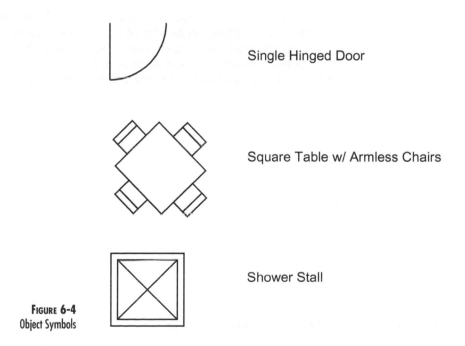

Single Hinged Door

Square Table w/ Armless Chairs

Shower Stall

FIGURE 6-4
Object Symbols

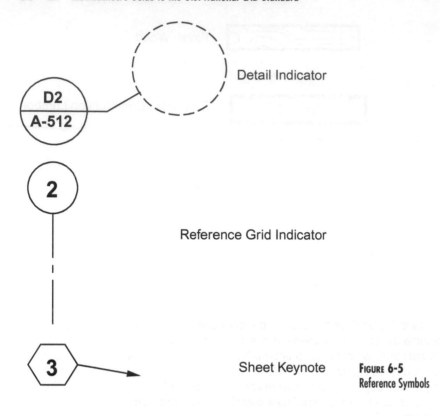

Detail Indicator

Reference Grid Indicator

Sheet Keynote

FIGURE 6-5
Reference Symbols

IMPLEMENTATION ISSUES

The first step to take during the symbols adoption process is also the easiest: inclusion of the 14 NCS text symbols. These can be adopted in the blink of an eye because most workplaces are already using the exact same format, and a CAD drawing does not have to be created for them. Once the text symbols have been adopted, however, the next steps will take more effort. When these steps are taken one at a time, the symbols implementation process will be much easier.

′   foot (feet)

″   inch (inches)

&   and

@   at

number, pound

FIGURE 6-6
Text Symbols

Before implementing reference, object, identity, line, and material symbols, a few other NCS components need to be incorporated into the workplace. For example, if the symbols are adopted before the AIA CAD Layer Guidelines are in place, the CAD layer names in each symbol will need to be reviewed and modified to conform to the proper formats in the **data fields** included in the AIA CAD Layer Guidelines. There are four layer name fields: discipline designators, **major group, minor groups,** and **status.** This is a good reason to make the AIA CAD Layer Guidelines the most important NCS component to adopt before taking on the symbols adoption process.

Another NCS component to adopt prior to symbols is file naming, because for them to be created, stored, and imported into CAD software, these two-dimensional symbols have to be given an electronic file name. Unless formats for file names from the UDS Drawing Set Organization are used to identify them, the names will need to be changed later. Using NCS-compliant file names will be very worthwhile; otherwise, it will take more time later to rename them.

Two other NCS components that need to be adopted prior to the symbols are the pen widths from the UDS Drafting Conventions Module and the NCS colors from Plotting Guidelines. These are almost as important as adopting the AIA CAD Layer Guidelines and file naming because their adoption makes it possible to create the symbols in accordance with the proper line widths and display colors. Doing so also precludes having to go back later and change them. The colors and pen widths also need to be coordinated with the proper CAD layer name.

After incorporating these NCS components, a systematic, prioritized approach should be used to implement the UDS Symbols Module. That is, a hierarchy needs to be established to identify and prioritize the symbols from most important to least important. Even though each discipline will prioritize the adoption order for symbols differently, we recommend adopting the reference symbols early on because they are common to all disciplines and are fairly easy to create.

We also recommend adopting the drawing block title, section indicators, detail indicators, and elevation indicators, because they are among the most commonly shared among the disciplines. After that, the remaining reference symbols should be incorporated, because the majority of them are also very easy to use and most are used by multiple disciplines.

After text and reference symbols, the remaining symbols can be adopted to suit the needs in the workplace. That said, keep in mind that some of these types of symbols will be more difficult to create than others. For example, line symbols and material symbols will be much easier to create than many of the object and identity symbols.

Certain reference symbols, such as elevation and section indicators, incorporate the sheet identification in the lower portion of the symbol. However, where user-defined designators are used, such as in large building projects, with multiple plan sheets, the sheet identification will not fit into the recommended size symbol. After testing several solutions to resolve this problem, we recommend breaking the symbol to allow the entire sheet identification to be shown. (For more about the overall implementation process, see Chapter 11, "Implementation.")

REVIEW OF KEY CONCEPTS IN THIS CHAPTER

1. Symbols are organized in the NCS first by MasterFormat 2004 Level 2 number and then by symbol classification.
2. The NCS classifies symbols into one of six types: identity symbols, line symbols, material symbols, object symbols, reference symbols, or text symbols.
3. The UDS Symbols Module should be implemented into the workplace after other NCS components have been adopted. These include the AIA CAD Layer Guidelines, NCS colors (Plotting Guidelines), and pen widths (UDS Drafting Conventions Module), because doing so will avoid having to go back and modify the symbols later.

FREQUENTLY ASKED QUESTIONS

Q: *Why was the CD that contained CAD files for each of the symbols discontinued after NCS version 2.0? Are they available somewhere else?*

A: When the UDS Symbols Module was first created, CSI was concerned that it would take time for CAD vendors to make them available in their software. In response to this issue, an optional CD was made available with NCS version 2.0 that contained CAD-formatted versions of each symbol.

Then, when NCS version 3.0 was adopted, more than 50 new symbols were added, and another 25 were either changed or deleted. Coupled with the fact that all 1,235 symbols (yes, we counted them) in NCS version 3.1 would have required their file names to be coordinated with MasterFormat 2004, the costs associated with updating the CD were deemed not affordable, and so it was discontinued.

At the time of this writing, the NCS symbols were not available from CAD software vendors, nor had any third-party software company picked them up. We expect a vendor out there somewhere will soon come to the rescue and provide them, but until then, many of the NCS symbols can be used or created without interfering with CAD production too much. This is discussed further in the "Implementation Issues" section above.

Q: *The UDS Symbols Module includes a symbol for the north arrow. Is it the only north arrow symbol allowed?*

A: Unlike the other symbols in the module, the authors of the UDS Symbols Module intended for the north arrow symbol to only serve as an example and allow other formats to be used. Unfortunately, they didn't do as good a job of explaining this as they could have (we confess, we blame ourselves, too).

The primary reason the format is optional is that, traditionally, many workplaces have designed their own north arrow that is often used to give their organizations a unique identity. The concept that the north arrow symbol format is only an example is suggested in the discussion on drawing orientation and north arrows included in the UDS Drafting Conventions Module. Like the examples of typical schedules in Appendix B of the UDS Schedules Module, it is okay to make alterations. Whatever symbol you decide on for the north arrow, we recommend using the same one throughout the drawing set.

Q: *Most of the symbols in the UDS Symbols Module are different from the ones we use in our workplace. Where did they come from?*

A: Most of the symbols came from the CADD/GIS Technology Center (CGTC). At the time the UDS Symbols Module was being created, the CGTC had a collection of more than 1,200 symbols that had been gathered from various disciplines of design firms that were developing projects for the U.S. Department of Defense. At the time, the collection represented the most commonly used symbols; and since many of the first organizations to adopt the NCS were federal agencies, it was decided that if a conflict occurred, it was better to use the Tri-Services version because of the marketplace it represented.

Q: *Why doesn't the UDS Symbols Module identify the CAD layers and pen widths that should be used for the symbols?*

A: Assigning CAD layers to all the symbols in the NCS is not possible because many of them are shared among multiple disciplines. For example, a centerline is a line symbol used by most disciplines, as are drawing block titles, section indicators, concrete patterns, and text symbols, just to name a few.

Line widths have been identified for most of the reference and line symbols because they are scale-independent. Establishing line widths for scale-dependent symbols, such as material and object symbols, is not possible because pen widths of the same symbol will change, depending upon the drawing scale.

Q: *The original version of the UDS Symbols Module classified template symbols. What happened to them?*

A: When the UDS Symbols Module was adopted by amendment into NCS version 2, certain members of the NCS Project Committee felt the term "template symbol" was not definitive enough for the door swings, metal angles, appliances, and many of the other symbol types that many of us had created by hand with a plastic drafting template. The classification was changed by amendment to NCS version 2, to "object symbols." We like the original name better and are confident the revision would never have been made under the current NCSPC Rules of Governance.

Q: *Our client wants us to use a detail indicator symbol where the bottom of the symbol is divided in half to indicate each sheet in the drawing set, where the detail is taken from, as well as the sheet the detail appears on. Why isn't this symbol in the NCS?*

A: Using a reference symbol with a "split-bottom bubble" is not recommended for many reasons. One of the problems is that the premise of the symbol conflicts with the concept of how drawings should be used. Details are created from views such as sections, plans, and elevations. Drawing users should be looking at the larger-scale views first, then the details generated from them—not the other way around.

   Another problem is that the text required to indicate each sheet in the limited space of the symbol (one-quarter of the bubble—"the split bottom") can take quite a bit of creativity, and often results in cluttering the drawing block with text that has to extend beyond the symbol itself.

   Referencing each sheet the details are taken from simply requires too much handholding, which is just not needed by the constructors. Perhaps more importantly, it places additional liability issues on the designer if one of the references is not included (we are aware of at least one situation where a contractor was successful in filing a claim as a result of a reference that was overlooked).

   One last comment: Recording every sheet where a detail is referenced is an administration headache because it requires a great deal of time to accurately track each instance where the detail is referenced and is rarely 100% accurate. Time spent recording each instance of a detail's point of origin is time spent away from thoughts about design and constructability.

Q: *Can we use arrowheads instead of slashes for terminating dimension lines?*

A: No. The NCS requires the use of slashes for dimension line terminators; arrowheads are used for the termination of leaders.

Notations

GENERAL

It is the responsibility of the architect's instruments of service to communicate the design intent. But with the typical $100M project having more than 150,000 separate documents, the words used on construction drawings must be clear, complete, correct, and concise. This textual information is referred to as notations. The architect is responsible for coordinating the notations used throughout the drawing set to ensure they meet these requirements and are coordinated with the terms and language used in the project manual, form of agreement, and other contract documents.

The format requirements for notations are located in the UDS Notations Module of the Construction Specification Institute's Uniform Drawing System (UDS). This module was published by CSI in 2000, and it became part of the U.S. National CAD Standard (NCS) version 2.0 in 2001. The primary intent of the UDS Notations Module is to improve construction document quality by establishing format requirements for text notes that are located within the sheet's drawing area and note block. The standard provides consistent methodology for the creation, use, and appearance of notations. When incorporated into the workplace, these formats will help streamline communication among all the drawing users. This includes owners, designers, consultants, contractors, and material suppliers. During the creation of drawings, the formats can also be used as tools that can play a significant role in the quality control process. By improving document quality, NCS-compliant notations help reduce the effort needed to create drawings, bid projects, and construct and manage facilities.

The standards included in the UDS Notations Module provide methods to improve coordination between drawings and specifications in the project manual. The formats also make it possible to modify the documents more efficiently during the design and construction phases of the project. They also make it easier for contractors and material suppliers to locate information, which will necessitate fewer phone calls to design professionals, asking for help. Perhaps the most significant impact this NCS component offers is the potential to help designers, contractors, owners, and material suppliers to work better together as a team, by helping reduce errors and omissions.

TYPES OF NOTATIONS

The UDS Notations Module establishes the format requirements for five types of notations used on construction drawings:

- General notes
- General discipline notes
- General sheet notes

- Reference keynotes
- Sheet keynotes

None of the requirements for these note types was created by the authors of the Uniform Drawing System; rather, like many of the formats throughout the NCS, they were developed from construction drawing methodologies that had been in use in workplaces for many years.

General notes, general discipline notes, and general sheet notes are very similar in nature. They only appear in a sheet's note block, and each type of note applies to very specific sheets within the drawing set. Reference keynotes and sheet keynotes consist of a symbol that is located in drawing blocks and keyed to a notation in the sheet's note block. However, reference keynotes link elements on the drawings to specific documents in the project manual, whereas sheet keynotes identify items that are *not* referenced to the project manual.

Reference keynotes and sheet keynotes must be located in drawing blocks according to the hierarchy established in the UDS Drafting Conventions Module. Each of these types of notations will be discussed in greater detail below, including many of the implementation issues associated with them.

GENERAL NOTES

The first type of general notations are general notes. These notes have been around for a very long time and were probably invented within moments after lines were placed on the world's first construction drawing. General notes are just what their name implies: notations that are general in nature. They apply to all drawings within the drawing set, and therefore must be located within General discipline (G-series) sheets. When general notes are used on a sheet, they are located at the top of the note block, above all other note types. They must appear under a heading bar, and the layout of the note block must meet specific requirements of the UDS Notations Module. For some typical examples of these types of notes refer to Figure 7-1. The format requirements for the layout of the note block heading bar, margins, text height, text alignment, and note block border line widths are indicated in the UDS Notations Module.

General notes are also used for code information that is applicable to the entire project. The specific location and appearance of the information is discussed further in Chapter 8, "Code Conventions." An example of code information appearing as general notes is illustrated in Figure 7-2.

GENERAL DISCIPLINE NOTES

General discipline notes are almost identical to general notes, except they only apply to a specific discipline within the drawing set. They are identified with the same name of the discipline they apply to. For example, general discipline notes that apply to the Civil discipline (C-series) sheets are called general civil notes; general discipline notes that apply to the Mechanical discipline (M-series) sheets are called general mechanical notes.

Since these types of notes only apply to each of the sheets within a single discipline, they are located on sheet type designator 0-series (General) sheets. For example, general architectural notes would be located on sheet A-001; general electrical notes would be located on sheet E-001; and general plumbing notes would be located on sheet P-001. These notations are also located at the top of the note block, under a heading bar. When they appear on the same sheet with general notes, they must be located below them, with their own heading bar. Like general notes, the

GENERAL NOTES

1. ABBREVIATIONS: REFERENCED FROM VERSION 3.1 OF THE U.S. NATIONAL CAD STANDARD

2. LOCATION AND APPEARANCE OF REGULATORY INFORMATION: iN ACCORDANCE WITH VERSION 3.1 OF THE U.S. NATIONAL CAD STANDARD.

3. DEFINITIONS:
   FURNISH: SUPPLY AND DELIVER TO PROJECT SITE, READY FOR INSPECTION.
   INSTALL: PLACE IN POSITION FOR SERVICE OR USE,
   PROVIDE: FURNISH AND INSTALL, COMPLETE AND READY FOR INTENDED USE.

4. SCHEDULE DISRUPTION OF UTILITY SERVICES TO THE SITE AND BUILDING WITH THE OWNER AT LEAST 48 HOURS IN ADVANCE.

5. EXISTING BUILDING SPACES MAY NOT BE USED FOR STORAGE.

6. DUST CONTROL: EXECUTE WORK BY METHODS TO MINIMIZE RAISING DUST FROM CONSTRUCTION OPERATIONS. PROVIDE POSITIVE MEANS TO PREVENT AIR-BORNE DUST FROM DISPERSING INTO ATMOSPHERE.

7. VERIFY LOCATIONS OF SURVEY CONTROL POINTS PRIOR TO STARTING WORK. PROMPTLY NOTIFY ARCHITECT OF ANY DISCREPANCIES DISCOVERED.

FIGURE 7-1   Examples of General Notes

GENERAL NOTES

1.   APPLICABLE CODES:
     BUILDING AND STRUCTURAL: 2003 STATE OF NEW MEXICO COMMERCIAL BUILDING CODE (2003 INTERNATIONAL BUILDING CODE, AS AMENDED)

     PLUMBING: 2003 STATE OF NEW MEXICO PLUMBING CODE (2003 UNIFORM PLUMBING CODE AND ALL APPENDICES, AS AMENDED)

     MECHANICAL: 2003 STATE OF NEW MEXICO MECHANICAL CODE (2003 UNIFORM MECHANICAL CODE, AS AMENDED)

     ELECTRICAL: 2002 STATE OF NEW MEXICO ELECTRICAL CODE (2002 NATIONAL ELECTRICAL CODE, AS AMENDED)

     ENERGY: 2003 STATE OF NEW MEXICO ENERGY CONSERVATION CODE (2003 INTERNATIONAL ENERGY CONSERVATION CODE, AS AMENDED)

     ACCESSIBILITY: ICC/ANSI A117.1-2003

FIGURE 7-2   Code Information Presented as General Notes

GENERAL STRUCTURAL NOTES

1. CLEAN FORMS AS ERECTION PROCEEDS TO REMOVE FOREIGN MATTER WITHIN FORMS.

2. WELDING OF REINFORCEMENT IS NOT PERMITTED.

3. DO NOT DISPLACE VAPOR RETARDER. REPAIR VAPOR RETARDER DAMAGED DURING PLACEMENT OF CONCRETE REINFORCING WITH VAPOR RETARDER MATERIAL. LAP OVER DAMAGED AREAS MINIMUM 12 INCHES AND SEAL WATERTIGHT.

4. SAW CUT JOINTS WITHIN 18 HOURS AFTER PLACING.

5. ALLOW FOR ERECTION LOADS, AND PROVIDE SUFFICIENT TEMPORARY BRACING TO MAINTAIN STRUCTURE IN SAFE CONDITION, PLUMB, AND IN TRUE ALIGNMENT UNTIL COMPLETION OF ERECTION AND INSTALLATION OF PERMANENT BRACING.

6. GROUT SOLIDLY BETWEEN COLUMN PLATES AND BEARING SURFACES, COMPLYING WITH MANUFACTURER'S INSTRUCTIONS FOR NONSHRINK GROUT. TROWEL GROUTED SURFACES SMOOTH, SPLAYING NEATLY TO 45 DEGREES.

FIGURE 7-3 Examples of General Discipline Notes

heading bar, margins, text height, text alignment, and note block border line widths for note blocks containing general discipline notes must comply with the requirements of the UDS Notations Module. Examples of these types of notes are shown in Figure 7-3.

GENERAL SHEET NOTES

General sheet notes are similar to general notes and general discipline notes, but they only apply to the sheet on which they appear. Therefore, they can be found in note blocks on any sheet in the drawing set. These types of notes are also located at the top of the note block. When they appear on the same sheet with general notes and/or general discipline notes, they are located below them. Like each of the other types of general notations, the layout of the note block containing general sheet notes must be formatted according to the requirements in the UDS Notations Module. For examples of these types of notes, refer to Figure 7-4.

USE OF GENERAL NOTATIONS ON SMALLER PROJECTS

FYI: Many of the illustrations included in the UDS Notations Module were originally created on table napkins during visits to Murphy's Irish Pub, a popular watering hole located in Alexandria, Virginia.

Locating general notations in drawing sets for smaller projects will be different than for larger projects. Since smaller projects require fewer sheets, it is usually a waste of resources to create a General discipline (G-series) sheet just for general notes. Likewise, it would be excessive to create a sheet type designator 0-series (General) sheet for the location of general discipline notes, if there were no other need for the sheet. The NCS provides options for smaller projects by allowing general notes and general discipline notes to be located on other sheet types.

```
┌──────────────────────────────────────────────────────────────────────┐
│  GENERAL  SHEET  NOTES                                                 │
├──────────────────────────────────────────────────────────────────────┤
│  1. DIMENSIONS TO PARTITIONS ARE TO FACE OF STUD UNLESS NOTED          │
│     OTHERWISE.                                                         │
│                                                                        │
│  2. SPACE STUDS AT 16 INCHES ON CENTER.                                │
│                                                                        │
│  3. FINISH ALL GYPSUM BOARD IN ACCORDANCE WITH ASTM C 840, LEVEL 3.    │
│                                                                        │
│  4. HANG CEILING SUSPENSION SYSTEM INDEPENDENT OF WALLS, COLUMNS,      │
│     DUCTS, PIPES AND CONDUIT.                                          │
│                                                                        │
│  5. SUSPENDED CEILINGS AND SOFFITS: SPACE FRAMING AND FURRING MEMBERS  │
│     AT 12 INCHES ON CENTER.                                            │
│                                                                        │
│  6. SEE SHEET A—601 FOR ROOM FINISH SCHEDULE.                          │
│                                                                        │
└───────────────────────────────────────────────/\─────────────────────┘
```

FIGURE 7-4   Examples of General Sheet Notes

The UDS Notations Module allows each type of general notation to be combined within the same note block when sheets in the drawing set are limited, provided they are located at the top of note blocks in accordance with the following hierarchy:

First Priority: General notes
Second Priority: General discipline notes
Third Priority: General sheet notes

An example of this concept is when a civil site plan (Sheet C-101) or an architectural floor plan (A-101) is the first sheet in a small drawing set.

Combining general notations in the same note block is not limited to small projects. When larger projects do not include the G-series (General) sheets, where general notes are located, or sheet type designator 0-series (General) sheets, where general discipline notes are located, they can be placed with notations on other sheets. This methodology helps to conserve resources, so we strongly recommend using it whenever possible. In this situation, general notes should be located on the first sheet in the drawing set; general discipline notes should be located on the first sheet in the discipline. For examples of combining general notations on the same sheet, refer to Figure 7-5.

Reference Keynotes

Reference keynotes identify elements in the drawing area with a symbol that is keyed to a text notation in the note block. The symbol contains five components, as indicated in Figure 7-6.

The **root** of the reference keynote symbol identifies a specific document, or specification section, within the project manual, where information about the item being identified can be found. This methodology is commonly referred to as **linking.** Even though reference keynotes are primarily used for linking products or materials to specification sections, they can also used to identify and link other types of items such as:

GENERAL NOTES

1. CONTRACTOR TO PAY PERMIT FEES AS REQUIRED BY LOCAL AUTHORITIES HAVING JURISDICTION.

2. DEFINITIONS:
   FURNISH: SUPPLY AND DELIVER TO PROJECT SITE, READY FOR INSPECTION.
   INSTALL: PLACE IN POSITION FOR SERVICE OR USE.
   PROVIDE: FURNISH AND INSTALL, COMPLETE AND READY FOR INTENDED USE.

3. ABBREVIATIONS: REFERENCED FROM VERSION 3.1 OF THE U.S. NATIONAL CAD STANDARD.

GENERAL ARCHITECTURAL NOTES

1. VISUAL REQUIREMENTS: DO NOT CUT AND PATCH IN A MANNER THAT WOULD, IN THE ARCHITECT'S OPINION, REDUCE THE BUILDING'S AESTHETIC QUALITIES.

2. DO NOT CUT AND PATCH WALLS AND CEILINGS IN A MANNER THAT WOULD RESULT IN VISUAL EVIDENCE OF CUTTING AND PATCHING.

3. REFER TO SECTION 01 70 00 FOR ADDITIONAL CUTTING AND PATCHING REQUIREMENTS.

GENERAL SHEET NOTES

1. PROVIDE 6 MIL THICK PLASTIC MOISTURE BARRIER OVER FLOORING BELOW SKYLIGHTS AND WINDOW UNITS INDICATED TO BE REMOVED; SEAL SEAMS AND TERMINIATIONS OF BARRIER WATER TIGHT WITH WATER-RESISTANT TAPE.

2. EXTEND MOISTURE BARRIER BEYOND FLOORING PERIMETER AS REQUIRED FOR PROTECTION AGAINST WIND-DRIVEN RAIN AND MOISTURE.

3. TURN EDGE OF MOISTURE BARRIER UP AT TERMINATIONS AS REQUIRED TO PREVENT WATER FROM TRAVELING BEYOND PERIMETER.

4. REMOVE STANDING WATER FROM MOISTURE BARRIER AS IT ACCUMULATES.

5. PROVIDE PLYWOOD BARRIER OVER FLOORING LOCATED BELOW SKYLIGHTS INDICATED TO BE REMOVED; PROVIDE PLYWOOD PANELS IN SUFFICIENT THICKNESS TO PROTECT FLOORS AND MOISTURE BARRIER FROM FALLING TOOLS AND OBJECTS.

FIGURE 7-5
Combining General Notations on the Same Sheet

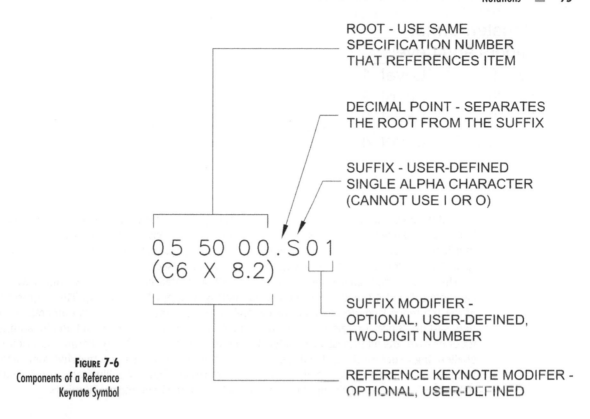

ROOT - USE SAME SPECIFICATION NUMBER THAT REFERENCES ITEM

DECIMAL POINT - SEPARATES THE ROOT FROM THE SUFFIX

SUFFIX - USER-DEFINED SINGLE ALPHA CHARACTER (CANNOT USE I OR O)

05 50 00.S01
(C6 X 8.2)

SUFFIX MODIFIER - OPTIONAL, USER-DEFINED, TWO-DIGIT NUMBER

REFERENCE KEYNOTE MODIFER - OPTIONAL, USER-DEFINED

FIGURE 7-6
Components of a Reference
Keynote Symbol

- Soil boring locations
- Alternates
- Temporary dust barriers
- Existing construction
- Selective site demolition items

This concept will be discussed later in this chapter.

Each reference keynote symbol that appears in the drawing area is keyed to a text notation under the reference keynote heading bar in the note block. Reference keynotes are always located beneath any general notations that appear in the note block. To minimize the effort needed for revisions that may later occur, the notation must be brief, generic, and not include proprietary information. This will allow many changes to be made only in the project manual and will help to minimize changes on the drawings. Some examples of this concept include:

- Instead of "4-PLY HOT-MOPPED ASPHALT ROOFING," use, "BUILT-UP ROOFING."
- Instead of "R30 EXTRUDED TYPE IV POLYSTYRENE BOARD INSULATION," use, "ROOF INSULATION."
- Instead of "INTEGRAL COLORED, MOISTURE-RESISTANT, SPLIT-FACE FLUTED CONCRETE BLOCK," use, "CONCRETE MASONRY UNIT—TYPE A."

Reference Keynote Roots

The root of the reference keynote symbol has undergone significant changes since the UDS Notations Module was first adopted by the NCS. The changes became necessary when CSI incorporated the 2004 edition of MasterFormat into the UDS modules in NCS version 3.1. The MasterFormat 2004 update expanded the format for the location of construction information from 16 divisions

MasterFormat
Numbers and Levels

08	00	00	Level 1
08	11	00	Level 2
08	11	13	Level 3
08	11	13 .16	Level 4

FIGURE 7-7
MasterFormat 2004 Numbering Structure

to 50 divisions. The specification section numbering system for Level 1, Level 2, and Level 3 numbers was expanded from five digits to six and includes a provision for eight-digit, Level 4 numbers that feature a decimal (the decimal is referred to by MasterFormat as a "dot"). Figure 7-7 shows typical examples of the MasterFormat 2004 specification section numbers.

The most complicated issue MasterFormat 2004 created for reference keynotes was the new eight-digit, Level 4 specification section numbering (i.e., NN NN NN.NN). This requires the root of the reference keynote symbol to be expanded to accommodate the extra numerals used by the new system. Since the reference keynote symbol already had a decimal and an alphanumeric suffix of its own, the additional decimal (dot) and numerals added by MasterFormat 2004 raised some challenging issues for the updated symbol. The resulting appearance is somewhat confusing at first, but becomes clear once the methodology is understood. Figure 7-8 illustrates some examples of reference keynote symbols that incorporate each level of MasterFormat numbers.

ROOT (LEVEL 1 NUMBER)
05 00 00 . A

ROOT (LEVEL 2 NUMBER)
05 51 00 . A

ROOT (LEVEL 3 NUMBER)
05 51 33 . A

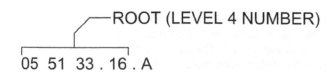
ROOT (LEVEL 4 NUMBER)
05 51 33 . 16 . A

FIGURE 7-8
Reference Keynote Symbols Using MasterFormat 2004 Numbers

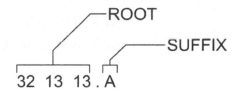

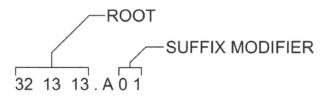

FIGURE 7-9
Reference Keynote Suffix and Suffix Modifier

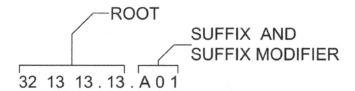

Reference Keynote Suffix

The **suffix** in the reference keynote symbol is mandatory and serves to provide unique identifiers for elements that are being referenced to the same document in the project manual. The suffix is a user-defined alpha character (with the exception of the letters O and I, which cannot be used to avoid confusing them with numerals). Since only 24 letters from the alphabet are available, two user-defined numerals, called the **suffix modifier,** can be added after the alpha character in order to provide an almost limitless supply of identifiers for each specification section. Two numerals between 01 and 99 must be used for the suffix modifiers. Figure 7-9 provides an example of the reference keynote suffix and suffix modifier.

Reference Keynote Modifiers

The reference keynote modifier is a user-defined, optional component consisting of textual information located in parentheses below the reference keynote symbol. The text describes unique characteristics about an item, such as size, finish, quantity, and locations. The modifiers help to avoid having to create a unique reference keynote for every variation of the same item. For example, instead of creating a reference keynote for every size and configuration of a steel angle, a single reference keynote can be used for all steel angles, with a reference keynote modifier added to identify unique size and configuration requirements.

Because space for information within the reference keynote modifier is rather limited, use of abbreviations and text symbols will help save space. When using abbreviations, they must comply with the format requirements included in the UDS Terms and Abbreviations Module. If text symbols are used, they must comply with the UDS Symbols Module. Reference keynote modifiers play a significant role during the creation of the reference keynote office master, discussed later in this chapter. Figure 7-10 illustrates some examples of reference keynote modifiers.

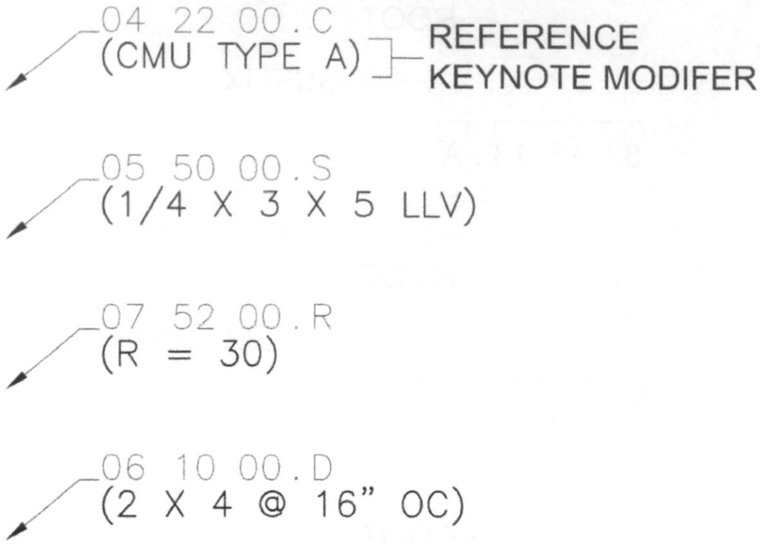

04 22 00.C
(CMU TYPE A) ⎤— REFERENCE
                   KEYNOTE MODIFER

05 50 00.S
(1/4 X 3 X 5 LLV)

07 52 00.R
(R = 30)

06 10 00.D
(2 X 4 @ 16" OC)

Figure 7-10
Examples of Reference Keynote Modifiers

Reference Keynote Appearance Options

Two of the most important issues resulting from the MasterFormat 2004 updates are the read-ability of the numbers in the reference keynote symbol and the space needed for the symbol in the drawing and note blocks. MasterFormat 2004 offers three options for the graphic display for-mat of the numbers. Displaying the first six numerals of the specification number with a space between the Level 1 and Level 2 numbers, and again between the Level 2 and the Level 3 num-bers, as illustrated in Figure 7-7, is the recommended configuration. However, when this format is combined with the reference keynote suffix and suffix modifier, the symbol becomes very elon-gated and consumes more space in the drawing and note blocks. When a Level 4 MasterFormat number is used, the symbol needs even more space, and readability is even more difficult. An ex-ample of some of the readability concerns can be seen in Figure 7-11.

If the readability or space requirements of the reference keynote format is a concern, other al-ternatives are available that will help address these issues. MasterFormat allows two other op-tions for the graphical display of the Level 1, Level 2, and Level 3 numbers. The first option is to leave the space between the Level 1 and Level 2 numbers and remove the space between the Level 2 and Level 3 numbers, as illustrated in Figure 7-12. The second option is to remove the space between the Level 1 and Level 2 numbers and between the Level 2 and Level 3 numbers, as indicated in Figure 7-13. Even though the second option (Figure 7-13) requires less space in the drawing and note blocks, the resulting symbol is more difficult to read, so we do not recom-mend using it. The first option (Figure 7-12) also saves space and is easier to read; therefore, we recommend it when choosing between these two options.

When considering options for the appearance of the reference keynote, the arrangement of the MasterFormat level numbers in the root of the reference keynote symbol should match the arrangement of the specification section numbers in the project manual. For example, if the nu-merals in the specification section numbers have a space between the Level 1 and Level 2 num-bers, such as 04 2223, the arrangement of the numerals in the root of reference keynote symbol should also have a space between the Level 1 and Level 2 numbers (e.g., 04 2223). Using dif-ferent arrangements for the appearance of the numbers should be avoided because the UDS No-tations Module requires the root of the reference keynote to be the same specification number that references the item.

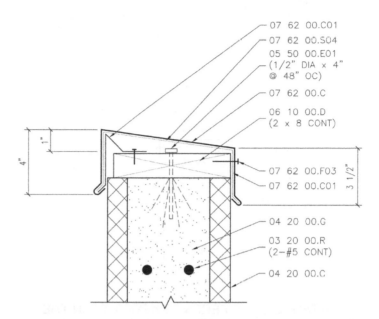

APPEARANCE OF REFERENCE KEYNOTES IN THE DRAWING BLOCK (SPACE BETWEEN LEVEL 1 AND 2, AND BETWEEN LEVEL 2 AND 3 NUMBERS)

REFERENCE KEYNOTES

DIVISION 03 — CONCRETE
03 20 00.R   REINFORCING STEEL

DIVISION 04 — MASONRY
04 20 00.C   CONCRETE MASONRY UNIT
04 20 00.G   GROUT

DIVISION 05 — METALS
05 50 00.E01 EXPANSION ANCHOR

DIVISION 06 — WOOD, PLASTICS, AND COMPOSITES
06 10 00.D   DIMENSION LUMBER

DIVISION 07 — THERMAL AND MOISTURE PROTECTION
07 62 00.C   COPING
07 62 00.C01 CLEAT
07 62 00.F03 FASTENER
07 62 00.S04 SPLICE PLATE

FIGURE 7-11
Reference Keynotes with Appearance of Root as Recommended by MasterFormat

APPEARANCE OF REFERENCE KEYNOTES IN THE NOTE BLOCK (SPACE BETWEEN LEVEL 1 AND 2, AND BETWEEN LEVEL 2 AND 3 NUMBERS)

Another option that some organizations are using for reference keynote roots is employed during the schematic phase of the project, when specific products and materials have not yet been determined. When these types of notes are needed, the appropriate five-character alphanumeric UniFormat number can be used for the root. This methodology also can be used to identify objects created by CAD software programs. However, if an elemental organizational format for the numbers is being considered, we recommend postponing the use of UniFormat until upcoming

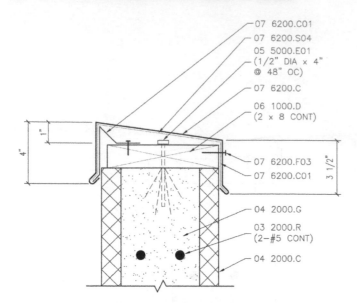

APPEARANCE OF REFERENCE KEYNOTES IN THE
DRAWING BLOCK (SPACE BETWEEN LEVEL 1 AND
LEVEL 2 NUMBERS ONLY)

REFERENCE KEYNOTES

DIVISION 03 – CONCRETE
03 2000.R   REINFORCING STEEL

DIVISION 04 – MASONRY
04 2000.C   CONCRETE MASONRY UNIT
04 2000.G   GROUT

DIVISION 05 – METALS
05 5000.E01   EXPANSION ANCHOR

DIVISION 06 – WOOD, PLASTICS, AND COMPOSITES
06 1000.D   DIMENSION LUMBER

DIVISION 07 – THERMAL AND MOISTURE PROTECTION
07 6200.C   COPING
07 6200.C01   CLEAT
07 6200.F03   FASTENER
07 6200.S04   SPLICE PLATE

APPEARANCE OF REFERENCE KEYNOTES IN THE
NOTE BLOCK (SPACE BETWEEN LEVEL 1 AND
LEVEL 2 NUMBERS ONLY)

FIGURE 7-12
Option 1: Reference Keynotes with Space between the Level 1
and Level 2 Numbers Only

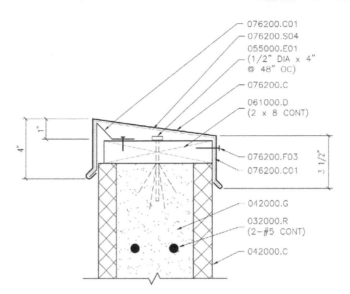

076200.C01
076200.S04
055000.E01
(1/2" DIA x 4"
@ 48" OC)

076200.C

061000.D
(2 x 8 CONT)

076200.F03
076200.C01

042000.G

032000.R
(2-#5 CONT)

042000.C

1"
4"
3 1/2"

APPEARANCE OF REFERENCE KEYNOTES IN THE
DRAWING BLOCK (NO SPACES BETWEEN NUMBERS)

REFERENCE KEYNOTES

DIVISION 03 — CONCRETE
032000.R   REINFORCING STEEL

DIVISION 04 — MASONRY
042000.C   CONCRETE MASONRY UNIT
042000.G   GROUT

DIVISION 05 — METALS
055000.E01   EXPANSION ANCHOR

DIVISION 06 — WOOD, PLASTICS, AND COMPOSITES
061000.D   DIMENSION LUMBER

DIVISION 07 — THERMAL AND MOISTURE PROTECTION
076200.C   COPING
076200.C01   CLEAT
076200.F03   FASTENER
076200.S04   SPLICE PLATE

FIGURE 7-13
Option 2: Reference Keynotes with Spaces between the
MasterFormat Levels Removed

APPEARANCE OF REFERENCE KEYNOTES IN THE
NOTE BLOCK (NO SPACES BETWEEN NUMBERS)

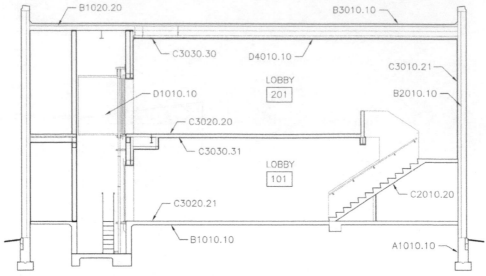

APPEARANCE IN THE DRAWING BLOCK

REFERENCE KEYNOTES

SUBSTRUCTURE
A1010.10   CAST—IN—PLACE CONCRETE FOUNDATION WALL

SHELL
B1010.10   CAST—IN—PLACE CONCRETE FLOOR SLAB
B1020.20   PRECAST HOLLOW CORE PLANK ROOF DECK
B2010.10   CONCRETE MASONRY WALLS
B3010.10   MEMBRANE ROOFING

INTERIORS
C2010.20   CAST—IN—PLACE CONCRETE STAIR
C3020.21   GYPSUM PLASTER WALL FINISH
C3020.20   CARPETING
C3020.21   QUARRY TILE
C3030.30   ACOUSTICAL TILE CEILING
C3030.31   GYPSUM PLASTER CEILING FINISH

SERVICES
D1010.10   HYDRAULIC ELEVATOR
D4010.10   FIRE SPRINKLERING

APPEARANCE IN THE NOTE BLOCK

Figure 7-14   Reference Keynotes Using UniFormat Numbers

changes are released by CSI. (For more information about the pending changes, visit www.csinet.org.) An example of reference keynotes using the UniFormat numbering system is demonstrated in Figure 7-14.

Some organizations employ a methodology for the reference keynote suffix that assigns the alpha portion of the suffix to certain user-defined categories. There are many options available. One system we've seen organizes the suffixes into product

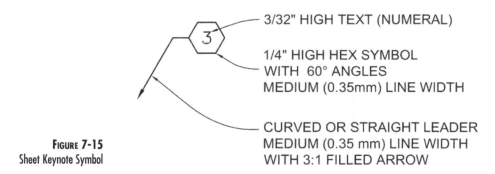

3/32" HIGH TEXT (NUMERAL)

1/4" HIGH HEX SYMBOL
WITH 60° ANGLES
MEDIUM (0.35mm) LINE WIDTH

CURVED OR STRAIGHT LEADER
MEDIUM (0.35 mm) LINE WIDTH
WITH 3:1 FILLED ARROW

FIGURE 7-15
Sheet Keynote Symbol

or material categories that are common to other sections. For example, each fastener-related product from each specification section can be identified with the same alpha character in the reference keynote suffix. Of the many options available for defining the reference keynote suffix, we still haven't found a system we like nearly as much as the one we recommend, which is discussed later in this chapter.

SHEET KEYNOTES

Sheet keynotes identify items in a drawing, but they are not linked to documents or specification sections in the project manual. Some of the uses for sheet keynotes include:

- Identifying hidden conditions
- Describing installation requirements
- Identifying elements from other disciplines

> **FYI:** The selection of the hexagon symbol to identify Sheet Keynotes was not completely arbitrary. Many of the alternatives such as circles, triangles, and rectangles could conflict with other symbols and object lines in the drawing area.

The sheet keynote symbol consists of a hexagon, with a number that is keyed to a notation in the sheet keynote portion of the note block, as illustrated in Figure 7-15.

Sheet keynote symbols are located in the graphic and notation area of drawing blocks. The sheet keynotes are located beneath reference keynotes in the note block, and the heading bar that identifies them includes a representation of the hexagon symbol. Figure 7-16 provides an example of sheet keynote symbols in the drawing block and sheet keynotes in the note block.

IMPLEMENTATION ISSUES

Implementation of the UDS Notations Module is best accomplished in stages, and the easiest portions of the module should be adopted first. Based on the least amount of effort that will be required to incorporate the formats into the workplace, we recommend prioritizing them in the following order:

1. General notations (all three types)
2. Sheet keynotes
3. Reference keynotes

Because the notations are located either on a drawing and/or in the note block areas, they should not be implemented until after the format requirements included in the UDS Sheet Organization Module have been adopted. The overall NCS adoption process is discussed in Chapter

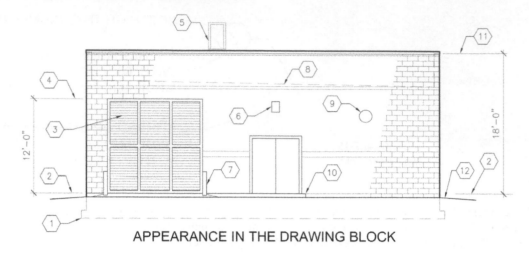

APPEARANCE IN THE DRAWING BLOCK

⬡ SHEET KEYNOTES

1. DASHED LINE INDICATES FOUNDATION – SEE STRUCTURAL SHEETS.
2. FINISH FLOOR – SEE CIVIL SHEETS FOR CONTROL DATUM.
3. LOUVER – SEE MECHANICAL SHEETS.
4. TOP OF LOUVER.
5. LADDER BEYOND.
6. ELECTRICAL LIGHT FIXTURE – SEE ELECTRICAL SHEETS.
7. BOLLARD–SEE STRUCTURAL SHEETS.
8. DASHED LINE INDICATES ROOF LINE.
9. EXHAUST FAN – SEE MECHANICAL SHEETS.
10. PAVING – SEE CIVIL SHEETS.
11. TOP OF MASONRY.
12. FINISH GRADE – SEE CIVIL SHEETS.

APPEARANCE IN THE NOTE BLOCK

Figure 7-16 Appearance of Sheet Keynotes

11, "Implementation." Specific implementation issues associated with each type of notation are discussed below.

The Notations Coordinator

Before notations are implemented, a **notations coordinator** needs to be identified. The notations coordinator will be responsible for:

- Creating the sheet keynote office master.
- Creating the reference keynote office master.
- Creating the format for the numerals in the reference keynote symbol and coordinating it with the appearance of the specification numbering system in the project manual office master (specifications master).

- Creating notation terminology in the reference keynote office master and coordinating it with terms in the project manual master and the UDS Terms and Abbreviations Module.
- Maintaining the reference keynote office master and the sheet keynote office master.

In a sense, the notations coordinator becomes empowered as the office's notation "czar," because the process he or she oversees needs to be strictly adhered to if it is going to succeed. A single coordinator will be much more efficient than a committee, because it will streamline the decision-making process. That said, the notations coordinator will also need to work with other members of the workplace because their input will be also be necessary if the process is going to succeed.

The best candidates for notations coordinators possess a variety of qualifications. Some of the most important characteristics include:

- Specifications writer, or strong background with specifications process
- Excellent knowledge of construction documents
- Familiarity with NCS components
- Familiarity with sheet keynote software
- Familiarity with CAD software
- Familiarity with reference keynote software
- Membership on the NCS Project Committee

Implementation of General Notations

The requirements for general notations are so similar to those already being used by most architects and engineers prior to the arrival of the NCS, they can be adopted with very little effort. The biggest obstacle to overcome is the creation of the note block in strict accordance with the formats included in the illustrations in the UDS Notations Module. The appearance of each of the note block formats was given previously in Figures 7-1 through 7-5.

Another implementation concern is the coordination of each type of general notation with consultants. However, since the project management efforts related to these issues are similar to those that existed before the advent of the NCS, the coordination concepts are virtually unchanged. Usually, it doesn't require too much effort to make sure each consultant understands how to classify, format, and locate each type of general notation according to the NCS.

Implementation of Sheet Keynotes

We recommend implementing sheet keynotes after adopting each of the general notation types, because the process will require a few more resources. However, since many workplaces are already familiar with them, sheet keynotes are often adopted at the same time as general notes, general discipline notes, and general sheet notes. Adopting the sheet keynote format requirements for the note block, as indicated in Figure 7-16, is made easier once the note block format for each of the general notations is in place. The major issue for many design professionals to come to terms with is replacing their current symbols (circles, ellipses, triangles, and rectangles) with the hexagon shape required by the NCS. This is a common issue for many other NCS format requirements, which are discussed further in Chapter 11.

Sheet keynote software is available in CAD software packages, including one or two that are available from third-party or add-on software companies. Typically, the software provides a means to generate the hexagon symbol and leader and the sequential numbers used for each note. One of the best features sheet keynote software provides is the capability to generate a table for the notations in the sheet keynote portion of the note block. The table is created automatically from each sheet keynote symbol that appears in the sheet's drawing area. The best benefit of using sheet keynote software is that it helps to reduce errors by ensuring that each sheet keynote appearing in the sheet's drawing area is included in the note block, and vice versa.

Another benefit sheet keynote software provides is the option to create a sheet keynote office master that can be used as a template for generating sheet keynote project masters. The sheet keynote office master can be created from the most common notations used on multiple projects and customized as needed for each project. Creating a sheet keynote office master, which takes a small amount of time, offers the following benefits:

- Consistent identification of the same items from sheet to sheet throughout the project
- Reduction of spelling and terminology errors

The benefits of sheet keynote office masters are so undeniable that we recommend creating a sheet keynote office master that can be used as a template for *all* projects, even if sheet keynote software is not used.

One of the best benefits of a sheet keynote office master is that it will result in the use of the same sheet keynotes for the same items throughout the drawing set. For example, if a sheet keynote symbol is used on an exterior architectural elevation appearing on Sheet A-201 to identify the top of masonry, a sheet keynote symbol with the same number can be used to identify the top of masonry on a building section appearing on Sheet A-301. This will help streamline communication from sheet to sheet, as drawing users become more familiar with the consistent use of the same sheet keynotes throughout the drawing set.

Even though the project sheet keynote office master may contain many notes, usually only a few of them will be needed for any given sheet in the drawing set. Therefore, because unused numbers should not be included, many of the sheet keynotes from the master will not appear in the sheet's note block. The numbers that are used must appear sequentially, similar to the way reference keynotes must appear. An example of how sheet keynotes would typically appear in a note block when using a sheet keynote project master is demonstrated in Figure 7-17. For an example of a sheet keynote office master that can be used as a template for architectural sheets, see Appendix C.

Templates that are created from the sheet keynote office master can be customized for the specific needs of each project. Just be aware that as more notes are added to the master, the more cumbersome it can become to manage and use. When the list becomes too long, the hassles associated with finding notes will quickly outweigh any benefits a master might offer. Therefore, when creating a sheet keynote office master, include only those sheet keynotes that are common to a majority of projects. Once it is exported into the project as a template, additional, project-specific notes can be added to it.

Another management concept we recommend for the creation and administration of a sheet keynote office master is to organize the notations alphabetically. This will eliminate having to determine a hierarchy based upon notes that are "most used," or organizing them according to some other system. Organizing the notes alphabetically provides an automatic location for notes as they are added to the master. The alphabetical order also enables CAD technicians to locate the notations faster from CAD menus and to insert them onto the drawings faster. It also establishes a hierarchy for inserting new notes into the master.

Implementation of Reference Keynotes

Adopting NCS-compliant reference keynotes into the workplace will require a significant amount of effort—more than any of the other types of notations. Adopting these types of notations will require (1) the involvement of more personnel and (2) time to train CAD staff. Furthermore, those who have not used reference keynotes before will need some time to learn the methodology of how materials, products, and other items are identified on the drawings. Thus, even though reference keynotes will dramatically improve the quality of the construction documents, we recommend scheduling their implementation after other NCS components have been adopted. (More information on the overall NCS adoption schedule is discussed in Chapter 11.)

```
      ◇  SHEET KEYNOTES

   8.  DASHED LINE INDICATES FINISH FLOOR.
  10.  DASHED LINE INDICATES FOUNDATION — SEE STRUCTURAL SHEETS.
  13.  DASHED LINE INDICATES ROOF LINE.
  24.  ELECTRICAL LIGHT FIXTURE — SEE ELECTRICAL SHEETS.
  29.  EXHAUST FAN — SEE MECHANICAL SHEETS.
  32.  FINISH FLOOR — SEE CIVIL SHEETS FOR CONTROL DATUM.
  34.  FINISH GRADE — SEE CIVIL SHEETS.
  48.  PAVING — SEE CIVIL SHEETS.
  57.  SLOPE PAVING AWAY FROM BUILDING — SEE CIVIL SHEETS.
  60.  TOP OF MASONRY.
```

FIGURE 7-17   Appearance of Sheet Keynotes from a Sheet Keynote Project Master

When the notations coordinator has been identified, a reference keynote process has to be established. A major component in the process is reference keynote software. There are a number of options available, some of which are standard features of CAD software packages; or, third-party, add-on software is available that can work quite well. Our evaluation is that the reference keynote tools included with CAD software we have looked at are either too cumbersome or cannot provide a compliant format. We prefer the add-on software, because it is much easier to use and is very affordable. (See the Frequently Asked Questions section at the end of this chapter for further discussion about third-party, add-on notation software.)

Without software that is easy to use, it makes little sense to adopt the reference keynote system, so we do not recommend implementing this component of the NCS without it. When considering which software to use, make sure that it meets the following requirements:

■ Easy to configure and use
■ Compliant with MasterFormat 2004 (including Level 4 numbers for the reference keynote root)
■ Capable of providing optional appearances for MasterFormat 2004 numerals (as indicated in Figures 7-11, 7-12, and 7-13)
■ Provides NCS-compliant suffixes and suffix modifiers
■ Capable of providing reference keynote modifiers (as indicated in Figure 7-10)
■ Compliant with UniFormat (as indicated in Figure 7-14, if needed)
■ Notations created automatically in the note block conform to NCS requirements
■ Master can be quickly updated without extensive CAD knowledge

Creating Reference Keynote Office Masters

After identifying the notations coordinator and selecting the CAD keynoting software that will be used, the next step is to create a reference keynote office master. But first, a decision has to be made regarding the appearance of the MasterFormat 2004 number that will be used for the reference keynote root, as indicated by the options in Figures 7-11, 7-12, and 7-13. As discussed earlier in this chapter, the arrangement of the numerals in the root should match the arrangement of the MasterFormat 2004 numerals in the project manual.

To save space in drawing and note blocks, compressed variations of the MasterFormat number are provided in Figure 7-12 (Option 1) and Figure 7-13 (Option 2). If this is a concern, we recommend the single space numeral configuration shown in Figure 7-12 (Option 1), because the character format in the symbol is easier to remember as eyes focus back and forth from the drawings to the note block. When space in the drawings and note block is a concern, we also recommend avoiding the use of Level 4 MasterFormat numbers as much as is practical. This strategy will, however, require additional coordination with specifiers, but restricting the use of reference keynotes with Level 4 MasterFormat numbers will certainly result in symbols that are easier to read and require less space. (For a comprehensive list of reference keynotes that do not use MasterFormat Level 4 numbers, refer to the reference keynote office master in Appendix D.)

Reference Keynote Suffix Recommendations

Creating and maintaining a reference keynote office master is a dynamic process—that is, it is never completed and will need to be updated regularly. The frequency of the updates will depend on the quantity of projects and the variation of materials and products they normally include. For example, a reference keynote office master created by a consultant such as a structural engineer will usually consist, primarily, of notations for concrete, masonry, metal, and wood materials. An architectural reference keynote master will contain notations for a wider variety of materials and might also include items from other documents in the project manual. Once the reference keynote master is created, the list of notations will continue to expand to accommodate additional materials and products that need to be specified, and the master will need to be updated accordingly. Unless a system of organizing the list is established, the notations will eventually become difficult to maintain and use.

The appearance of the suffix for the reference keynote symbol can be formatted according to a variety of methodologies, as long as they comply with the minimum requirements of the UDS Notations Module: The first character (the suffix) must be an alpha character (excluding the letters I and O); and numerals (suffix modifiers) must be two characters (00 cannot be used). As long as the suffix meets these criteria, the methodology used to create reference keynote suffixes can be user-defined. For example, an approach for assigning suffixes to components located in specification section 08 4413 Glazed Curtain Walls could be as simple as assigning a suffix, without suffix modifiers, to each component in alphabetical order, as follows:

08 4413.A   GLAZING GASKET
08 4413.B   ALUMINUM FRAMING MEMBER
08 4413.C   PERIMETER SEALANT

Note that this methodology would require the introduction of suffix modifiers when symbols were needed for more than 24 materials from the same specification section (remember, only 24 letters of the alphabet are allowed—as just stated above, I and O cannot be used).

The numbering convention system we recommend for creating a reference keynote master is one that allows the reference keynote suffix to be determined by the first alphabetic character in the notation's term. Using the arrangement of MasterFormat 2004 numbers given in Figure 7-12 (Option 1), some examples of this system are as follows (alphabetic characters that determine the reference keynote suffix are highlighted in bold):

07 6200.S   **S**HEET METAL FLASHING
09 6800.C   **C**ARPET
10 1100.M   **M**ARKERBOARD
22 4000.E   **E**LECTRIC WATER COOLER
26 5100.R   **R**EFLECTOR LAMP

When a term in the notation begins with the letter I or O, the next compliant letter in the term should be used for the suffix. This exception is required because, again, the NCS does not allow I and O to be used in the reference keynote modifier, because they can be confused with numerals. Fortunately, this exception does not need to be used very often, as the number of terms for materials and products that begin with the letters I and O represent a very small minority. The following examples illustrate how to assign reference keynote suffixes for terms beginning with I and O, using this alphabetized system:

01 1000.W	OWNER-FURNISHED, OWNER-INSTALLED ITEM
05 2100.P	OPEN WEB STEEL JOIST
08 3323.V	OVERHEAD COILING DOOR
09 2116.M04	IMPACT-RESISTANT GYPSUM BOARD
26 5100.N	INTERIOR LUMINAIRE

Assigning reference keynote suffixes according to the first compliant alphabetic character in the term offers many advantages, some of which include:

- Suffix is determined automatically.
- CAD technicians can easily locate notations from even the longest master lists.
- Notations coordinators can identify locations for new notations faster.
- Helps to prevent creation of duplicate keynotes within the same section.
- Association of same alphabetic characters for the term and keynote suffix helps streamline identification of reference keynotes in the note block.

For an example of a reference keynote office master that has been created using this methodology, refer to Appendix D.

Creating Reference Keynotes

To avoid confusion, terms in reference keynotes must match exactly the wording in the project manual. This convention is consistent with the requirements of the UDS Terms and Abbreviations Module. It is also important that the wording of the terms matches that of the preferred terms listed in the UDS Terms and Abbreviations Module. When creating reference keynotes we recommend following this step-by-step procedure:

Step 1: Identify each term in the document or specification section that will be included in the master. Select only generic, nonproprietary terms.

Step 2: Compare the selected terms with those in the UDS Terms and Abbreviations Module, and replace any nonpreferred terms in the specification section with the preferred term.

Step 3: Assign each term with the appropriate reference keynote root (the number of the document or specification section where the activity, product, or material is referenced).

Step 4: Assign reference keynote suffixes according to the first compliant alphabetic character in the terms.

Step 5: When terms begin with the same letter of the alphabet, assign a reference keynote suffix modifier, beginning with 01, to differentiate each notation.

When the specification section contains materials that are similar in nature, assign each of them to the same generic term and use the reference keynote modifier to identify unique characteristics. For example, if a specification section includes a variety of similar products, such as deck screws, self-tapping screws, nails, and staples, assign each of them with a common term such as "fastener." The reference keynote modifier can then be used to identify the specific fastener being referenced. This technique should be used for each specification section to help keep the list of notations in the reference keynote office master to a minimum, which will be easier to maintain.

Other Reference Keynotes to Include in the Master

One of the most often overlooked uses for reference keynotes is associated with items that are not products or materials. They are items located in the following MasterFormat 2004 divisions:

Division 00—Procurement and Contracting Requirements
Division 01—General Requirements
Division 02—Existing Conditions

There are many uses for reference keynotes with 00, 01, and 02 division numbers, some of which include identification of the following items:

- Survey benchmarks (Document 00 31 21)
- Soil boring locations (Document 00 31 32)
- Work provided by owner (Section 01 10 00)
- Alternates (Section 01 23 00)
- Temporary dust barriers (Section 01 50 00)
- Existing items to remain (02 41 00)

Making use of reference keynotes for these divisions will make it easier to locate information about the items in the project manual. Sheet keynotes should not be used to identify these types of items, because they should not be used to identify items referenced in the project manual; moreover, doing so will result in an excessive number of notations in a sheet keynote master.

Reference Keynotes and the Detail Library

Another benefit of using reference keynotes in the workplace is that they make it much easier to create and maintain detail libraries. This is because reference keynotes stay the same from project to project—they do not need to be changed. Each detail should be identified according to either the MasterFormat or UniFormat file-naming system included in the UDS Drawing Set Organization Module. We prefer to identify library files with MasterFormat numbers because more users are familiar with them. We also recommend organizing the detail library according to the MasterFormat division numbers, and then assigning them with a file name that is derived from the section number that is best associated with the reference keynotes used to identify components in the detail.

For example, a jamb detail for a hollow metal door frame might include other components such as masonry (Division 04) or wood (Division 06), but since the primary intent of the detail is to illustrate a hollow metal door frame, we assign a file name based on the appropriate number from Division 08—Openings, such as 081113 (notice that spaces between the numerals are not used for NCS-compliant file names). Many details will share the same section number, so user-defined characters need to be added at the end of the file name, so that each library file (or detail) will have its own unique file name.

A table of contents should be created for the detail library, which includes the file name of each detail and the detail's name. We recommend identifying the detail in the table of contents with the same term that will be used in the title area of the drawing block. Figure 7-18 lists examples of some library file names for library details for Division 08 Openings.

To facilitate the quality control process, we recommend including the detail's file name beneath the title area of the detail when it is inserted into the drawing area. The file name will identify the detail as one from the library and will help to differentiate it from similar details that may have been inadvertently copied onto the sheet from another project. The file name can be removed before going to final plots. However, we often leave the file names with the details on the final plots because it helps to track them later. This makes it easier to keep the library updated if constructability issues are discovered during the construction administration phase or if other ed-

LIBRARY FILE NAME	DRAWING TITLE
081113-01.dwg	Hollow Metal Frame - Head
081113-02.dwg	Hollow Metal Frame - Jamb
081113-02A.dwg	Hollow Metal Frame - Jamb
081113-03.dwg	Hollow Metal Frame - Sill
083323-01.dwg	Overhead Coiling Door - Head
083323-02.dwg	Overhead Coiling Door - Jamb
083323-03.dwg	Overhead Coiling Door - Sill
085113-01.dwg	Aluminum Window - Head
085113-01A.dwg	Aluminum Window - Head
085113-01B.dwg	Aluminum Window - Head
085113-02.dwg	Aluminum Window - Jamb
085113-03.dwg	Aluminum Window - Sill
089100-01.dwg	Fixed Louver - Head
089100-02.dwg	Fixed Louver - Sill

FIGURE 7-18
Examples of Detail Library File Names

its are identified on the plotted sheets. Refer to Figure 7-19 for examples of standard details using these concepts.

Incorporating Reference Keynotes into the Quality Control Process

Reference keynotes are a valuable resource, hence can play a significant role in the quality control process. The foundation of the process rests on the reference keynotes that appear in each sheet's note block. The note block is used as a checklist to ensure that:

- Each document and specification section referenced by the reference keynote has been created.
- Materials, activities, and products identified by the terms in the reference keynotes are included in the documents or specification section referenced.

Instigating this methodology throughout the construction document phase of the project will help avoid last-minute modifications to specifications and the drawings and will help eliminate errors.

Another part of the process involves the project manual table of contents (TOC). Once the TOC has been created, it needs to be distributed to the entire design team. If the TOC is revised, team members must be provided with an update as soon as the modifications have been made. This process is valuable because it will help to ensure that products and materials are only identified on the drawings with reference keynotes whose roots match the documents and specification sections used in the TOC. Until the TOC is distributed, reference keynotes should not be placed on drawings. This methodology will also improve coordination between the specifier and those creating the drawings.

Toward the end of the project, a final quality control step can be accomplished by clerical staff or coworkers (even if they have not been involved with the project). Just before sending the drawings for their final plots, we recommend that someone make one last comparison between the final project manual TOC and each of the document and specification section numbers referenced by the reference keynotes in the note block. It is surprising how many times one or two conflicts are discovered this way, just before going to print.

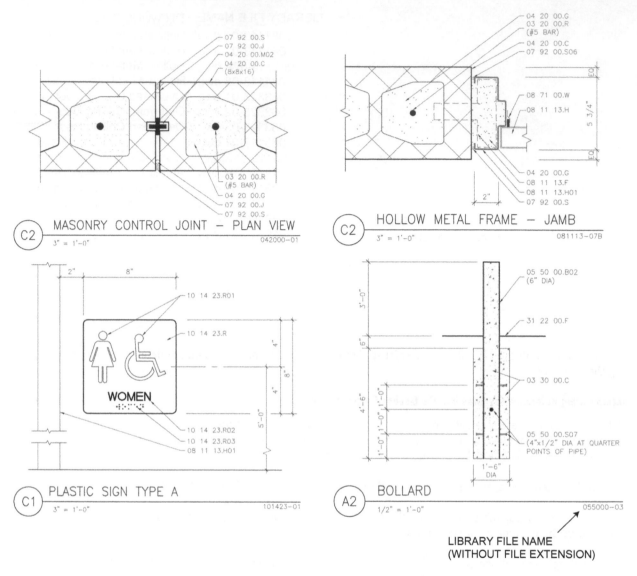

FIGURE 7-19
Examples of Standard Details (Library Files) Using Reference Keynotes

General Note for Reference Keynotes

AIA A201-1997 General Conditions of the Contract for Construction advises the contractor that the arrangement of the drawings and the organization of the specifications into divisions, sections, and articles is not intended to be used to subdivide the work or to establish the amount of work to be performed by any trade. To reinforce these instructions, we recommend including a general note that makes a similar statement regarding the use of reference keynotes. The notation should also provide a brief explanation of the reference keynote system, for anyone who might not be familiar with their usage. The general note, which should be included in the General discipline (G-series) sheets, should read similar to the example in Figure 7-20.

```
┌─────────────────────────────────────────────────────────────────────────┐
│  GENERAL NOTES                                                            │
├───────────────────────────────────────────────────────────────────────  │
│     1. THESE DRAWINGS UTILIZE A REFERENCE KEYNOTE SYSTEM CONSISTING OF A   │
│        6-DIGIT NUMERICAL ROOT FOLLOWED BY A PERIOD AND AN ALPHANUMERIC     │
│        SUFFIX (SUCH AS 05 50 00.A01).                                      │
│                                                                           │
│        EACH REFERENCE KEYNOTE THAT APPEARS ON THE SHEET IS LISTED IN THE   │
│        REFERENCE KEYNOTES PORTION OF THE NOTE BLOCK, ALONG WITH A TEXT     │
│        NOTE THAT DESCRIBES THE GRAPHIC.                                    │
│                                                                           │
│        THE 6-DIGIT NUMERICAL ROOT CORRESPONDS TO THE SPECIFICATION SECTION │
│        NUMBER LOCATION WHERE THE OBJECT OR MATERIAL IS SPECIFIED. THE      │
│        ALPHANUMERIC SUFFIX IS NOT ASSOCIATED WITH ANY SPECIFIC REFERENCE IN│
│        THE SPECIFICATION SECTION.                                         │
│                                                                           │
│        CERTAIN REFERENCE KEYNOTES MAY INCLUDE MODIFIERS (CONTAINED WITHIN  │
│        PARENTHESES) LOCATED BENEATH THE REFERENCE KEYNOTE. THE MODIFIER    │
│        IDENTIFIES TYPE, SIZE, THICKNESS, AND OTHER ADDITIONAL CHARACTERISTICS│
│        ABOUT THE ITEM.                                                     │
│                                                                           │
│        THE REFERENCE KEYNOTING SYSTEM SHALL NOT CONTROL THE CONTRACTOR     │
│        IN DIVIDING THE WORK AMONG SUBCONTRACTORS OR                        │
│        IN ESTABLISHING THE EXTENT OF WORK TO BE PERFORMED BY ANY TRADE.    │
│                                                                           │
└──────────────────────────────────────────\   /──────────────────────────┘
                                             \ /
                                              V
```

FIGURE 7-20   General Note Explaining Use of Reference Keynotes in the Drawing Set

REVIEW OF KEY CONCEPTS IN THIS CHAPTER

1. The purpose of the UDS Notations Module is to provide a consistent methodology for the creation and use of notations that appear in drawing and note blocks.
2. There are five types of NCS-compliant notations: general notes, general discipline notes, general sheet notes, reference keynotes, and sheet keynotes.
3. Office masters should be created for reference keynotes and sheet keynotes.
4. The use of CAD notation software will help streamline the notation process and help reduce errors.
5. Reference keynotes should not be implemented without the use of proper CAD notation software.
6. Sheet keynotes and each of the general notation types can be adopted earlier in the NCS implementation process; reference keynotes should not be implemented until later.
7. Reference keynotes will provide many benefits to the quality control process.

FREQUENTLY ASKED QUESTIONS

Q: *The UDS Notations Module only includes format requirements for general notations, reference keynotes, and sheet keynotes. What about text notations? Can we use them in the drawings?*

A: This is a common question. According to the NCS, there are only five types of notations, and text notations are not listed as one of them. Therefore, to be in strict accordance with the NCS, text notations should be avoided; only reference keynotes should be used to identify activities, products, materials, or other items that are included in the project manual.

Q: *The keynoting feature in our CAD software is very cumbersome to use and requires too much effort to manipulate to get the appearance of the symbols to match those in the NCS. Which third-party, add-on software companies are capable of providing us with an easier way to create our sheet keynotes and reference keynotes?*

A: The two products we like best are CadPLUS SpecNoter, available from National MultiTech LTD (www.cadplus.com) and Keynotes 1.0 available from DotSoft (www.dotsoft.com). These products are much easier to use than others we have seen, including those from major CAD software companies.

Q: *We've heard that contractors and material suppliers really dislike reference keynotes. Is this true?*

A: No. In fact, quite the contrary. The contractors and material suppliers we've interviewed have embraced reference keynotes because their use makes it easier to find information and requirements. Though many find the system a little confusing at first, they learn the process very quickly. We also recommend including a brief explanation of the system during the prebid conference, and the preconstruction conference, to make sure everyone understands the concept. We keep looking for those contractors you've heard about. We haven't found them yet.

Q: *Doesn't it take a long time to create a reference keynote office master?*

A: The effort involves a substantial investment of manpower to get started, but it is one that pays huge dividends afterward. Once the system is up and running, it is fairly easy to maintain, especially with the proper CAD software.

Q: *Our office wants to use a different symbol for the sheet keynote. Is this okay?*

A: The hexagon shape is the only one allowed; anything else is not compliant. This issue is similar to many other NCS format requirements—they become easier to adopt once we stop resisting change.

Q: *Can decimal format be used for the numerals in the sheet keynote symbol?*

A: Decimal formats for the numbers in the sheet keynote symbol can be used. Just be aware that the 1/4″ high symbol and 3/32″ text size requirements will probably restrict the use of anything more than N.N format (there usually will not be enough room inside the symbol for NN.N format).

Q: *Wouldn't an abbreviations legend be preferable to using a general note such as, "Abbreviations: Referenced from NCS version 3.1?"*

A: Not necessarily. This note is consistent with others throughout the construction documents that reference standards published by organizations such as ASTM, ANSI, UL, IBC, and many others. In addition, every abbreviations legend we've seen either does not contain all of the abbreviations used and/or it contains unused abbreviations. Until CAD software can create the legends automatically when each abbreviation is placed on a sheet, we like the general note idea better.

Code Conventions

GENERAL

The architect's primary responsibility as a licensed design professional is to protect the health, safety, and welfare of the public. In carrying out these duties, the architect must make sure that code-related information that appears on the drawings is communicated to all drawing users in a useable and understandable manner. He or she must also coordinate these requirements with all design disciplines.

Format requirements for regulatory information used in construction drawings are located in the UDS Code Conventions Module of the Construction Specification Institute's (CSI) Uniform Drawing System (UDS). Since publication and adoption into the second version of the UDS in 2001, the UDS Code Conventions Module has been subject to only a handful of revisions by the U.S. National CAD Standard Project Committee (NCSPC).

Generally, each of the components that make up the NCS, such as the UDS Drawing Set Organization Module, the UDS Drafting Conventions Module, and the UDS Symbols Module, are the result of interpretations of guidelines and standards that have been used by the construction industry for many years. The only exception is the UDS Drafting Conventions Module, which represents new information or standards for locating code-related information on drawings.

The UDS Code Conventions Module establishes requirements for the use of regulatory information on the drawings. Since regulatory requirements are unique to each authority having jurisdiction (AHJ), the formats in the NCS establish an overall methodology by which to identify, locate, and illustrate the general types of information needed. The appendices in the UDS Code Conventions Module provide examples of tables and graphics that can be used to present the necessary information.

BENEFITS OF NCS CODE CONVENTIONS

The primary focus of the UDS Code Conventions Module is to establish consistency in identifying regulatory information that appears in construction drawings. Consistent identification of regulatory information will aid drawing users during the project cycle and the facility cycle. The guidelines in the UDS Code Conventions Module provide tools for determining the type of regulatory information needed, the format for its appearance, and its proper location in the drawings and project manual.

Benefits for Architects and Engineers

Regulatory information that complies with the format requirements of the U.S. National CAD Standard (NCS) will benefit design professionals during the various phases of the design stage by providing a means to easily communicate regulatory requirements to members of the design team while developing the construction drawings during the construction document stage.

Using consistent formats for the type, location, and appearance of the information streamlines communications to bidders (or proposers) and code officials during the procurement and permit application stages of the project. The guidelines in the UDS Code Conventions Module provide architects and engineers with the means to identify critical code information for contractors and material suppliers during the construction phase. Emerging design professionals in the construction industry will discover the UDS Code Conventions Module also provides an easy-to-read reference guide for plan review, code regulations, and the design process.

Benefits for Contractors and Material Suppliers

When code-related information is formatted on the drawings to comply with the NCS, it makes it easier for contractors and material suppliers to identify code issues during the procurement and construction stages of the project. Subsequently, this will help to provide owners with more accurate pricing and help to ensure that the finished project will comply with the necessary governing regulations. When code information is easy to identify and communicate, contractors and material suppliers make fewer errors, hence save the costs and time required to correct them.

Benefits for Code Officials

Documents that comply with the UDS Code Conventions Module provide code officials with a means to easily locate regulatory requirements during the permit application stage. NCS-compliant drawings include thorough and complete information that is consistent for all projects, no matter what size. As the requirements are adopted by more designers, code officials will become more familiar with the format, which will mean plans submitted for permit can be reviewed in less time and building permits will be issued sooner.

Benefits for Owners and Facility Managers

FYI: During the development of the UDS Code Conventions Module, it was determined that more than 46,000 U.S. governmental agencies have jurisdiction over the regulatory information that appears on construction documents.

NCS-compliant documents help owners and facility managers to identify critical code information during the postconstruction stage of the project cycle, which then helps them to better coordinate code-related elements with proposed modifications that may be needed in the future. Perhaps the most important result of construction documents organized according to the UDS Code Conventions Module is that it streamlines the transfer of regulatory information from owners and facility managers to the next group of designers who will be involved with later stages of the facility cycle.

IDENTIFICATION OF REGULATORY INFORMATION

Local authorities having jurisdiction establish their own requirements for the governing regulations that are required to appear in construction documents; therefore, it is only possible to provide general guidelines for the identification of each type of information that might be needed. To furnish a standard that can provide consistent identification, location, and appearance for each different type, the UDS Code Conventions Module groups related regulatory information into 12 generic categories. The categories are as follows:

1–General
2–Site
3–Building
4–Life Safety-Egress
5–Fire Protection-Passive

6–Accessibility
7–Energy
8–Structural
9–Fire Protection-Active (also known as fire suppression)
10–Plumbing
11–Mechanical
12–Electrical

Each category contains key types of related information that might be necessary to include in a set of construction documents. For example, some of the regulatory information listed in Category 7–Energy includes: energy conservation, thermal performance of the facility envelope, thermal performance of materials, mechanical and electrical loads, and air infiltration.

LOCATION AND FORMAT FOR REGULATORY INFORMATION BASED UPON CATEGORY GROUP				
Category Group	Regulatory Information	Drawing Location		Suggested Format
		Level 1 Project	Level 2 Project	
2 - Site	Site-Related Design Criteria			
	Location on site (distances to lot lines/existing buildings)	C-1xx	CS-1xx	Graphic
	Site grading/water run-off	C-1xx	CG-1xx	Graphic
	Irrigation	L-1xx	LI-1xx	Graphic
	Erosion control details	C-5xx	CG-5xx	Graphic
	Environmental impact statements	Project manual	Project manual	Text
	Zoning drawings	G-0xx	GI-0xx	Text
	Zoning use (allowable/actual)	G-0xx	GI-0xx	Text
	Site coverage (allowable/actual)	G-0xx	GI-0xx	Text
	Building height (allowable/actual)	G-0xx	GI-0xx	Text
	Parking/loading requirements (required/actual)	G-0xx	GI-0xx	Text
	Signage type, area, and height (allowable, actual)	G-0xx	GI-0xx	Text
	Fire districts	G-0xx	GI-0xx	Text
	Historical preservation	G-0xx	GI-0xx	Text

FIGURE 8-1   Example of a Table (Category Group 2) Included in the UDS Code Conventions Module

The 12 categories for governing regulations included in the UDS Code Conventions Module are organized into tables, which provide a list of the types of regulatory information required, a location for the information, and the suggested format for its appearance. In addition to organizing the different kinds of information required, the tables can also be used as a checklist to coordinate the code requirements throughout the set of construction documents. Figure 8-1 provides an example of how a typical category table is organized.

Drawing locations for code information are identified in the tables for sheets with Level 1 discipline designators (identified as a Level 1 Project) and for sheets with Level 2 discipline designators (identified as a Level 2 Project). (Refer to Chapter 1, "Drawing Set Organization," for more

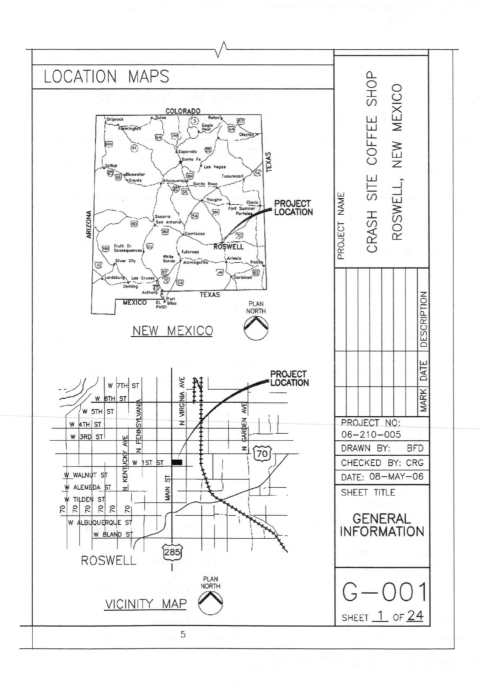

FIGURE 8-2
Example of Graphic-Formatted
Regulatory Information

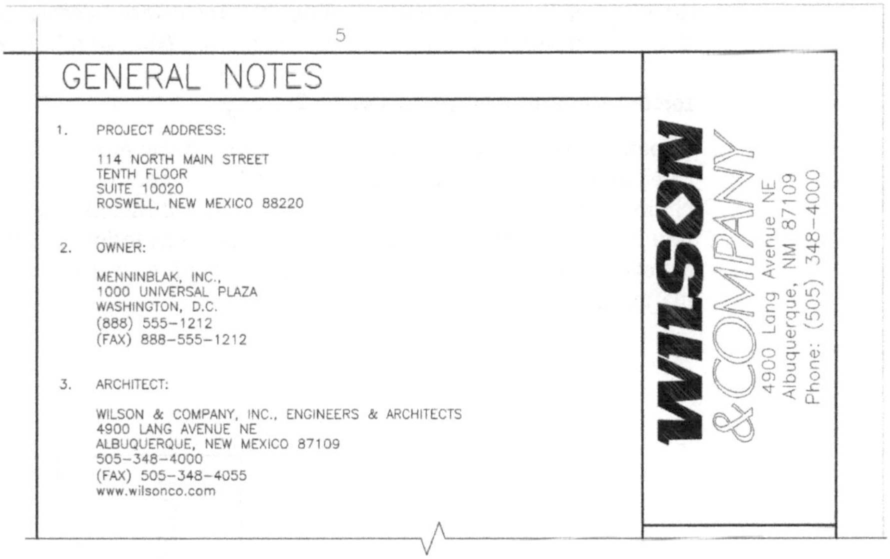

FIGURE 8-3
Example of Text-Formatted
Regulatory Information

information on discipline designators.) In some instances, the information is indicated as provided in either the drawings or the project manual. For example, a project address can be located in either of the following locations:

- Sheet G-001
- Sheet GI-001
- Project Manual (PM)

The presentation format for each regulatory item is indicated in the category group tables as one of two different types: graphic or text. Graphic examples consist of drawings, diagrams, **details,** and other presentation techniques that illustrate necessary requirements. Examples of graphic formats include project location maps, accessibility routes, details of fire-resistance assemblies, and single-line electrical diagrams. The tables indicate that most of the graphic-formatted regulatory information is to be located on the drawings. An example of graphic-formatted regulatory information is illustrated in Figure 8-2.

Text format indicated in the tables consists of words used to describe the regulatory information. Examples include the project address, a listing of applicable ordinances and jurisdictions, design loads, and wiring methods and materials. The location of text formats for regulatory information can be in the drawings, the project manual, or both. The proper locations are indicated accordingly in the category group tables. Figure 8-3 demonstrates an example of text-formatted regulatory information.

LOCATION AND APPEARANCE OF REGULATORY INFORMATION IN THE CONSTRUCTION DOCUMENTS

Regulatory information is located in the construction documents according to the category group tables included in the UDS Code Conventions Module. To provide consistent requirements for the location of the information, the tables require that certain types of information be included only on the drawings; other types of information should be included only in the project manual. In some instances, however, the guidelines in the NCS allow the information to be provided in either the drawings or the project manual. When the regulatory information can be located in either location, we recommend using one location, but *not both,* to minimize the potential for errors.

Locating Regulatory Information on the Drawings

Depending on the category type and the items being presented, regulatory information will be located on either sheet type designator 0-series (General) sheets or on certain sheets in specific disciplines, such as the Architectural, Structural, and Mechanical sheets. In addition to the location requirements, Appendix K of the UDS Code Conventions Module includes illustrations for the appearance of certain types of graphic information so that users can see clearly how the information may be presented.

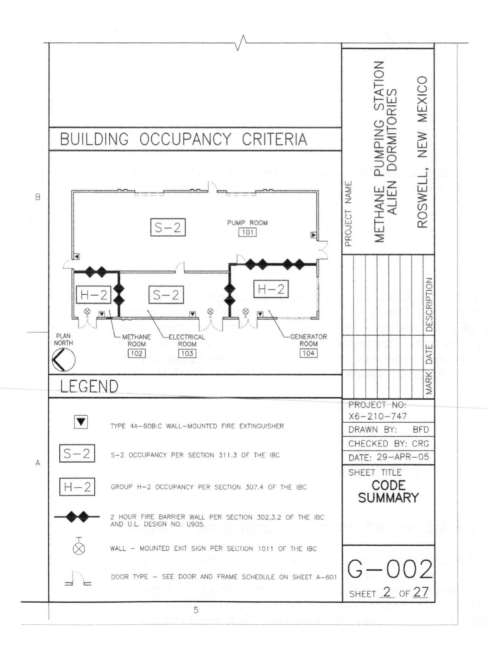

FIGURE 8-4
Example of Regulatory Information Appearing on General Discipline (G-Series) Sheets in Graphic Format

Since all of the items included in the Category 1 General table applies to all sheets in the set, this information needs to be located on Level 1 discipline designator sheets, such as G-001, or Level 2 discipline designator sheets, such as GI-001. On smaller projects without Sheet Type Designator 0-series (General) sheets, the information can be included on the first sheet in the drawing set. General regulatory information includes the name of the design professional(s), a listing of applicable codes, construction type, occupant loads, fire-resistance ratings, and so on. Regulatory information will be presented in either graphic or text format, in accordance with the requirements listed in the tables.

Regulatory information that must be presented in graphic format is located in the drawing area of the sheet. For example, floor plans used to indicate regulatory information such as occupancy types, fire-resistive construction, fire extinguisher locations, travel distances to exits, and exiting signs should be identified as described in Chapter 2, "Sheet Organization." An example of the presentation of regulatory information applicable to the entire drawing set in graphic format is illustrated in Figure 8-4.

When the NCS indicates that regulatory information should be presented in text format (a notation), it should appear as a general note, located within the sheet's note block, as detailed in Chapter 7, "Notations." Since general notes, by definition, apply to all sheets in the drawing set, this would include, for example, a list of governing regulations, allowable floor area calculations, plumbing fixture counts, occupancy loads, and allowable floor areas and building heights. To see how regulatory information appears on Sheet Type Designator 0-series (General) sheets, refer to Figure 8-5.

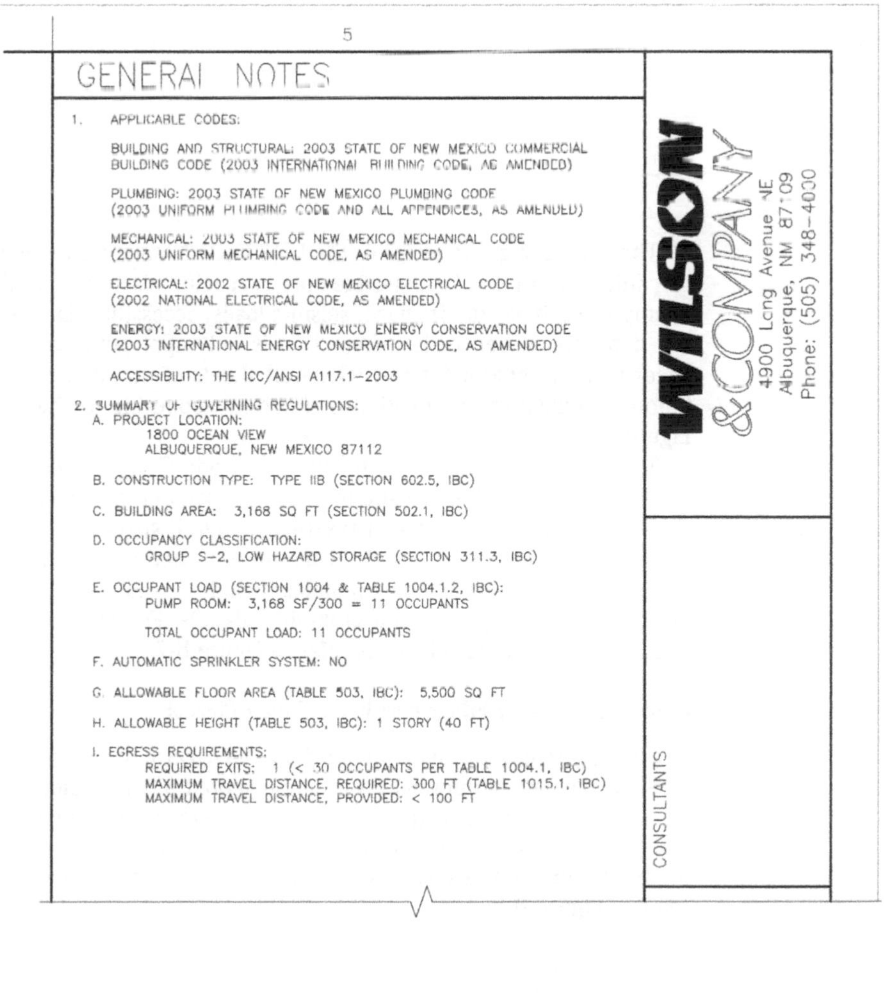
5

GENERAL NOTES

1. APPLICABLE CODES:

BUILDING AND STRUCTURAL: 2003 STATE OF NEW MEXICO COMMERCIAL BUILDING CODE (2003 INTERNATIONAL BUILDING CODE, AS AMENDED)

PLUMBING: 2003 STATE OF NEW MEXICO PLUMBING CODE (2003 UNIFORM PLUMBING CODE AND ALL APPENDICES, AS AMENDED)

MECHANICAL: 2003 STATE OF NEW MEXICO MECHANICAL CODE (2003 UNIFORM MECHANICAL CODE, AS AMENDED)

ELECTRICAL: 2002 STATE OF NEW MEXICO ELECTRICAL CODE (2002 NATIONAL ELECTRICAL CODE, AS AMENDED)

ENERGY: 2003 STATE OF NEW MEXICO ENERGY CONSERVATION CODE (2003 INTERNATIONAL ENERGY CONSERVATION CODE, AS AMENDED)

ACCESSIBILITY: THE ICC/ANSI A117.1-2003

2. SUMMARY OF GOVERNING REGULATIONS:

A. PROJECT LOCATION:
1800 OCEAN VIEW
ALBUQUERQUE, NEW MEXICO 87112

B. CONSTRUCTION TYPE: TYPE IIB (SECTION 602.5, IBC)

C. BUILDING AREA: 3,168 SQ FT (SECTION 502.1, IBC)

D. OCCUPANCY CLASSIFICATION:
GROUP S-2, LOW HAZARD STORAGE (SECTION 311.3, IBC)

E. OCCUPANT LOAD (SECTION 1004 & TABLE 1004.1.2, IBC):
PUMP ROOM: 3,168 SF/300 = 11 OCCUPANTS

TOTAL OCCUPANT LOAD: 11 OCCUPANTS

F. AUTOMATIC SPRINKLER SYSTEM: NO

G. ALLOWABLE FLOOR AREA (TABLE 503, IBC): 5,500 SQ FT

H. ALLOWABLE HEIGHT (TABLE 503, IBC): 1 STORY (40 FT)

I. EGRESS REQUIREMENTS:
REQUIRED EXITS: 1 (< 30 OCCUPANTS PER TABLE 1004.1, IBC)
MAXIMUM TRAVEL DISTANCE, REQUIRED: 300 FT (TABLE 1015.1, IBC)
MAXIMUM TRAVEL DISTANCE, PROVIDED: < 100 FT

FIGURE 8-5
Example of Regulatory Information Appearing on General Discipline (G-Series) Sheets in Text Format

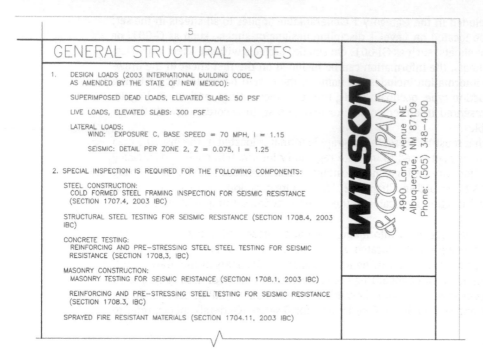

FIGURE 8-6
Example of Regulatory
Information Applicable to Sheets
in a Specific Discipline Appearing
on General (0-Series) Sheets

The category group tables in the UDS Code Conventions Module include locations for regulatory information that is applicable only to specific disciplines in the drawing set. This can include examples such as site drainage, seismic loads, accessible signage, roof storm water drainage, and fire dampers. When code information is only applicable to sheets in a discipline, locate it on sheet type designator 0-series (General) sheets of that discipline. For an example of the presentation of regulatory information that is only applicable to sheets in a specific discipline, refer to Figure 8-6.

The category group tables in the UDS Code Conventions Module also indicate locations for regulatory information specific to a single discipline that needs to be presented on sheets other than the sheet type designator 0-series (General) sheets. When information has to be presented in formats such as plans, details, diagrams, or schedules, the tables indicate the proper sheet type designator for them. Typical examples include erosion control details, accessible toilet facilities, plumbing riser diagrams, and grounding details. For an example of regulatory information presented on these types of sheets refer to Figure 8-7.

Locating Regulatory Information in the Project Manual

The category group tables included in the UDS Code Conventions Module provide for some types of regulatory information to be presented in the project manual. This type of information, which is presented in text format, includes items such as environmental impact statements, fire-stopping design test numbers, special inspection requirements, piping materials, and wiring methods and materials. For an example of regulatory information included in the project manual, refer to Figure 8-8.

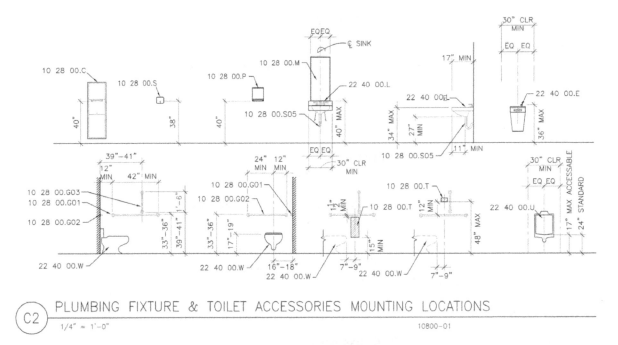

C2 PLUMBING FIXTURE & TOILET ACCESSORIES MOUNTING LOCATIONS
1/4" = 1'-0"   10800-01

Figure 8-7 Example of a Specific Type of Regulatory Information Appearing on a Sheet Within a Discipline

Implementation Issues

Before adopting the formats in the UDS Code Conventions Module, many of the other NCS components should be implemented first, to ensure that the regulatory information is located properly; following this guideline will also help to prevent going back and reformatting some of the graphics to comply with some of the NCS requirements for CAD drawings. For example, the 12 category group tables in the UDS Code Conventions Module identify regulatory information locations in the drawings according to the discipline and sheet type designator formats included in the UDS Drawing Set Organization Module. Prior adoption of the AIA CAD Layer Guidelines, the UDS Drafting Conventions Module, and the Tri-Service Plotting Guidelines will allow graphics to be formatted according to CAD layers, line widths, and line types that comply with the NCS. Therefore, we recommend scheduling implementation of the UDS Code Conventions Module near the end of the NCS implementation process.

If it is desired to incorporate formats in the UDS Code Conventions Module earlier in the process, the locations for the code information portion of the module can be adopted once the discipline designators and sheet identification requirements included in the UDS Drawing Set Organization Module have been implemented. This will allow regulatory information to be included in the proper location within the drawing set, even if the components used to create the graphics such as line types and CAD layer names have not yet been implemented.

Adopting the drawing format requirements for code conventions will be easier to do once standard sheets and drawings have been created that include the regulatory information commonly used on most projects. These sheets and drawings can then be used as templates and modified to suit the specific requirements of each project. (For more information regarding implementation of the UDS Code Conventions Module, refer to Chapter 11, "Implementation.")

Code requirements from Section 08 14 16 - Flush Wood Doors:

2.02 INSTALLATION:
    A. Install fire-rated doors in accordance with NFPA 80 requirements

Code requirements from Section 08 71 00 - Door Hardware:

2.02 GENERAL REQUIREMENTS FOR DOOR HARDWARE PRODUCTS
    A. Applicable provisions of Federal, State, and local codes.

    B. ANSI/ICC A117.1, American National Standard for Accessible and Usable Buildings and Facilities.

    C. Hardware for Smoke and Draft Control Doors: Provide hardware that enables door assembly to comply with air leakage requirements of the applicable code.

Code requirements from Section 31 23 16 - Excavation:

3.02 EXCAVATING
    A. General: Excavate and overexcavate in accordance with 29 CFR - The Code of Federal Regulations Title 29, sub part P. Shoring and slope stability are the sole responsibility of the Contractor.

FIGURE 8-8
Example of Regulatory Information Included in the Project Manual

REVIEW OF KEY CONCEPTS IN THIS CHAPTER

1. Consistent formats for the types and locations of regulatory information will benefit many drawing users, help to expedite plan review by code officials, and streamline the transfer of code-related information during the project cycle and the facility cycle.
2. Regulatory information is grouped into 12 categories, which include related regulatory information. The UDS Code Conventions Module provides a table for each category that indicates locations and appearance guidelines for the presentation of regulatory information.
3. The appearance of regulatory information can be presented in two types of formats: graphic and text.
4. Adoption of the UDS Code Conventions Module should be scheduled later in the NCS implementation process in order to take advantage of other format requirements that will be needed for the location and creation of regulatory information.

FREQUENTLY ASKED QUESTIONS

Q: *Does the NCS require a certain minimum amount of regulatory information to be included in a set of construction documents?*

A: Since design professionals must comply with many different policies of local authorities having jurisdiction, the NCS does not require a minimum amount of regulatory information to be included in the construction documents. When regulatory information is included, it should comply with the guidelines established in the UDS Code Conventions Module, unless it would conflict with the requirements of local officials.

Q: *Does regulatory information need to be presented in strict accordance with the formats included in the appendices of the UDS Code Conventions Module?*

A: The appendices in the UDS Code Conventions Module include tables, schedules, and graphics for certain types of regulatory information that could appear in the construction documents. However, these are only examples, and their purpose is simply to demonstrate how regulatory information could be formatted and used. They may be modified or simply used as guidelines to create other user-defined formats. Whether or not the graphic formats are used, they should be created using line types, symbols, and other drafting conventions that comply with those in the NCS.

Q: *Are code officials familiar with the requirements for regulatory information in the NCS?*

A: Code officials and plan reviewers will become more familiar with the locations and formats for regulatory information included in the UDS Code Conventions Module as more drawing sets submitted to them comply with the NCS. To help the officials become more aware of the NCS formats, a note can be included with the general notes, which states, "Location and appearance of regulatory information: In accordance with version 3.1 of the U.S. National CAD Standard.

AIA CAD Layer Guidelines

GENERAL

For now, most CAD software is dependent upon the use of layers. Although we expect that to change in the future, CAD layering is a critical part of the work of the architect in producing graphic construction documents. The format requirements for CAD layers are located in the AIA CAD Layer Guidelines: U.S. National CAD Standard version 3.0. The CAD Layer Guidelines were first published 1990 and were included in the first version of the U.S. National CAD Standard (NCS), released in 1999. Since its debut, the document has been subjected to numerous revisions and expansion within the layer lists and formatting requirements. These revisions include:

- Discipline designators now match UDS Drawing Set Organization module
- Expanded layer lists
- Change in field codes for status field for four characters to a single character
- Addition of a second optional minor group
- Any major group can now be used with any discipline designator
- Any minor group can be used with any major group
- Minor group field codes may now be alpha, numeric, or tilde (~) characters

HISTORY OF THE AIA CAD LAYER GUIDELINES

The CAD Layer Guidelines, published by the American Institute of Architects (AIA) in 1990, was the first national drawing standard. In 1999, the document was incorporated into the NCS version 1.0, when the title was changed to the AIA CAD Layer Guidelines: Second Edition, which led to some confusion. When NCS version 2.0 was published, the document title was changed to AIA CAD Layer Guidelines: NCS Version 2.0, and the format of the document changed from portrait to landscape page orientation to match the UDS modules. The edition included many changes from the previous editions, including: changes to the **status** field codes from a four-character to a single-character designation; addition of a second optional minor group; and expanded layer list for drawing views, civil, structural, mechanical, plumbing, and telecommunications. A new layer list for Surveying/Mapping was added, as well as a commentary on compliance with the International Organization for Standardization (ISO) CAD Standard. Formatting requirements were also revised to allow the use of any major group with any discipline designator and minor group with any major group.

In 2004, the AIA CAD Layer Guidelines: U.S. National CAD Standard version 3.0 was published, layer lists were further expanded, and a new layer list for Process was added. This edition also changed the minor group designations. The NCS version 3.1 published in 2005 includes no changes to the AIA CAD Layer Guidelines version 3.

LAYER-NAMING FORMAT

The basic concept of the AIA CAD Layer Guidelines is found in the layer-naming format, which is organized as a hierarchy of data fields, with some fields being mandatory and some optional. The data fields include the discipline designator, major group, two minor groups, and status. Each data field is separated from the next by a hyphen (-). A layer name may be as simple as A-WALL or as complex as AI-WALL- FULL-DIM-N. Users determine the sophistication of the layer-naming scheme based on the complexity of their drawings. Most firms establish an office standard for layer naming and apply this standard to all projects. Figure 9-1 illustrates the data fields that may be incorporated into a layer name.

Discipline Designator (Mandatory)

The discipline designator data field uses either a Level 1 or Level 2 discipline designator, as described in Chapter 1, "Drawing Set Organization." In NCS version 1.0, the discipline designator was intended to designate the discipline that authored the information. This followed the concept of "agent responsible" in the ISO CAD Standard. In NCS version 2.0, this concept was changed to indicate the category of subject matter, not the author of the layer. Therefore, the discipline designation for a toilet fixture might be shown as P, for Plumbing, even though it is shown on an Architectural sheet.

Depending on the level of discipline designator used, the data field is either a one- or two-character data field, separated from the major group data field by a hyphen (-) as indicated below:

A-WALL   Typical layer name with a Level 1 discipline designator
AD-WALL   Typical layer name with a Level 2 discipline designator

Figure 9-2 provides a complete listing of the Level 1 discipline designators, and Figure 9-3 provides an abbreviated list of Level 2 discipline designators. In both cases, the Level 1 and Level 2 discipline designators match the discipline designators used in sheet identification, providing for added consistency throughout a set of construction documents.

Major Group (Mandatory)

The major group data field consists of a four-character designation for a major facility element: system or assembly, drawing view, or annotation. The major group field codes are not user-defined; they must be one of the listed major group field codes shown in the layer lists. Any major group field code may be combined with any discipline designator as long as the original definition of the major group does not change and it forms a reasonable combination. Figures 9-4, 9-5,

A A - A A A A - A A A A - A
Discipline Designators (mandatory)

A A - **A A A A** - A A A A - A A A A - A
Major Group (mandatory)

A A - A A A A - **A A A A - A A A A** - A
One or Two Minor Groups (optional)

A A - A A A A - A A A A - A A A A - **A**
Status (optional)

FIGURE 9-1
Layer Name Data Fields

Ａ Ａ - A A A A - A A A A - A A A A - A

**Discipline Designators – Coordinated
with UDS Module 01**

Level 1 Discipline Designators (Mandatory):

G	General		
H	Hazardous Materials	F	Fire Protection
V	Survey / Mapping	P	Plumbing
B	Geotechnical	D	Process
W	Civil Works	M	Mechanical
C	Civil	E	Electrical
L	Landscape	T	Telecommunications
S	Structural	R	Resource
A	Architectural	X	Other Disciplines
I	Interiors	Z	Contractor/Shop Drawings
Q	Equipment	O	Operations

FIGURE 9-2
Level 1 Discipline Designators, Complete

and 9-6 illustrate three options for denoting the major group, depending on facility system, drawing view, or annotation.

Minor Group (Optional)

The minor group is a four-character field that further defines the major group. In NCS version 2.0, the layer-naming structure was expanded to include a second optional minor group that can be used to further define the first minor group. The minor group is separated from the major group by a hyphen; and if two minor groups are used, they are also separated from each other by the use of a hyphen. Figure 9-7 gives an example of minor group identifiers.

Ａ Ａ - A A A A - A A A A - A A A A - A

**Discipline Designators – Coordinated
with UDS Module 01**

Examples of Level 2 Discipline Designators (Optional):

AS Architectural Site
AD Architectural Demolition
CG Civil Grading
CP Civil Paving
SF Structural Framing
DP Process Piping
EL Electrical Lighting

FIGURE 9-3
Level 2 Discipline Designators, Abbreviated

A A-<u>**A A A A**</u>-A A A A-A A A A-A
Major Group (Mandatory)

A – **W A L L**

Major Group Identifies:

<u>Major Building Systems:</u>

WALL	Walls
DOOR	Doors
LITE	Lighting Fixtures
FIXT	Plumbing Fixtures

FIGURE 9-4
Major Group Identifiers

NCS History: During the creation of NCS version 1.0, the U.S. Army representative pushed for adoption of ISO 13567 into the standard, but the Project Committee decided to stay with the AIA document.

User-defined minor groups may be identified with a combination of four alphabetic and/or numeric characters; and, if need be, a tilde (~) may be used as one or more placeholders. Any minor group can be used with any major group as long as the original definition of the minor group does not change. See Figure 9-8 for samples of user-defined minor groups.

The layer lists included in the NCS provides the most commonly used minor group field codes by discipline designator. It also includes the minor group field codes for drawing view and annotation layers.

Status (Phase) (Optional)

The final data field is the status. This field code is separated from the other field codes by a hyphen and is a single character that indicates the status of the work or construction phase. Figure 9-9 illustrates the status field and codes included in the NCS.

A A -<u>**A A A A**</u>-A A A A -A
Major Group (Mandatory)

A – **E L E V**

Major Group Identifies:

<u>Drawing Views </u>(for Layers that are organized primarily by drawing type rather than by major building system):

SECT	Sections
ELEV	Elevations
DETL	Details

FIGURE 9-5
Major Group Identifiers

A A- $\boxed{\text{A A A A}}$ - A A A A - A
Major Group (Mandatory)

A – **A N N O**

Major Group Identifies:

FIGURE 9-6
Major Group Identifiers

<u>Annotations </u>(text, dimensions, notes, sheet borders, detail references):

A A-A A A A - $\boxed{\text{A A A A - A A A A}}$ - A
Minor Groups (Optional)

A – W A L L - **F U L L**

Minor Group Further Differentiates Major Group:

FULL	Full Height
PART	Partial
IDEN	Identification
PATT	Pattern

FIGURE 9-7
Minor Group Identifiers

A A -A A A A- $\boxed{\text{A A A A - A A A A}}$ - A
Minor Groups (Optional)

A – W A L L - **F U L L – I N T R**

Minor Group can be User-Defined:

May be four alphabetic and/or numeric characters (0-9) or a "~" may be used as a placeholder.

FIGURE 9-8
User-Defined Minor Groups

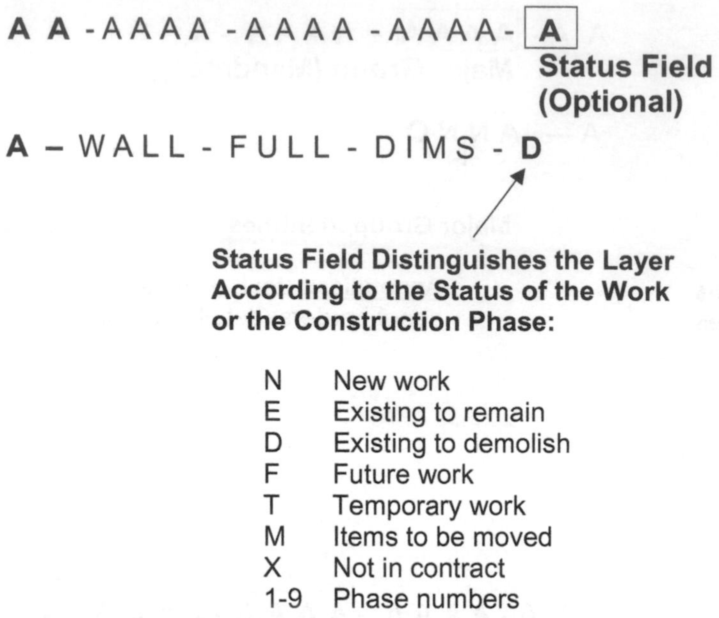

A A - A A A A - A A A A - A A A A - [A]

**Status Field
(Optional)**

A – W A L L - F U L L - D I M S - **D**

**Status Field Distinguishes the Layer
According to the Status of the Work
or the Construction Phase:**

N	New work
E	Existing to remain
D	Existing to demolish
F	Future work
T	Temporary work
M	Items to be moved
X	Not in contract
1-9	Phase numbers

FIGURE 9-9
Status Fields and Codes

LAYER LISTS

The NCS contains a prescribed list of typical layer names organized by drawing view, annotation, or discipline designator. Following is the organization of these layer lists.

Drawing View Layer List
Annotation Layer List
General Layer List
Hazardous Materials Layer List
Survey and Mapping Layer List
Geotechnical Layer List
Civil Works Layer list
Civil Layer List
Landscape Layer List
Structural Layer List
Architectural Layer List
Interiors Layer List
Equipment Layers list
Fire Protection Layer List
Plumbing Layer List
Process Layer List
Mechanical Layer List
Electrical Layer List
Telecommunications Layer List
Resource Layer List
Other Disciplines Layer List
Contractor/Shop Drawings Layer List
Operations Layer List

The NCS lists are not intended to represent a complete listing of all possible layer names, but those most commonly used, along with the methodology for creating a user-defined layer name. In version 2.0, the NCS created what came to be known as the "free agent" rule, which clarified that any reasonable combination of discipline designator, major group, and minor group would be permitted. The architect must use his or her professional judgment to determine whether a proposed combination of data fields forming a layer name is reasonable. In some cases, the combination simple does not make sense and is therefore nonconforming to the NCS guidelines or it changes the original definition of the major or minor group. One of the earlier complaints of layer naming was that the layer names reflected an architectural bias. The NCS Project Committee has worked hard to encourage more participation from nonarchitectural groups, such as engineering organizations, owners, facility mangers, and other industry groups, to respond to the layer-naming convention needs of more users. As more organizations participate in the process, these layer names are evolving.

COMMENTARY: U.S. NCS AND ISO 13567

Very early in the development of the AIA CAD Layer Guidelines, the AIA CAD Layer Task Force considered many of the concepts used in ISO Standard 13567, Organization and Naming of Layers for CAD. For example, the ISO field code "agent responsible" was first called "discipline code" in the AIA document and had the same definition as the ISO term. The term was later changed in NCS version 2.0 to "discipline designator" to match the UDS term, used for sheet identification, and the definition was changed to describe the category of the subject matter rather than the discipline that created the information.

There exist many similarities between the two formats, particularly in regard to the naming and use of data fields that make up a layer name; but there is an important difference, too: the NCS uses more prescribed field codes, where the ISO format is more user-defined for each field. Therefore, the ISO approach is not single language-dependent, whereas the NCS is, because it is English-based.

The commentary on ISO 13567 in the NCS describes how to make the layer name, as prescribed in the AIA CAD Layer Guidelines, conform conceptually with the ISO format. For firms that are performing international work, this may be important but for most us it is just interesting information.

IMPLEMENTATION ISSUES

Implementing the AIA CAD Layer Guidelines must be one of the earliest steps in the NCS implementation process, because most of the steps that follow either require the creation of new CAD files or revisions to existing ones. Even though the formats in this component may take more effort for some to incorporate into the workplace, it will save time in the long run if it is scheduled near the starting point of the process—changing layer names later on will take even more effort. For those workplaces that are already using something similar to the layer-naming requirements, it shouldn't be much of a problem at all. Quite often, the major obstacle is overcoming a resistance to change the formats we have grown so accustomed to. However, the same can be said for the entire implementation process.

Before changing to the layer-naming conventions in the AIA CAD Layer Guidelines, the Level 1 and Level 2 discipline designators from the UDS Drawing Set Organization Module need to be adopted, because they are used for the first component, or data field, of the CAD layer name. Rarely is this a problem, because most of the Level 1 discipline designators have been adopted from conventions already being used in the construction industry.

Once the discipline designators have been brought onboard, the next task is to review the formats for the major group field and compare them to those currently being used in the workplace. Several of the abbreviations used in the major group fields have been around for a number of years, so many CAD users will already be familiar with them. For those CAD users who have used them before, the time needed to revise current formats to comply with those in the NCS should be minimal.

Another factor that can make it easier to adopt the formats for major groups is the free-agent rule. This provision, which was incorporated into NCS version 2.0, can be a big help. Essentially, it allows any major group to be used with any discipline designator, as long as the definitions of the characters used in each of the fields remain the same. An example of using this rule would be changing a layer name for a title block from A-ANNO-TITL to G-ANNO-TITL. Even though G-ANNO-TITL is not on the identified layer list for the General discipline in the AIA CAD Layer Guidelines, it is still in accordance with the NCS—and is probably a better layer name anyway because title blocks are for use by all the disciplines in the drawing set.

The remaining two data fields in CAD layer names are optional: the minor group fields and the status field. These fields are only used when needed, and many of them can be avoided completely. Adopting the format requirements for these parts of the layer name should be even easier than the previous fields, especially when one considers that minor group data fields can be user-defined.

An important tool worth considering during the AIA CAD Layer Guidelines implementation process is the creation of a CAD layer naming office master. The master is created on paper first, and then used to help establish the fundamental CAD layers that will be needed for the initial setup of each sheet type, according to the sheet type designators identified in the UDS Drawing Set Organization Module. These include:

Sheet type designator 0: General
Sheet type designator 1: Plans
Sheet type designator 2: Elevations
Sheet type designator 3: Sections
Sheet type designator 4: Large-Scale Views
Sheet type designator 5: Details
Sheet type designator 6: Schedules and Diagrams

An example of layer names for an architectural sheet type designator 1-series (Plans) sheet needed in a multidiscipline drawing set might include the following:

A-ANNO-DIMS	Dimensions
A-ANNO-IDEN-DOOR	Door identification symbols (includes user-defined minor group, DOOR)
A-ANNO-IDEN-ROOM	Room identification symbols
A-ANNO-IDEN-WIND	Window identification symbols (includes user-defined minor group, WIND)
A-ANNO-KEYN	Sheet keynotes
A-ANNO-NOTE-GNSH	General sheet notes (name includes user-defined minor group, GNSH)
A-ANNO-NLPT	Nonplotting graphic information
A-ANNO-ASYB	Reference symbols
A-ANNO-TTLB-TEXT	Text in the title block (includes user-defined minor group, TEXT)
A-DOOR	Doors
A-GLAZ	Windows
A-WALL	Walls
A-WALL-PATT	Wall hatch patterns

G-ANNO-TITL	Drawing or detail titles (name makes use of the free-agent rule, which allows any major group to be used with any discipline, as long as the definitions of the characters used in the fields remain the same)
G-ANNO-TTLB	Title block and sheet borders (this name also makes use of the free-agent rule)

Once the layer names for each sheet type have been identified, a CAD template can be created as a library file. It can then be copied as a project file and modified as needed to suit the user's needs for a project.

For an example of **CAD layer-naming office master** that can be used as an architectural template for each sheet type designator, see Appendix E.

Review of Key Concepts in this Chapter

1. The AIA CAD layer-naming format contains four data fields separated by hyphens.
2. Recent revisions to the AIA CAD Layer Guidelines such as user-defined minor groups have resulted in a format that is much more flexible and easier to use.
3. Only the discipline designator data field and the major group data field are mandatory; user-defined data fields are not allowed in either of these fields.
4. The NCS contains sample layer lists, of the commonly used layer names.
5. If the AIA CAD Layer Guidelines are adopted very early in the implementation plan, it will help save time because additional man-hours will not be needed later to correct NCS symbols, CAD drawings, and details created with incorrect layer names.

Frequently Asked Questions

Q: *We like to group all of our demolition layer names together because our CAD users can locate them easier that way. Can we use D (demolition) for the first field in the layer name?*

A: Not unless you want to confuse all those in the Process discipline, because D is the discipline designator for Process. Since there is no "Demolition" discipline, here are the two best alternatives:

1. Use D for the Level 2 discipline designator. For example, a wall that is going to be demolished can be assigned to a layer similar to AD-WALL. This methodology will keep all the architectural demolition layer names together.
2. Use a D in the status field. An example of how this would be used for an architectural wall that is going to be demolished would be: A-WALL-D. Be aware, though, that this methodology will probably not work as well for most CAD users because CAD software is often unable to group all the different demolition layers together using this method.

Q: *The CAD software that we are considering purchasing appears to include default CAD layer names that are in compliance with the NCS. How do we know if they are?*

A: At the time of this writing, none of the software manufacturers were providing CAD layer names in accordance with the NCS. At least one was basing its CAD layering system on outdated second-edition AIA CAD layer names that had been replaced many years ago. However, at the same time, Bentley Systems Inc., makers of MicroStation, became the first NCS-licensed CAD vendor and announced development of an NCS plug-in for its products. We anticipate Bentley's product will become the first CAD software product to provide compliant CAD layer names.

Most likely, if the CAD software isn't NCS-licensed, the default CAD layer names used probably do not comply with the NCS. The best way to find out is to contact the manufacturer and ask.

Q: *The layer names in the Process Layer List are the only place I can find that includes layer names with a tilde (~), instead of four alpha and/or numeric characters in the minor group. Can they be used in other disciplines also?*

A: The tilde is indicated in the Process Layer List simply because it was incorporated into the NCS in response to requests by those in the Process discipline who were frustrated by trying to convert the shorter abbreviations used for many of the names used in their industry to four characters. For example, H2 (H_2) is a common abbreviation for hydrogen, but changing it from two characters to four caused too much confusion. Since all minor groups must consist of four characters, a placeholder was needed for the unused characters. Hence, the advent of the use of the tilde into the U.S National CAD Standard.

Even though the tilde is only shown in the Process layer list, it can be used in minor groups for any discipline. The AIA CAD Layer Guidelines require all minor groups of all disciplines to consist of four alphabetic and/or numeric characters (0-9) and/or the tilde (~).

Plotting Guidelines

GENERAL

Until we are able to truly develop a paperless set of project construction documents, the printing of drawings and specifications will be critical to every project. And we suspect that even in a paperless world, someone will always need a printed report, whether graphic or text, for some purpose. Therefore, it is necessary that standards and guidelines be developed that allow users of different software and hardware to create similar printed output. Since this output is commonly the legal instruments of service of the design professionals, it is critical that it be able to be consistently reproduced from the electronic file.

> **FYI:** During an early NCS Project Committee meeting, representatives from Tri-Service and the U.S. Coast Guard were excused from the meeting to coordinate their two plotting guidelines documents. At the conclusion of their meeting, the Tri-Service Plotting Guidelines document emerged.

The format requirements for printed output of electronic CAD files are located in the Tri-Service Plotting Guidelines, which were developed by the **U.S. Coast Guard** and published by the **Tri-Service CADD/GIS Technology Center.** The Tri-Service Plotting Guidelines were adopted into the first version of the U.S. National CAD Standard (NCS), in 1999, and they were not subjected to a single revision by the National CAD Standard Project Committee (NCSPC) through NCS version 3.1. In fact, the NCSPC has resisted every change that has been proposed to the Tri-Service Plotting guidelines through two revision cycles. However, later in this chapter, we will discuss why this component of the standard will soon be subjected to significant changes.

BENEFITS OF NCS PLOTTING GUIDELINES

The primary intent of Tri-Service Plotting Guidelines is to provide consistent black-and-white and color plots from various CAD programs. This is made possible by a table originally created by the U.S. Coast Guard, which assigns each CAD display color to a single NCS color number, line width, and plotting color. Even though the table is based upon AutoCAD and MicroStation CAD software, it allows other CAD software manufacturers to map their colors and line widths to those in the tables.

THE CADD/GIS TECHNOLOGY CENTER

The Tri-Service CADD/GIS Technology Center was created by the U.S. Department of Defense (DOD) in 1993, to reduce redundant CAD standardization efforts within the Army, Navy, and Air Force. The organization is located in Vicksburg, Mississippi, at the U.S. Army Engineer Research and Development Center, Information Technology Laboratory. Since publishing the Tri-Service

Plotting Guidelines, its name has been changed to the CADD/GIS Technology Center for Facilities, Infrastructure and Environment, or simply, the CADD/GIS Technology Center (CGTC). A large portion of the CGTC's mission is to standardize CAD requirements for architecture, engineering, and construction (A/E/C) design and construction documents, and its efforts in this regard were primarily targeted toward the numerous architecture and engineering (A/E) firms doing vertical construction design work (buildings) for the DOD. The CGTC created its own A/E/C CADD Standard in 1995 (version 1.0) and, working in conjunction with the U.S. Coast Guard, published the Tri-Service Plotting Guidelines in 1999.

To incorporate the Tri-Service Plotting Guidelines into version 1.0 of the NCS, CGTC representatives coordinated their efforts with the AIA, CSI, and NIBS. Even though the guidelines are part of the NCS, they are in the public domain, and portions of the plotting guidelines may also be found in the CGTC's current A/E/C CADD Standard (version 2.0). Its standard includes references to each of the other NCS components. (More information about the CGTC is available at the organization website: http://tsc.wes.army.mil).

PLOTTING GUIDELINES TABLE

The Tri-Service Plotting Guidelines consists of a table that was established to ensure consistency in plotting and to minimize problems exchanging electronic files among drawing users. Though the table was created to be applicable to most commercially available CAD software packages, it is based on AutoCAD Release 13 and MicroStation Version 95 software, because of their dominance, at the time, throughout the DOD. Thus, the table, though proprietary to AutoCAD and MicroStation, is set up to allow other CAD vendors to develop color mapping to either or both MicroStation and/or AutoCAD.

The table in the Tri-Service Plotting Guidelines consists of the following seven categories:

- NCS Color Number
- Pen Plotter Pen (millimeters)
- Laser/Electric Inkjet (inches)
- Plot Color
- MicroStation Color Number
- MicroStation Line Weight
- AutoCAD Color Number

The categories in the table are cross-referenced to each other to provide a means of translation between the various elements and CAD software systems. For an example of how the table is organized, refer to Figure 10-1.

Colors

Graphics and text used on drawings are displayed on a computer monitor in various colors to differentiate the elements from one another. The table in Tri-Service Plotting Guidelines includes a color number for each of the 255 colors used by AutoCAD. Each of the default AutoCAD colors is assigned a color number from 1 through 255. These 255 numbers are then used to create the NCS color numbers that have been given the same number as those used by AutoCAD. (Note, however, that the AutoCAD color number 0 is not included in the chart because it is not used by AutoCAD for plotting.) These numbers are then mapped to 255 MicroStation colors. The result is a table of NCS colors that can translate between AutoCAD, MicroStation, and other CAD vendors.

The table created by the CADD/GIS Technology Center was based on assigning wider lines to colors that appear brighter on a black background (black backgrounds are used by most CAD users). The reasoning is that, on a black computer screen background, brighter colors such as yel-

NCS PLOTTING GUIDELINES TABLE

NCS Color #	Pen Plotter pen mm	Laser/Elec. InkJet in.	Plot Color	MicroStation Color #	MicroStation line weight	AutoCAD Color #
1	0.18	0.007	Black	3	0	1
2	0.25	0.010	Black	4	1	2
3	0.35	0.014	Black	2	2	3
4	0.35	0.014	Black	7	2	4
5	0.50	0.020	Black	1	3	5
6	1.00	0.039	Black	5	7	6
7	1.40	0.055	Black	0	10	7
8	0.35	0.014	Halftone	9	2	8
9	2.00	0.079	Black	14	15	9
10	0.18	0.007	Black	10	0	10
11	0.25	0.010	Black	19	1	11
12	0.35	0.014	Black	27	2	12
13	0.50	0.020	Black	35	3	13
14	0.70	0.028	Black	43	5	14
15	1.00	0.039	Black	51	7	15
16	1.40	0.055	Black	59	10	16
17	0.70	0.028	Halftone	67	5	17
18	0.35	0.014	Halftone	75	2	18
19	2.00	0.079	Black	83	15	19
20	0.18	0.007	Rust	6	0	20
21	0.25	0.010	Rust	30	1	21
22	0.35	0.014	Rust	22	2	22
23	0.50	0.020	Rust	46	3	23
24	0.70	0.028	Rust	38	5	24
25	1.00	0.039	Rust	62	7	25
26	1.40	0.055	Rust	54	10	26
27	0.70	0.028	Rust	78	5	27
28	0.35	0.014	Rust	70	2	28
29	2.00	0.079	Rust	94	15	29
30	0.18	0.007	Black	86	0	30
31	0.25	0.010	Black	110	1	31
32	0.35	0.014	Black	102	2	32
33	0.50	0.020	Black	126	3	33
34	0.70	0.028	Black	118	5	34
35	1.00	0.039	Black	142	7	35
36	1.40	0.055	Black	134	10	36
37	0.70	0.028	Halftone	158	5	37
38	0.35	0.014	Halftone	150	2	38
39	2.00	0.079	Black	174	15	39
40	0.18	0.007	Gold	166	0	40
41	0.25	0.010	Gold	190	1	41
42	0.35	0.014	Gold	182	2	42

FIGURE 10-1
Organization of the Tri-Service Plotting Guidelines Table

low or magenta appear wider than blue or gray colors, even when they are the same pixel width. Therefore, colors such as blue or gray are assigned to thinner line widths, which can be used for elements such as hatch patterns and backgrounds. Brighter colors are assigned to wider lines that can be used for items such as sheet borders, building footprints, and large text.

In addition to providing a means for mapping AutoCAD and MicroStation colors to each other, each color is assigned to two types of line width categories. One category is identified as a Pen

FYI: "Line width" is the preferred term, because it more accurately describes the two-dimensional characteristic of a line, whereas terms such as "line weight" and "line thickness" should be avoided because they imply three-dimensional characteristics of mass and volume

Plotter Pen (with line width expressed in millimeters); the other category is the MicroStation line weight (with line widths expressed according to the numbering system used by MicroStation).

Line Widths

Most commercial CAD programs can provide an almost limitless supply of line widths, sometimes referred to as "pen widths." However, for any CAD standard to be effective, a uniform number of line widths needs to be established so that drawings can be shared and printed more easily. According to the CGTC, during the development of the Tri-Service Plotting Guidelines, a decision was made to follow a standard established by the International Organization for Standardization (ISO) for line widths. The standard, published in 1982 was the ISO 128 Technical Drawings—General Principles of Presentation—Part 20: Basic Conventions for Lines. The decision made sense at the time because it avoided the creation of another standard by adopting one that had already been in use.

The line widths in the Tri-Service Plotting Guidelines were also coordinated with the line width table in the Uniform Drawing System (UDS) Drafting Conventions Module, which also includes a description for the typical use of each width. The eight line widths are as shown in Figure 10-2.

FYI: A miscommunication between CSI and the CADD/GIS Technology Center resulted in only five line widths being included in the original UDS Drafting Conventions Module, whereas the Plotting Guidelines was published with eight. The three missing lines were added by amendment when the UDS Drafting Convention was incorporated into NCS version 2.0

Plot Colors

In addition to providing a means to establish line widths for the colors displayed by CAD software, the table in the Tri-Service Plotting Guidelines also includes mapping between CAD display colors and plot colors. Each of the CAD software colors is mapped to one of the following 14 plot colors:

Black
Halftone
Rust
Gold
Olive

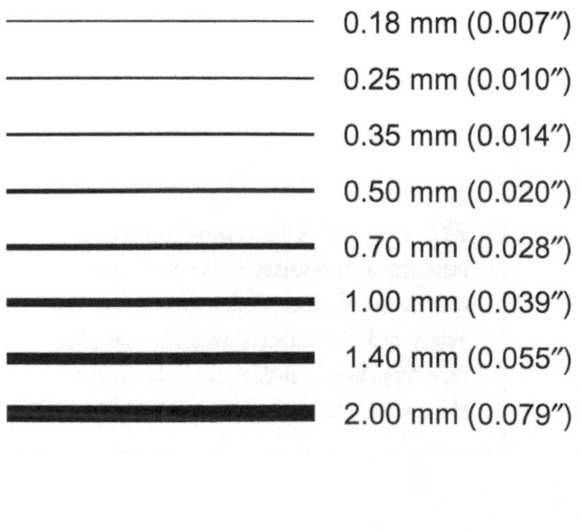

0.18 mm (0.007")

0.25 mm (0.010")

0.35 mm (0.014")

0.50 mm (0.020")

0.70 mm (0.028")

1.00 mm (0.039")

1.40 mm (0.055")

2.00 mm (0.079")

FIGURE 10-2
NCS Line Widths

Green
Forest green
Teal
Cyan
Blue
Navy
Purple
Magenta
Red

The Tri-Service Plotting Guidelines makes no attempt to provide a definition of the colors via a ratio of the percentage of Red-Green-Blue (RGB percent ratio) or other means. (Plot colors are discussed more later in this chapter, under "Future of the Tri-Service Plotting Guidelines.")

Laser/Electric Inkjet Settings

The table in the Tri-Service Plotting Guidelines also includes values, in inches, for laser and inkjet printers, which are mapped to the AutoCAD, MicroStation, and NCS colors. There are eight values, as follows:

0.007"
0.010"
0.014"
0.020"
0.028"
0.039"
0.055"
0.079"

Each of these values is, simply, an imperial conversion from the eight metric pen plotter settings, as follows:

0.007" (0.18 mm)
0.010" (0.25 mm)
0.014" (0.35 mm)
0.020" (0.50 mm)
0.028" (0.70 mm)
0.039" (1.00 mm)
0.055" (1.40 mm)
0.079" (2.00 mm)

These conversions provide CAD users with a consistent set of values, which makes it possible to set line widths as either metric or imperial measurements.

FUTURE OF THE TRI-SERVICE PLOTTING GUIDELINES

Since becoming a component of the first NCS version in 1999, the Tri-Service Plotting Guidelines is the only NCS component that did not undergo a single modification through NCS version 3.1. But, as mentioned earlier here, this is all about to change. Shortly after the NCSPC began the NCS version 3 ballot process, the CADD/GIS Technology Center submitted a letter to NIBS, recommending that the Tri-Service Plotting Guidelines be considered obsolete and asking for it to be removed from the NCS. The request was received too late to be incorporated into the NCS ballot, however, so the Tri-Service Plotting Guidelines remained unchanged, as just noted, through NCS version 3.1.

The CGTC made the request to withdraw the Tri-Service Plotting Guidelines for a variety of reasons. Perhaps the most compelling was due to dramatic changes that have occurred in CAD software since the component was originally created. For example, in 1999, when the component became part of the NCS, AutoCAD users had to assign colors to graphics and text and then use pen tables to assign line widths to each color. Recent changes to AutoCAD's software have made it possible to assign AutoCAD line widths to individual elements, regardless of color.

In addition to the aforementioned changes to CAD software, there are also problems with a number of the 255 colors listed in the table. Many of them are so dark they would not be visible on computer monitors when used on a black background. Another concern is that even though most CAD software and computer systems are capable of displaying from 16 to 256 colors, most drawings can be created using 16 or less. The downside is that the more colors used, the greater the effort necessary to create, plot, and exchange CAD files.

In addition to the issues related to display colors, there are also concerns with the 14 plot colors that are listed in the table. The colors have no definition (Red-Green-Blue percent ratio), meaning that their exact configuration is undefined and completely open to interpretation. More importantly, there is a question as to whether plot colors should even be included in the NCS. When users need to plot in color, they usually need more flexibility than that which is available in the table, because the printed output required is often very unique to the user's specific needs. Thus, this element needs to be removed from future updates to the Tri-Service Plotting Guidelines.

Another issue is the need to allow flexibility of color use. Many workplaces distinguish features on their drawings with colors that have to be drawn in a variety of pen widths. For example, a civil engineering firm may want to set up its screen colors for utility lines according the American Public Works Association (APWA) Uniform Color Code. In this case, red would be used to indicate electric power lines, yellow for gas lines, and blue for potable water lines. Other workplaces, such as the U.S. Geological Survey (USGS), must use very specific colors and pen widths for the topographical and satellite image maps they create.

Another problem with the Tri-Service Plotting Guidelines table is that some of the display colors are mapped to halftone plot colors. Providing for screened output is beneficial; however, providing only 50 percent of screened output (halftone translates to one-half, or 50 percent) does not offer enough variety. If screened output is going to be included in the standard, other screen percentages should be added to give users greater flexibility, depending upon their needs.

Recently, another subject also has drawn much attention: the quantity of line widths included in the table. Since the release of the Tri-Service Plotting Guidelines, some members of the NCSPC have proposed that a thinner line width be added to the standard, either 0.10 mm or 0.13 mm. The effort has been resisted by the NCSPC, including some members from the CADD/GIS Technology Center. In fact, an amendment to incorporate a 0.10 mm line width into NCS version 3.0 was defeated; but we do not expect this issue to go away, because a reasonable argument can be offered on both sides of the issue—and, lately, it seems the argument for the thinner line is gaining momentum.

CAD technicians and others who want to use a line width thinner than the 0.18 mm pen included in the Tri-Service Plotting Guidelines claim it would enable them to more clearly differentiate elements, and that it would be useful for lighter backgrounds and hatch patterns. Those who oppose adding a thinner line to the table are concerned about the reproduction quality of a thinner line on plots and certain media types such as Ozalid and photocopy reproductions. Ironically, this issue may be resolved by something that has nothing to do with either of these arguments: the International Organization for Standardization (ISO). In 1996, the ISO updated and published ISO 128-20 Technical Drawings—General Principles of Presentation—Part 20: Basic Conventions for Lines, to include a 0.13 mm line width. If the NCS is to remain synchronized with ISO, it is certainly plausible that the NCS would also adopt the 0.13 pen width.

In response to the need to update the Tri-Service Plotting Guidelines, the NCSPC has formed a Printed Output Task Team to explore a wide range of plotting-related issues. In addition, the CADD/GIS Technology Center has created new tables for display colors, line widths, and screened colors. The tables are included in version 2.0 of its A/E/C CADD Standard, which can be obtained free of charge at the CGTC website (http://tsc.wes.army.mil). Note, however, that though the CGTC standard is based on NCS components, the new tables have dropped plot colors. The A/E/C CADD Standard also recommends that CAD drawings be created using only the eight colors included in its standard. Provisions are included, however, for the 255 colors listed in the current Tri-Service Plotting Guidelines, to accommodate users who need more colors. Without a doubt, dramatic changes are in store for this component of the NCS.

IMPLEMENTATION ISSUES

The eight pen widths included in the Tri-Service Plotting Guidelines are very easy to comprehend. It will not take much effort to create pen tables in CAD software that match the colors and line widths in the table. Thereafter, however, many workplaces will be faced with a tremendous challenge in trying to implement the new pens and colors, because, in all likelihood, they will be much different from those currently in use. CAD technicians and designers grow very accustomed to the tables they use, so changing them is not easy for many. Doing so will require most workplaces to replace at least some of their pens with those closest to them in the table. If more than eight widths are currently being used, the additional pens will need to be converted to one of the eight in the NCS.

Once the pen widths have been updated, they will have to be assigned to the NCS color numbers in the table. This will probably be the most difficult step in the adoption process for many CAD users because it will change the appearance of their drawings on the display monitor. To be successful, it will help to focus on the bigger picture, specifically, on the benefits that all members of the project team will gain by making this transition.

Another implementation hurdle to overcome, in addition to the colors and pens listed in the Tri-Service Plotting Guidelines table, is the use of the lines. This information is not found in the Plotting Guidelines table, but in other components of the NCS. In particular, a table included in the UDS Drafting Conventions Module identifies the use of many line widths such as those used to create title block borders, property lines, match lines, and schedules. The UDS Drafting Conventions Module also includes many figures that illustrate how lines are used for different drawing types. (For more on this issue, refer to Chapter 4.)

Proper use of line types is also explained in the UDS Symbols Module. Graphic depictions of the symbols are represented, along with the types of lines that must be used, such as continuous, dashed, centerline, and so on. A description accompanying many of the symbols also identifies the metric line widths, taken from the table of common line types in the UDS Drafting Conventions Module. These are not specified in millimeters directly, but instead are cross-referenced to the description of the line from the table of common line types included in the UDS Drafting Conventions Module. The five lines, described in the graphics of the symbols as either fine, thin, medium, wide, or extra-wide, equate to those in the Tri-Service Plotting Guidelines, as follows:

Fine lines: 0.18 mm
Thin lines: 0.25 mm
Medium lines: 0.35 mm
Wide lines: 0.50 mm
Extra wide lines: 0.70 mm

Adopting the pens and colors from the Tri-Service Plotting Guidelines, and implementing the lines as described in the UDS Drafting Conventions and UDS Symbols Modules, will require an appreciable investment of time and effort for many workplaces. First, it will take time to make the changes to drawings already in use, such as title blocks and standard details, which, in all probability, were established using pens different from those in the NCS. Then, it will require making a psychological adjustment to how these changes will affect the appearance of the drawings. Therefore, it will probably be easier for most workplaces to implement the Tri-Service Plotting Guidelines one step at a time, in this order: pen widths first, then the colors, and, finally, the line usage from the UDS Drafting Conventions and UDS Symbols Modules. Moreover, it will probably be less disruptive to production to convert existing drawings on an as-needed basis, rather than trying to transform all of them at the same time.

Certainly, the format requirements in the Tri-Service Plotting Guidelines can be adopted after other NCS components are implemented, but we recommend putting this component into practice early in the implementation process and prior to sharing drawing files with consultants and other users. In all likelihood, at least some of the pens currently being used in the workplace will match those in the Tri-Service Plotting Guidelines table, which should make the conversion process a little smoother. And there is no reason to delay the adoption of the pen widths due to a concern that the Tri-Service Plotting Guidelines will undergo changes in future NCS updates, as we do not anticipate that any of the current line widths will be replaced. (For more information regarding implementation of the Tri-Service Plotting Guidelines, refer to Chapter 11, "Implementation.")

REVIEW OF KEY CONCEPTS IN THIS CHAPTER

1. The purpose of the Tri-Service Plotting Guidelines is to provide consistent black-and-white and color plots from various CAD programs.
2. The Tri-Service Plotting Guidelines was published by the Tri-Service CADD/GIS Technology Center and incorporated into NCS version 1.0 in 1999. Tri-Service is now known as the CADD/GIS Technology Center.
3. The format requirements in the Tri-Service Plotting Guidelines are located in a table that translates AutoCAD and MicroStation display colors to the same line widths and common NCS colors.
4. General use of each line type is included in the UDS Drafting Conventions Module. The symbols in the UDS Symbols Module also identify use of lines.
5. Technological changes to CAD software and CAD user needs have occurred since the creation of the Tri-Service Plotting Guidelines. This should result in changes to this component of the NCS in future updates.
6. Implementing the line widths and display colors in the Tri-Service Plotting Guidelines may be disruptive to many workplaces. However, it will streamline the overall NCS adoption process if this component is scheduled earlier, rather than later, in the NCS implementation plan.

FREQUENTLY ASKED QUESTIONS

Q: *Why aren't pen widths narrower than .18 mm included in the NCS?*
A: When the Tri-Service Plotting Guidelines was originally being developed, it was coordinated with the 1982 edition of ISO 128-20 Technical Drawings—General Principles of Presentation—Part 20: Basic Conventions for Lines. Back then, ISO 128-20 included eight pen widths, and each of them was incorporated into the Tri-Service Plotting Guidelines: 0.18 mm, 0.25 mm, 0.35 mm, 0.50 mm, 0.70 mm, 1.00 mm, 1.40 mm, and 2.0 mm.

These eight pen widths are the only ones that comply with the NCS, and they cannot be modified, nor can others be used. Please note, however, that the 1996 edition of ISO

128-20 added a 0.13 mm pen width, and there is a possibility that it might be included in a future NCS update, if the NCS Project Committee members can be convinced that it should be.

Q: *Why does the Tri-Service Plotting Guidelines only establish line widths set to colors and fail to assign them to objects and elements?*

A: When the Tri-Service Plotting Guidelines was first established, AutoCAD assigned line widths to colors, not objects. Since AutoCAD can now assign line widths to colors and objects, we anticipate that future versions of the Tri-Service Plotting Guidelines will address this issue.

Q: *Do the colors and line assignments in version 2.0 of the CADD/GIS Technology Center's A/E/C CADD Standard (published in September 2001) supersede those in the Tri-Service Plotting Guidelines, which was published by the CADD/GIS Technology Center in 1999?*

A: No, they could only be adopted into the NCS by the ballot amendment process, in accordance with the NCS Project Committee Rules of Governance.

Q: *Why does the table in the Tri-Service Plotting Guidelines only map colors to AutoCAD and MicroStation? What about other CAD software?*

A: The Tri-Service Plotting Guidelines was published by the Tri-Service CADD/GIS Technology Center, an organization created by the U.S. Department of Defense to oversee CAD technologies in use throughout the DOD. The standard was based on AutoCAD and Micro-Station software because of their dominance, at the time, throughout the DOD. The table is set up to allow other CAD vendors to develop color mapping to either or both MicroStation and AutoCAD.

Implementation

GENERAL

Since publication of the first version of the U.S. National CAD Standard (NCS) in 1999, it has been distributed to more than 4,000 workplaces throughout North America and other countries. The 2005 release of NCS version 3.1 in electronic format made access to the standard much easier and resulted in even more organizations and companies coming onboard. Unfortunately, the NCS does not include a manual of instructions or a module to explain how to adopt the standard into the workplace. Consequently, once architects and engineers have installed the NCS CD-ROM into their computers, they are faced with many implementation questions, among them:

- Where do we start?
- How disruptive will the process be?
- How long will it take?
- What will it cost to complete the implementation?

The purpose of this chapter is to answer these questions and introduce some of the successful strategies that can be taken by various types of workplaces. It will also address some of the significant challenges that users will face during the process and will offer strategies that can be used to meet them. Finally, the chapter will provide tips that can help save time and keep the workplace productive while the formats in the standard are being adopted.

THE BEST REASON TO ADOPT THE NCS

Companies and organizations are motivated to adopt the National CAD Standard for a variety of reasons. Some of the most common include:

- To meet compliance requirements of future clients
- To keep up with technology
- To improve the transfer of information
- To gain a marketing advantage on the competition
- To gain endorsements from AIA, CSI, NIBS, and other industry organizations

Although it is probably true that many organizations have been motivated to adopt the NCS for some of these reasons alone, another important advantage to implementing the standard is one that is often overlooked, even though it can impact the workplace in more positive ways than the others: increased productivity.

Problems with In-house Office Standards

Companies and organizations that have developed their own in-house office standards realize how much effort is required to create, maintain, and enforce them. Many are incomplete, contain contradictions, or have not been coordinated with the rest of the office's construction documents. Quite often, an in-house standard is used only sporadically, or by only a few members of the workplace.

Once an in-house standard has been developed, it can take a great deal of effort to motivate consultants to use them, especially when they are less than inspired to adopt yet another set of drawing formats from one of their clients. Organizations with branch offices or multiple disciplines are often faced with a dilemma of having to impose the formats favored by one group over those being used by one of the others. When new employees join an organization, they are often faced with the challenge of casting off the standard used at their previous workplace for the one being used in the new one.

It's fair to say that when most architects were sitting in their college design studios they were not envisioning the necessity of one day having to create and maintain an in-house office drafting standard. This is probably one of the reasons that so many of these efforts have resulted in less than favorable results—that is, designers want to use their talents *designing,* not creating and updating drafting standards. This attitude is understandable, even commendable.

The NCS does just that: it enables architects, engineers, and CAD technicians to focus on design, not on developing and updating drawing standards. This will benefit both their clients and companies, because the time and labor it would take to assemble and maintain an in-house standard instead can be applied to improving the quality of their designs, as well as the quality of the construction documents used to create them. When facility managers require the architects they hire to use the NCS, it helps them to focus more on managing and planning, instead of managing their own standards.

The NCS can also be a convenient scapegoat, in that it will be easier for consultants and coworkers in other offices to accept it, because it is, simply, the standard being used throughout the industry, as opposed to one created for a single workplace. Organizations need only adopt a standard that has already been developed and that will be maintained and updated by the National CAD Standard Project Committee (NCSPC) to respond to rapidly changing technology. When allowed more time to spend on design and productivity, organizations will see a reduction in errors and omissions. The bottom line is that adopting the NCS will give companies the opportunity to make their workplaces more enjoyable and more profitable.

IMPLEMENTATION OBSTACLES

For an implementation plan to succeed, a number of obstacles need to be removed from the workplace before the first format is even adopted. Most of these barriers are found within the workplace itself, and some of the most challenging are within the minds of those who work there. The most difficult obstacles to overcome can be summed up in one simple phrase: resistance to change.

Adopting the NCS will require a willingness to change many formats and work processes, some of which have been in place for many years. Accepting these changes will not be easy for many. But there will be little, if any, chance of succeeding unless the following basic principles are recognized and agreed to:

- The adoption of the NCS must be supported by upper management.
- Recognition that most resistance is created from psychological barriers.
- Success will require involvement from the workforce.
- The workforce will need training.
- Communication, teamwork, and a spirit of cooperation will be the keys to success.

Of these principles, none is as important as the support of upper management. Without it, adoption and implementation of the NCS cannot succeed. The decision makers in an organization must be willing to commit the manpower needed, and must be open to the changes that will result, before a workplace should attempt to adopt any of the components in the NCS. And before upper management can endorse the effort they must be willing to take a risk and, just as important, believe the reward will be worth the investment. In all likelihood, having this philosophy is how they became decision makers in the first place. Once the leaders recognize how the NCS can benefit revenues, by increasing accuracy and improving quality, they will usually find it much easier to support the effort.

The second biggest barrier that needs to be conquered is the psychological one. Most of the formats that appear in the NCS are not brand new; in fact, they were adapted from those already being used in the industry. When the contributing organizations of the NCS components were faced with selecting one industry format over another, sometimes the decision was purely arbitrary, because a compelling argument one way or the other did not exist. This is why, when put under a microscope, it is tempting to argue about many of the procedures. As authors of this book, and coauthors of many of the documents that were incorporated into the NCS, we can honestly say that we ourselves didn't agree with all of the decisions the committees made either—and we served on them. But for a national standard like this one to succeed, we all must acknowledge that none of us can have it all our own way. This applies to workplaces also. Those adopting the standard must be willing to compromise and exchange a few of their favorite drawing methodologies for something else, even if they find it less appealing.

Beginning the Implementation Process

Before opening the first page of the NCS, a number of decisions need to be made that will make the adoption process much easier. The first is to identify a person, or a committee, that will be responsible for the effort. In smaller workplaces, the committee might be one or two people. In larger workplaces, more help will be beneficial, as it will serve to get more people involved, thus providing a more encompassing sense of ownership.

An implementation committee will be responsible for many decisions, so they will need to work closely with upper management and staff to keep the process running smoothly. Some of their most important responsibilities should include:

- Developing an implementation plan
- Drawing up an implementation schedule
- Identifying software and procedures that will be used
- Training staff and consultants
- Assisting the notations coordinator
- Promoting awareness among clients, constructors, and materials suppliers
- Staying informed about NCS changes and updates

With those duties in mind, the personnel to consider for the implementation committee should include the following:

- Project managers with expertise in construction documents
- Specifiers
- Senior CAD technicians

In workplaces with multiple disciplines, a representative from each discipline should also be included. That said, be aware that the larger the committee, the more difficult it will be to reach consensus on decisions. Therefore, we also recommend that one person be identified to chair the committee, and he or she must be empowered to break deadlocks when they occur.

The first thing that each member of the implementation committee needs to do is to join the NCS Project Committee (NCSPC). There are two primary reasons this is essential.

- There is no cost to join and no meetings that must be attended, but by being a member of the NCSPC, each member of the implementation committee will be able to stay up to date about the latest NCS developments through a free e-mail service. These communications from the NCSPC will affect implementation decisions that need to be made, and knowledge of impending changes will help save time by allowing the implementation schedule to be adjusted in accordance with upcoming changes—as opposed to in response to a change that has already occurred.
- As members of the NCSPC, implementation committee members will also be able to participate in the development of the standard, and exchange their own ideas.

The many positive benefits the NCSPC offers to the workplace is why upper management should make it mandatory for any members serving on the NCS implementation committee to join the NCSPC. (For more information about the NCSPC, and how to join it, refer to the Introduction of this book.)

The next task the implementation committee should accomplish is to identify goals for the implementation process. These objectives, which will vary for each organization, will make it easier to get the process started. Some typical examples, taken from real-life situations, include:

- Begin the process without having to "know it all."
- Learn the system at a comfortable pace.
- Minimize costs and downtime.
- Incorporate formats gradually into projects.
- Receive benefits early.

In larger organizations with a number of departments or multiple disciplines, it's a good idea to select one or two groups to serve as implementation "guinea pigs." The best groups to target are usually smaller, rather than larger. It's also important to assure that the leaders of these initiation groups be supportive of the effort; and group members should include at least some who are open-minded to adopting a new work process. One of the benefits of this strategy is that as positive results are achieved, the group can help spread the word to the rest of their coworkers.

It's important that the implementation committee be aware of a misconception that exists about the process: that is, that learning the various NCS components is difficult and that only experts can understand how it works. In fact, many of the processes are very easy to adopt, and some of them can be implemented quickly. With that in mind, the best implementation strategy is to adopt the easiest formats first, and schedule those that require more effort later. The benefit of this step-by-step approach is twofold: first, it provides a sense of accomplishment early; second, each implemented format will make the next one go more smoothly. Furthermore, adopting this strategy will help the implementation committee meet their biggest challenge: developing the implementation plan.

Another strategy that will speed up the implementation process is to start out by including only small portions of the NCS in a project. As more formats are adopted, they can be included in projects later on. To make the most effective use of this strategy, the implementation committee should, first, identify a project that can be used as the first test case, and, second, select only a few aspects of the standard to incorporate into this project. This approach is, in effect, a methodology that makes it possible to adopt the standard at a more comfortable pace, rather than trying to learn all of it at the same time and trying to implement it on the first project. This step-by-step method will also provide results and benefits sooner, and will help to minimize costs and downtime.

Developing an NCS Implementation Plan

Many of the formats in the NCS were based on drawing methodologies that have been used in workplaces throughout the country. So, to develop a plan, the implementation committee needs to review the standard and identify those formats that are most similar to the ones already being used. The initial review of the NCS does not need to be exhaustive, nor does it need to be all-inclusive. One or two of the more recognized formats will usually result in a successful start-up, because members of the workplace will be more willing to accept and adopt more familiar concepts. As more of the concepts in the NCS are analyzed, most organizations will discover that the list of items that resemble those already in use in their own drawing practice is longer than they anticipated.

One of the first procedures we recommend adopting can be accomplished without changing a single line on a drawing. Most workplaces already organize their drawing sets by disciplines, although usually not in the same order as the one prescribed in the NCS. Therefore, all it takes to comply with the standard is to reshuffle the hierarchy of the subsets into the required sequence. The greatest challenge with an issue like this is not the manpower or time needed, because they are really not a factor; rather, it is the psychological shift necessary to make the change itself—and it will be this same barrier that will need to be pushed aside time and time again during much of the implementation process.

One of the key decisions to make during the development of the implementation plan is when to schedule the adoption of the AIA CAD Layer Guidelines (CLG) and the Tri-Service Plotting Guidelines. Our recommendation is to schedule them earlier, because doing so will help to avoid having to reformat CAD drawings that may have been created with noncompliant layers and colors. For example, if a sheet template is created in accordance with the format requirements in the UDS Sheet Organization Module *before* adopting the formats from the AIA CAD Layer Guidelines and Tri-Service Plotting Guidelines, the layers, display colors, and line widths used in the template will have to be reviewed and reconfigured later. The smarter approach is to get the requirements right the first time. True, adopting these elements from the NCS early in the plan will require some work, but the effort will be worth it in the long run.

Example of an Implementation Plan

An example of an implementation plan is provided here to help implementation committees develop their own plans. It is based on the step-by-step approach described in the preceding sections in this chapter: it incorporates the strategy of using early adopted elements as tools to ease the implementation steps that follow. Note, however, that in all likelihood, portions of some of the steps will be started while another step is still being implemented. This is normal; the objective of the plan is simply to provide a means to measure progress.

This demonstration of how an implementation plan can be developed is one that should work satisfactorily in many workplaces as a point of reference from which to start. The plan presumes that a test project has been identified, as suggested above, and that our other recommendations, given in the "Beginning the Implementation Process" section earlier, have already been completed. Furthermore, the plan recommends using many test projects during the adoption process; to that end, many of the steps are those that should be included from one project to the next. Also, keep in mind that training will have to be scheduled between many of the steps, or between groups of steps, as necessary to meet the unique requirements of each workplace.

Finally, be aware that implementation plans like this one can also be created using a spreadsheet, using columns to specify the scheduled dates for each step and to identify issues that need to be resolved before the item can be implemented.

How to Interpret the Plan

The example implementation plan is set up as follows:

1. Each step identifies the action to be taken.
2. The NCS components that contain the requirements for the action being described are identified within square brackets—[ ].
3. Cross-references to chapters/appendixes in this book where more specific implementation information for the step can be found are contained within curly braces—{ }.
4. The comments identify the key implementation issues.
5. At the end of each step, an "effort rating" is provided to indicate the level of difficulty most workplaces should anticipate for the action. The scale is based on the presumption that the workplace has a basic understanding about the format being adopted and that employees are open-minded in regard to its implementation. (Note: If familiarity and attitude about the item being adopted is otherwise, the scale will have to be adjusted accordingly.) The effort scale is delineated as follows:

★	Very little effort required
★★	Some effort required
★★★	Moderate effort required
★★★★	Considerable effort required
★★★★★	Substantial effort required

NCS IMPLEMENTATION PLAN

Step 1: *Adopt discipline designators.* [UDS Drawing Set Organization Module] {Chapter 1} Comments: Replace current discipline designators with those in the UDS Drawing Set Organization Module. This may necessitate replacing a few noncompliant alpha characters currently in use with compliant discipline designators in the UDS. No other revisions to current drawing formats are required. Steps 1 and 2 can be combined on the first test project. This step will require some coordination with consultants.
Effort rating: ★★

Step 2: *Adopt order of subsets within the drawing set.* [UDS Drawing Set Organization Module] {Chapter 1} Comments: No revisions to current drawing formats will be required. This step can be included with step 1 on the first test project.
Effort rating: ★

Step 3: *Adopt format for sheet type designators, sheet sequence numbers, and sheet identification (sheet numbering).* [UDS Drawing Set Organization Module] {Chapter 1} Comments: Format of current title blocks and sheet layout may continue to be used. Most of the adoption effort will be associated with arranging the order of the sheets in the discipline subsets to comply with the hierarchy of the sheet type designators. References to sheets will be affected, due to the new sheet identification system. This step is usually a good one to include in the second test project. It will require close coordination with consultants. (Example lists of sheets for drawing sets are included in Appendixes A and B.)
Effort rating: ★★★

Step 4: *Adopt CAD layer names.* [AIA CAD Layer Guidelines] {Chapter 9 and Appendix E} Comments: Adopting this component of the NCS may require more effort than any other. However, adoption will be eased by using the free agent rule and user-defined minor fields. Creating a CAD layer-naming office master for each sheet type designator will help expedite the adoption process, because it can be used as CAD template for the initial setup of each sheet. This step, and the three that follow it, will probably cause the most disruption to the workplace during the NCS implementation process. (See Appendix E for a typical example of a CAD layer naming office master.) This step should usually be included with the third test project.

Effort rating: ★★★★★

Step 5: *Adopt line widths.* [Tri-Service Plotting Guidelines] {Chapter 10} Comments: Adopting this component is sure to cause some disruption and will almost always result in the need to replace some of the current line widths with one of the eight that comply with the standard. Ideally, this step should be combined with step 7; however, many workplaces may resist having to adopt both lines and colors at the same time. This step should usually be included on the fourth test project.

Effort rating: ★★★★★

Step 6: *Adopt recommended uses for line widths.* [UDS Drafting Conventions Module and UDS Symbols Module] {Chapters 4 and 6} Comments: Adopting the recommended use of lines will take time, but once done, can be put into practice almost immediately. Each of the two UDS modules associated with this step includes requirements for the use of lines. A test project for this step should be identified after step 5 has been completed.

Effort rating: ★★★★★

Step 7: *Adopt NCS color numbers.* [Tri-Service Plotting Guidelines] {Chapter 10} Comments: For many workplaces, this step will require as much effort as any others in the implementation process; therefore, the implementation committee needs to stay in close contact with the NCS Project Committee to stay abreast of potential changes that could occur to future versions of Tri-Service Plotting Guidelines. Ideally, this step should be combined with step 5.

Effort rating: ★★★★★

Step 8: *Adopt drawing area coordinate system.* [UDS Sheet Organization Module] {Chapter 2} Comments: Some workplaces will want to combine this step with step 13, adoption of the sheet title block, and step 11, adoption of the drawing block title. It might, however, be wiser to wait until after step 10 is completed so that the proper file names can be assigned to them. Until those steps are completed, the coordinate system can be implemented with current title blocks and drawing block title symbols. The coordinate system needs to be coordinated with consultants.

Effort rating: ★★★

Step 9: *Adopt text symbols.* [UDS Symbols Module] {Chapter 6} Comments: Other than the lines, layer names, and colors used to create them, this is probably one of the easiest NCS components to adopt.

Effort rating: ★

Step 10: *Adopt file naming.* [UDS Drawing Set Organization Module] {Chapter 1} Comments: The previous steps could be accomplished without any changes to file naming or to any of the electronic files currently used in the workplace. Subsequent implementation will impact electronic CAD files and other electronic files that will be incorporated into the implementation process. Adopting the file-naming formats now will avoid having to go back and change them later. This may be one of the most difficult steps for some offices and workplaces to take.

Effort rating: ★★★★

Step 11: *Adopt the following reference symbols: drawing block title, section indicators, detail indicators, and elevation indicators.* [UDS Symbols Module; UDS Drafting Conventions

Module] {Chapters 4 and 6} Comments: Once the earlier steps of adopting line widths, colors, CAD layer names, and file names have been accomplished, most of the effort to adopt symbols and other drawing formats will be much easier. Though most of these symbols will be very similar to those already in use in many workplaces, this step will require close coordination with consultants. This step could be combined with step 12.

Effort rating: ★★★

Step 12: *Adopt remaining reference symbols.* [UDS Symbols Module] {Chapter 6} Comments: Next to text symbols, the reference symbols are the easiest to adopt, but nevertheless, this step also requires close coordination with consultants. This step could be combined with Step 11.

Effort rating: ★★★

Step 13: *Adopt sheet title block.* [UDS Sheet Organization Module] {Chapter 2} Comments: Most workplaces will adopt the NCS title block that most closely resembles the one they are currently using (horizontal or vertical text format). Some organizations will, however, have a very difficult time replacing the title block they have been using.

Effort rating: ★★★

Step 14: *Adopt note block.* [UDS Notations Module] {Chapter 7} Comments: The note block format will be similar to those currently being used by many workplaces. Therefore, the biggest challenge will probably be adopting the notation headings and coordinating the notations with proper line spacing, margin widths, and indent requirements.

Effort rating: ★★

Step 15: *Adopt terms and abbreviations.* [UDS Terms and Abbreviations Module] {Chapter 5} Comments: This step will require input from the specifier and coordination with the specifications. It will also require close coordination with consultants. It should be adopted before implementing the formats in the UDS Schedules Module (step 20), and it needs to be implemented before adopting reference keynotes (steps 28 to 30).

Effort rating: ★★★★

Step 16: *Identify notations coordinator.* {Chapter 7} Comments: The notations coordinator will play a major role during the adoption of each of the notations in the UDS Notations Module; therefore, he or she has to be empowered to make decisions regarding the choice of terms that will be used in schedules and notations.

Effort rating: ★★★

Step 17: *Adopt general notes, general discipline notes, and general sheet notes.* [UDS Notations Module] {Chapter 7} Comments: These are the easiest of the notation formats to adopt, and thus could be combined with one of the previous steps, if desired. The notations coordinator should take a lead and identify the types of notes that will be used and where they will be located. This step requires coordination with consultants, to ensure consistent labels are used for general notations throughout the drawing set.

Effort rating: ★★

Step 18: *Create sheet keynote office master.* {Chapter 7} Comments: For this step, too, the notations coordinator should take the lead. (An example of a sheet keynote office master is located in Appendix C.)

Effort rating: ★★

Step 19: *Adopt sheet keynotes.* [UDS Notations Module] {Chapter 7} Comments: Here again, the notations coordinator should take the lead. The sheet keynote office master, from step 18, will be a useful tool when implementing this component of the NCS. Keynote software also can help with the implementation, but it is not critical. Adopting sheet keynotes should be coordinated with consultants, to ensure consistent use of symbols.

Effort rating: ★★★

Step 20: *Adopt schedules.* [UDS Schedules Module] {Chapter 3} Comments: The layout requirements will require very little effort to adopt. Most of the work is associated with the proper application of terms and abbreviations used in the schedules. This component will require the previous adoption of the UDS Terms and Abbreviations Module, as well as coordination with the specifier.

Effort rating: ★★★★

Step 21: *Adopt drawing orientation and use of north arrow, drawing block formatting, reference grid system, and methodology for use of cross-referencing, material indication, match lines, mock-up sets, and scale.* [UDS Drafting Conventions Module; UDS Symbols Module] {Chapters 4 and 6} Comments: Adopting the formats in the UDS Drafting Conventions Module will be different from the other modules because its focus is on the methodology of how the formats in the other UDS modules should be incorporated into the drawings. It will alter the appearance of the drawings due to the changes it will cause in the way drawings are currently being created. The UDS Symbols Module is included in this step because many of the techniques in the UDS Drafting Conventions Module focus on the use of symbols. This step includes some of the easier formatting techniques from the UDS Drafting Conventions Module.

Effort rating: ★★★★

Step 22: *Adopt remaining drafting conventions formats, including methodology for dimensioning and identification of spaces and objects and guidelines for sheet types.* [UDS Drafting Conventions Module; UDS Symbols Module]{Chapters 4 and 6} Comments: This step is a follow-up to step 21 and, as such, includes the use of symbols and some of the more difficult concepts in the UDS Drafting Conventions Module. (See comments in step 21.)

Effort rating: ★★★★

Step 23: *Adopt line symbols.* [UDS Symbols Module] {Chapter 6} Comments: The majority of line symbols represent utilities, but they also include others, such as hidden lines and centerlines. Once the graphic concepts in the UDS Drafting Conventions Module have been adopted, it will be easier to adopt these symbols—which are not to be confused with lines from the Tri-Service Plotting Guidelines component of the NCS. These symbols are some of the easiest in the module to adopt.

Effort rating: ★★

Step 24: *Adopt materials symbols.* [UDS Symbols Module] {Chapter 6} Comments: These symbols represent the hatch patterns used for materials such as brick, concrete, and insulation. There are not very many of them, and they can be adopted on an as-needed basis.

Effort rating: ★★

Step 25: *Adopt object symbols.* [UDS Symbols Module] {Chapter 6} Comments: These represent items such as doors, furniture, and steel beams. The most frequently used should be adopted first; the remaining can be adopted on an as-needed basis.

Effort rating: ★★

Step 26: *Adopt identity symbols.* [UDS Symbols Module] {Chapter 6} Comments: These symbols represent many different types of items such as welding symbols, valves, and controls. There are many of them and they should be adopted on an as-needed basis.

Effort rating: ★★★

Step 27: *Adopt location of regulatory information and presentation format requirements of regulatory information.* [UDS Code Conventions Module] {Chapter 8} Comments: Most of the effort to adopt this component of the standard will be associated with learning the proper locations for regulatory information. Fortunately, the tables in the module are relatively easy to use.

Effort rating: ★★★

Step 28: *Identify software that will be used for reference keynotes.* {Chapter 7} Comments: Implementing reference keynotes should not be attempted without notation software, whether from the CAD software or an add-on third-party product. The notations co-ordinator needs to take the lead on this step, and a senior CAD technician should also be involved. It is important to spend some time researching the products available to confirm which provide notations that comply with the format requirements of the standard—many cannot.

Effort rating: ★★★

Step 29:   *Create reference keynote office master.* {Chapter 7} Comments: This portion of the standard will take a great deal of effort initially; thereafter, it will be an ongoing process because, often, the master will need to be updated from one project to the next, and it will grow as more notes are added to it. The notations coordinator should take the lead in this effort, and input from the specifier is crucial to ensure that the terms in the notations are consistent with those in the specifications. The master also has to be coordinated with the preferred terms in the UDS Terms and Abbreviations Module. (An example of a reference keynote office master is included in Appendix D.)

Effort rating: ★★★★★

Step 30:   *Adopt reference keynotes.* [UDS Notations Module] {Chapter 7} Comments: This step is the last of those related to adopting reference keynotes. It will require staff training, both with the software being used and the reference keynote methodology. Work-places that have invested the time in setting up a reference keynote system will have been rewarded with improved document quality and fewer errors and omissions. A reference keynote system is an important tool to employ during the creation of a standard detail library.

Effort rating: ★★★★★

Step 31:   *Reformat standard detail library using NCS file names and previously adopted formats.* [UDS Drawing Set Organization Module] [Chapter 1} Comments: This step presumes that materials and products are identified using reference keynotes. If reference keynotes are not used, this step can be implemented after step 27.

Effort rating: ★★★★★

A Compliancy Tool for Owners and Facility Managers

When owners and facility managers are considering whether to require that their construction drawings comply with the NCS, they must also be prepared to address issues such as the following:

- How will compliancy be enforced? Do we have the technical expertise and manpower available to enforce it?
- Do we have specific formats we want the architect to use that do not comply with the NCS, such as title blocks or sheet numbering?
- Where the NCS allows optional formats (such as sheet size), do we want to mandate that a specific NCS option be used?

The Supplement to AIA Document G612—2001 Part D, included in Appendix F of this book, can be used by owners and facility managers to identify the scope of services related to the NCS for a project. It has been organized to coordinate with each of the NCS components, and it can be used to identify specific NCS compliancy requirements, as well as any formats the owner wants used that do not comply with the NCS. The form can also serve as a resource to discuss and further define the owner's specific NCS requirements with the architect. This form should be provided to the architect before he or she begins preparing the construction drawings—ideally, it should be provided prior to the execution of the owner-architect agreement.

Review of Key Concepts in this Chapter

1. The best reason to adopt the NCS is the positive effect it will have on productivity and profitability.
2. Upper management must support the implementation effort if it is to succeed.
3. One of the biggest obstacles to overcome during the implementation process is resistance to change.
4. A key component in the implementation process is the implementation committee.
5. Before beginning the implementation process, adopt an implementation plan.
6. Employ a step-by-step implementation strategy that will allow previously adopted steps to be used as tools to ease the next step in the implementation plan.

Frequently Asked Questions

Q: *What can owners and facility managers do to assure that the architects they hire provide them with NCS-compliant construction drawings?*

A: When owners and facility managers need their construction drawings to comply with the NCS, it is important that they inform the architect *prior* to the execution of the owner-architect agreement, because there are still a number of architectural firms that have yet to adopt the standard. Wording similar to that given in the following sample paragraphs can be used by owners and facility managers when they will require NCS compliancy on their projects:

Sample wording to use in the agreement between the owner and the architect (this can also be included in the owner's request for proposals (RFP)):

> *Construction drawing format: Construction drawings for this project are to be provided by the architect to the owner in accordance with version 3.1 of the U.S. National CAD Standard (NCS). At final completion, the architect shall provide the owner with electronic CAD files of the construction drawings formatted in accordance with version 3.1 of the NCS.*

Sample wording to use in the owner's request for proposals (RFP):

> *Expertise: Demonstrate, through narrative and/or graphics, the firm's knowledge of version 3.1 of the U.S. National CAD Standard (NCS). Discuss the firm's experience with the NCS, and projects that have been completed in accordance with NCS requirements. Demonstrate the firm's ability to provide the owner with construction drawings that comply with version 3.1 of the NCS, including the formatting of electronic CAD files. Identify personnel on your project team who have NCS expertise.*

Q: *What else can owners and facility managers do to help ensure the drawings being provided to them comply with the NCS?*

A: The following options are available to owners when they do not have the NCS experience or manpower necessary to enforce compliancy:

1. Rely on the architect's professional expertise. For many owners, this will require a "leap of faith," and some will not be willing to make it, especially if the architect has very limited experience with the NCS.
2. Provide the architect with the Supplement to AIA Document G612—2001 Part D (included in Appendix F of this book) prior to the design phase, to ensure that both parties clearly understand what will be expected. Ideally, this document should be provided to the architect prior to the execution of the owner-architect agreement.
3. Hire an NCS consultant. This option will usually require the owner and consultant to meet with the architect prior to the schematic design phase to review compliancy requirements. In addition to performing reviews of the construction drawings and CAD

files at intermittent points during the construction documents phase, the consultant can also act as a valuable resource to help resolve NCS formatting questions and issues the architect or owner may have during the design phase of the project.

Q: *How long does it take to implement the NCS into the workplace?*

A: Though the time needed will be different for each workplace, there are a few common variables. A general list of the most significant issues, in order of importance, is as follows:

1. Amount of support the effort will receive from upper management
2. Number of employees and departments in the workplace
3. Level of resistance toward change in the workplace
4. Amount of resources (manpower) that can be dedicated to the effort, including training
5. Level of conflict the effort will create with workloads

Assuming that adequate support and resources are available and that staff is not overly resistant to the change, smaller workplaces with little or no knowledge of the NCS components should be able to form an implementation committee in one to two weeks. If time is available, the committee should be able to create an implementation plan and conduct their first training in four to eight weeks. The time needed after that will be different in each workplace, but smaller workplaces should be able to adopt most of the requirements within 12 to 18 months.

Q: *The in-house drawing standards our client requires us to use do not comply with the NCS. Does it still make sense to use the NCS?*

A: When forced to use a client's in-house standard, identify any formats that are not restricted. For example, if the client's title block, sheet numbering, and organization of the disciplines within the drawing set are the only formats that do not comply with the NCS, most of the other NCS formats—such as the sheet coordinate system, schedules, terms and abbreviations, symbols, notations, and code conventions—can still be used. Our recommendation is to approach each project assuming that the NCS will be used, then trim it back only as needed to meet the client's requirements.

Q: *How do we convince our consultants to adopt the NCS?*

A: When consultants have little knowledge about the standard, use the same step-by-step implementation approach, and consider reducing the NCS formats they will be required to use on their first project with you. They can still comply with sheet format, sheet type designators, and sheet identification quite easily. Consultants need to know what their requirements will be before they enter into an agreement with the A/E. To help encourage consultants to adopt the standard, consider including them in the training programs that are conducted during the implementation process. When our consultants resist adopting the formats, we simply remind them that we are their client.

Q: *How do we select a project as our first NCS "guinea pig?"*

A: Usually, the smaller, the better. More specifically, other things to consider include:

- How many NCS formats will be included?
- What is the level of the client's resistance to the formats?
- Which formats will consultants be required to comply with?

Q: *Our department is adopting the NCS. How do we convince the other departments in our company to use it?*

A: It is not unusual to see the NCS adopted by one discipline within a larger office with multiple disciplines. Sometimes, one branch office from the same company has adopted it and another hasn't. If the decision makers from other departments are resisting the NCS, there is little you will be able to do. Groups from within the organization that are resisting adoption of NCS formats may not become motivated until they are suddenly faced with a client that requires it, or until they receive a memo from the decision makers instructing them to adopt it.

List of Sheets: Example for Level 1 Discipline Designators

SHEET IDENTIFIER	SHEET TITLE
G-001	GENERAL INFORMATION
G-101	CODE SUMMARY, FIRE EXITING, AND SEPARATION
G-102	PHASING PLAN
H-001	GENERAL HAZARDOUS MATERIALS NOTES AND SYMBOLS
H-101	HAZARDOUS MATERIALS SITE REMOVAL PLAN
H-101	FIRST-FLOOR HAZARDOUS MATERIALS REMOVAL PLAN
H-102	SECOND-FLOOR HAZARDOUS MATERIALS REMOVAL PLAN
V-101	SURVEY
B-101	SOIL BORING PLAN
B-301	SOIL BORING SECTIONS
C-001	GENERAL CIVIL NOTES AND SYMBOLS C-101
C-101	SITE DEMOLITION PLAN
C-102	DIMENSION CONTROL PLAN
C-103	GRADING PLAN
C-104	SITE PAVING PLAN
C-105	EROSION CONTROL PLAN
C-201	GRADING PROFILES
C-301	GRADING SECTIONS
C-302	PAVING SECTIONS
C-501	GRADING DETAILS
C-502	PAVING DETAILS
C-503	EROSION CONTROL DETAILS
W-001	GENERAL CIVIL WORKS NOTES AND SYMBOLS
W-101	VICINITY MAP
W-102	GEOMETRIC ROADWAY LAYOUT
W-103	ROADWAY PLAN AND PROFILE
W-104	SANITARY SEWER PLAN AND PROFILE
W-105	DOMESTIC WATER PLAN AND PROFILE
W-106	NATURAL GAS PLAN AND PROFILE
W-107	EROSION CONTROL PLAN
W-108	TRAFFIC CONTROL PLAN
W-109	PERMANENT SIGNING PLAN
W-110	SIGNAL PLAN
W-201	SIGN ELEVATIONS
W-301	ROADWAY SECTIONS
W-302	CULVERT PIPE END SECTIONS
W-501	PAVING DETAILS

W-502	STORM SEWER DETAILS
W-503	PERMANENT SIGNING DETAILS
W-504	SIGNAL AND LIGHTING DETAILS
W-505	CULVERT DETAILS
W-506	EROSION CONTROL DETAILS
W-507	SIDEWALK, CURB, AND GUTTER DETAILS
W-508	DROP INLET DETAILS
W-601	SUMMARY OF QUANTITIES
W-602	SURFACING SCHEDULE
W-603	CONDUITS, CABLES, AND FUNCTION DIAGRAMS
L-001	GENERAL LANDSCAPING NOTES AND SYMBOLS
L-101	IRRIGATION DEMOLITION PLAN
L-102	PLANTING REMOVAL PLAN
L-103	LANDSCAPE IRRIGATION PLAN
L-104	PLANT MATERIALS PLAN
L-401	LARGE-SCALE IRRIGATION PLAN
L-402	LARGE-SCALE PLANTING PLANS
L-501	IRRIGATION DETAILS
L-502	LANDSCAPE DETAILS
L-601	IRRIGATION SCHEDULES
L-602	IRRIGATION DIAGRAMS
L-603	PLANT MATERIALS SCHEDULES
S-001	GENERAL STRUCTURAL NOTES AND SYMBOLS
S-101	FOUNDATION PLAN
S-102	SECOND-FLOOR FRAMING PLAN
S-103	ROOF FRAMING PLAN
S-201	FOUNDATION WALL ELEVATIONS
S-202	REINFORCING ELEVATIONS
S-203	FRAMING ELEVATIONS
S-301	WALL SECTIONS
S-501	FOUNDATION DETAILS
S-503	FRAMING DETAILS
S-504	STAIR DETAILS
S-601	FOUNDATION SCHEDULE
S-602	REINFORCING SCHEDULE
S-603	COLUMN AND BEAM SCHEDULES
A-001	GENERAL ARCHITECTURAL NOTES AND SYMBOLS
A-101	ARCHITECTURAL SITE PLAN
A-102	FIRST-FLOOR DEMOLITION PLAN
A-103	FIRST-FLOOR PLAN
A-104	FIRST-FLOOR FINISH PLAN
A-105	FIRST-FLOOR REFLECTED CEILING PLAN
A-106	SECOND-FLOOR DEMOLITION PLAN
A-107	SECOND-FLOOR PLAN
A-108	SECOND-FLOOR FINISH PLAN
A-109	SECOND-FLOOR REFLECTED CEILING PLAN
A-110	ROOF PLAN
A-201	EXTERIOR ELEVATIONS
A-202	INTERIOR ELEVATIONS
A-203	SIGNAGE ELEVATIONS
A-301	BUILDING SECTIONS
A-302	WALL SECTIONS

A-401	LARGE-SCALE TOILET PLANS
A-402	STAIR PLANS AND SECTIONS
A-403	ELEVATOR PLANS AND SECTIONS
A-501	EXTERIOR DETAILS
A-502	INTERIOR DETAILS
A-601	DOOR AND FRAME SCHEDULE
A-602	ROOM FINISH SCHEDULE
I-001	GENERAL INTERIOR NOTES AND SYMBOLS
I-101	FIRST-FLOOR INTERIOR DEMOLITION PLAN
I-102	FIRST-FLOOR INTERIOR DESIGN PLAN
I-103	FIRST-FLOOR FURNISHINGS PLAN
I-104	FIRST-FLOOR INTERIOR GRAPHICS PLAN
I-105	FIRST-FLOOR INTERIOR DESIGN REFLECTED CEILING PLAN
I-106	SECOND-FLOOR INTERIOR DEMOLITION PLAN
I-107	SECOND-FLOOR INTERIOR DESIGN PLAN
I-108	SECOND-FLOOR FURNISHINGS PLAN
I-109	SECOND-FLOOR INTERIOR GRAPHICS PLAN
I-110	SECOND-FLOOR INTERIOR DESIGN REFLECTED CEILING PLAN
I-201	INTERIOR DESIGN ELEVATIONS
I-202	INTERIOR GRAPHICS ELEVATIONS
I-301	INTERIOR DESIGN SECTIONS
I-401	LARGE-SCALE INTERIOR DESIGN PLANS
I-501	INTERIOR DESIGN DETAILS
I-601	ROOM FINISH SCHEDULE
I-602	FURNISHING SCHEDULE
Q-001	GENERAL EQUIPMENT NOTES AND SYMBOLS
Q-101	EQUIPMENT DEMOLITION PLAN
Q-102	EQUIPMENT PLAN
Q-201	EQUIPMENT ELEVATIONS
Q-401	LARGE SCALE EQUIPMENT PLANS
Q-501	EQUIPMENT DETAILS
Q-610	EQUIPMENT SCHEDULES
F-001	GENERAL FIRE PROTECTION NOTES AND SYMBOLS
F-101	FIRST-FLOOR FIRE PROTECTION DEMOLITION PLAN
F-102	FIRST-FLOOR FIRE PROTECTION PLAN
F-103	FIRST-FLOOR FIRE SPRINKLER PLAN
F-104	SECOND-FLOOR FIRE PROTECTION DEMOLITION PLAN
F-105	SECOND-FLOOR FIRE PROTECTION PLAN
F-106	SECOND-FLOOR FIRE SPRINKLER PLAN
F-501	FIRE PROTECTION DETAILS
F-601	FIRE PROTECTION SCHEDULE
F-602	FIRE SPRINKLER RISER DIAGRAM
P-001	GENERAL PLUMBING NOTES AND SYMBOLS
P-101	PLUMBING SITE DEMOLITION PLAN
P 102	PLUMBING SITE PLAN
P-102	FIRST-FLOOR PLUMBING DEMOLITION PLAN
P-103	FIRST-FLOOR PLUMBING PIPING PLAN
P-104	FIRST-FLOOR PLUMBING EQUIPMENT PLAN
P-102	SECOND-FLOOR PLUMBING DEMOLITION PLAN
P-103	SECOND-FLOOR PLUMBING PIPING PLAN
P-104	SECOND-FLOOR PLUMBING EQUIPMENT PLAN
P-501	PLUMBING DETAILS

P-601	PLUMBING FIXTURE SCHEDULE
P-602	PLUMBING DIAGRAMS
D-001	GENERAL PROCESS NOTES AND SYMBOLS
D-101	PROCESS SITE PLAN
D-102	FIRST-FLOOR PROCESS DEMOLITION PLAN
D-103	FIRST-FLOOR PROCESS LIQUIDS PLAN
D-104	FIRST-FLOOR PROCESS GASES PLAN
D-105	FIRST-FLOOR PROCESS PIPING PLAN
D-106	FIRST-FLOOR PROCESS EQUIPMENT PLAN
D-107	FIRST-FLOOR PROCESS INSTRUMENTATION PLAN
D-102	SECOND-FLOOR PROCESS DEMOLITION PLAN
D-103	SECOND-FLOOR PROCESS LIQUIDS PLAN
D-104	SECOND-FLOOR PROCESS GASES PLAN
D-105	SECOND-FLOOR PROCESS PIPING PLAN
D-106	SECOND-FLOOR PROCESS EQUIPMENT PLAN
D-107	SECOND-FLOOR PROCESS INSTRUMENTATION PLAN
D-201	PROCESS EQUIPMENT ELEVATIONS
D-301	PROCESS BUILDING SECTIONS
D-302	PROCESS EQUIPMENT SECTIONS
D-401	LARGE-SCALE PROCESS PLANS
D-501	PROCESS DETAILS
D-601	PROCESS SCHEDULES
D-602	PROCESS DIAGRAMS
M-001	GENERAL MECHANICAL NOTES AND SYMBOLS
M-101	FIRST-FLOOR MECHANICAL DEMOLITION PLAN
M-102	FIRST-FLOOR MECHANICAL HVAC PLAN
M-103	FIRST-FLOOR CHILLED WATER PIPING PLAN
M-104	FIRST-FLOOR HEATING WATER PIPING PLAN
M-105	FIRST-FLOOR STEAM PIPING PLAN
M-106	FIRST-FLOOR INSTRUMENTATION PLAN
M-107	SECOND-FLOOR MECHANICAL DEMOLITION PLAN
M-108	SECOND-FLOOR MECHANICAL HVAC PLAN
M-109	SECOND-FLOOR CHILLED WATER PIPING PLAN
M-110	SECOND-FLOOR HEATING WATER PIPING PLAN
M-111	SECOND-FLOOR STEAM PIPING PLAN
M-112	SECOND-FLOOR INSTRUMENTATION PLAN
M-401	LARGE-SCALE MECHANICAL PLANS
M-501	MECHANICAL DETAILS
M-601	HVAC EQUIPMENT SCHEDULE
M-602	PIPING DIAGRAMS
E-001	GENERAL ELECTRICAL NOTES AND SYMBOLS
E-101	FIRST-FLOOR ELECTRICAL DEMOLITION PLAN
E-102	FIRST-FLOOR ELECTRICAL POWER PLAN
E-103	FIRST-FLOOR ELECTRICAL LIGHTING PLAN
E-104	FIRST-FLOOR ELECTRICAL INSTRUMENTATION PLAN
E-105	SECOND-FLOOR ELECTRICAL DEMOLITION PLAN
E-106	SECOND-FLOOR ELECTRICAL POWER PLAN
E-107	SECOND-FLOOR ELECTRICAL LIGHTING PLAN
E-108	SECOND-FLOOR ELECTRICAL INSTRUMENTATION PLAN
E-401	LARGE-SCALE ELECTRICAL POWER PLAN
E-501	ELECTRICAL DETAILS
E-601	ELECTRICAL SCHEDULES

E-602	ELECTRICAL DIAGRAMS
T-001	GENERAL TELECOMMUNICATIONS NOTES AND SYMBOLS
T-101	FIRST-FLOOR TELECOMMUNICATION DEMOLITION PLAN
T-102	FIRST-FLOOR AUDIOVISUAL PLAN
T-103	FIRST-FLOOR CLOCK AND PROGRAM PLAN
T-104	FIRST-FLOOR INTERCOM PLAN
T-105	FIRST-FLOOR MONITORING PLAN
T-106	FIRST-FLOOR DATA NETWORKS PLAN
T-107	FIRST-FLOOR TELEPHONE PLAN
T-108	FIRST-FLOOR SECURITY PLAN
T-109	SECOND-FLOOR TELECOMMUNICATION DEMOLITION PLAN
T-110	SECOND-FLOOR AUDIOVISUAL PLAN
T-111	SECOND-FLOOR CLOCK AND PROGRAM PLAN
T-112	SECOND-FLOOR INTERCOM PLAN
T-113	SECOND-FLOOR MONITORING PLAN
T-114	SECOND-FLOOR DATA NETWORKS PLAN
T-115	SECOND-FLOOR TELEPHONE PLAN
T-116	SECOND-FLOOR SECURITY PLAN
T-401	LARGE-SCALE ELECTRICAL POWER PLAN
T-501	ELECTRICAL DETAILS
T-601	ELECTRICAL SCHEDULES
T-602	ELECTRICAL DIAGRAMS
R-101	EXISTING SITE PLAN

List of Sheets: Example for Level 2 Discipline Designators

SHEET IDENTIFIER	SHEET TITLE
G-001	LOCATION AND AREA MAPS
GI-102	CODE SUMMARY FIRE EXITING AND SEPARATION
GC-001	GENERAL REQUIREMENTS NOTES
GC-101	SITE UTILIZATION PLAN
GC-102	PHASING PLANS
GC-601	CPM SCHEDULES
HL-001	GENERAL HAZARDOUS MATERIALS NOTES AND SYMBOLS—LEAD ABATEMENT
HL-101	HAZARDOUS MATERIALS SITE REMOVAL PLAN—LEAD ABATEMENT
HL-101	FIRST-FLOOR HAZARDOUS MATERIALS REMOVAL PLAN—LEAD ABATEMENT
HL-102	SECOND-FLOOR HAZARDOUS MATERIALS REMOVAL PLAN—LEAD ABATEMENT
VA-101	AERIAL SURVEY
BP-101	SOIL PERCOLATION BORING PLAN
BP-301	SOIL PERCOLATION BORING SECTIONS
CD-101	SITE DEMOLITION PLAN
CS-101	DIMENSION CONTROL PLAN
CG-102	GRADING PLAN
CG-104	EROSION CONTROL PLAN
CG-201	GRADING PROFILES
CG-301	GRADING SECTIONS
CG-501	GRADING DETAILS
CG-503	EROSION CONTROL DETAILS
CP-103	SITE PAVING PLAN
CP-302	PAVING SECTIONS
CP-502	PAVING DETAILS
WG-001	GENERAL CIVIL WORKS NOTES AND SYMBOLS
WG-101	VICINITY MAP
WG-102	GEOMETRIC ROADWAY LAYOUT
WG-103	ROADWAY PLAN AND PROFILE
WG-104	SANITARY SEWER PLAN AND PROFILE
WG-105	DOMESTIC WATER PLAN AND PROFILE
WG-106	NATURAL GAS PLAN AND PROFILE
WG-107	EROSION CONTROL PLAN
WG-108	TRAFFIC CONTROL PLAN
WG-109	PERMANENT SIGNING PLAN

WG-110	SIGNAL PLAN
WG-201	SIGN ELEVATIONS
WG-301	ROADWAY SECTIONS
WG-302	CULVERT PIPE END SECTIONS
WG-501	PAVING DETAILS
WG-502	STORM SEWER DETAILS
WG-503	PERMANENT SIGNING DETAILS
WG-504	SIGNAL AND LIGHTING DETAILS
WG-505	CULVERT DETAILS
WG-506	EROSION CONTROL DETAILS
WG-507	SIDEWALK, CURB, AND GUTTER DETAILS
WG-508	DROP INLET DETAILS
WG-601	SUMMARY OF QUANTITIES
WG-602	SURFACING SCHEDULE
WG-603	CONDUITS, CABLES, AND FUNCTION DIAGRAMS
LD-101	IRRIGATION DEMOLITION PLAN
LD-102	PLANTING REMOVAL PLAN
LI-103	LANDSCAPE IRRIGATION PLAN
LI-401	LARGE-SCALE IRRIGATION PLAN
LI-501	IRRIGATION DETAILS
LI-601	IRRIGATION SCHEDULES
LI-602	IRRIGATION DIAGRAMS
LP-104	PLANT MATERIALS PLAN
LP-402	LARGE-SCALE PLANTING PLANS
LP-502	LANDSCAPE PLANTING DETAILS
LP-603	PLANT MATERIALS SCHEDULES
SD-101	FOUNDATION DEMOLITION PLAN
SD-301	FOUNDATION DEMOLITION SECTIONS
SD-501	FOUNDATION DEMOLITION DETAILS
SD-601	FOUNDATION DEMOLITION SCHEDULE
SB-202	REINFORCING ELEVATIONS
SB-504	STAIR DETAILS
SB-602	REINFORCING SCHEDULE
SB-603	COLUMN AND BEAM SCHEDULES
SF-102	SECOND-FLOOR FRAMING PLAN
SF-103	ROOF FRAMING PLAN
SF-201	FOUNDATION WALL ELEVATIONS
SF-203	FRAMING ELEVATIONS
SF-503	FRAMING DETAILS
AS-101	ARCHITECTURAL SITE PLAN
AD-102	FIRST-FLOOR DEMOLITION PLAN
AD-106	SECOND-FLOOR DEMOLITION PLAN
AD-201	EXTERIOR DEMOLITION ELEVATIONS
AD-202	INTERIOR DEMOLITION ELEVATIONS
AD-301	BUILDING DEMOLITION SECTIONS
AE-105	FIRST-FLOOR REFLECTED CEILING ELEMENTS PLAN
AE-109	SECOND-FLOOR REFLECTED CEILING ELEMENTS PLAN
AE-203	SIGNAGE ELEVATIONS
AE-402	STAIR PLANS AND SECTIONS
AE-403	ELEVATOR PLANS AND SECTIONS
AE-601	DOOR AND FRAME SCHEDULE
AF-104	FIRST-FLOOR FINISH PLAN

AF-108	SECOND-FLOOR FINISH PLAN
AF-110	ROOF FINISH PLAN
AF-302	WALL FINISH SECTIONS
AF-401	LARGE-SCALE TOILET FINISH PLANS
AF-501	EXTERIOR FINISH DETAILS
AF-502	INTERIOR FINISH DETAILS
AF-602	ROOM FINISH SCHEDULE
AG-103	FIRST-FLOOR GRAPHICS PLAN
AG-107	SECOND-FLOOR GRAPHICS PLAN
ID-101	FIRST-FLOOR INTERIOR DEMOLITION PLAN
ID-106	SECOND-FLOOR INTERIOR DEMOLITION PLAN
IN-102	FIRST-FLOOR INTERIOR DESIGN PLAN
IN-105	FIRST-FLOOR INTERIOR DESIGN REFLECTED CEILING PLAN
IN-107	SECOND-FLOOR INTERIOR DESIGN PLAN
IN-110	SECOND-FLOOR INTERIOR DESIGN REFLECTED CEILING PLAN
IN-201	INTERIOR DESIGN ELEVATIONS
IN-301	INTERIOR DESIGN SECTIONS
IN-401	LARGE-SCALE INTERIOR DESIGN PLANS
IN-501	INTERIOR DESIGN DETAILS
IN-601	ROOM FINISH SCHEDULE
IF-103	FIRST-FLOOR FURNISHINGS PLAN
IF-108	SECOND-FLOOR FURNISHINGS PLAN
IF-602	FURNISHING SCHEDULE
IG-104	FIRST-FLOOR INTERIOR GRAPHICS PLAN
IG-109	SECOND-FLOOR INTERIOR GRAPHICS PLAN
IG-202	INTERIOR GRAPHICS ELEVATIONS
QD-101	DETENTION EQUIPMENT PLAN
QF-102	FOOD SERVICE EQUIPMENT PLAN
QF-201	FOOD SERVICE EQUIPMENT ELEVATIONS
QH-401	LARGE-SCALE HOSPITAL EQUIPMENT PLANS
QH-501	HOSPITAL EQUIPMENT DETAILS
QY-610	SECURITY EQUIPMENT SCHEDULES
FA-101	FIRST-FLOOR FIRE DETECTION AND ALARM PLAN
FA-104	SECOND-FLOOR FIRE DETECTION AND ALARM PLAN
FA-501	FIRE DETECTION AND ALARM DETAILS
FX-102	FIRST-FLOOR FIRE SUPPRESSION PLAN
FX-105	SECOND-FLOOR FIRE SUPPRESSION PLAN
FX-601	FIRE SUPPRESSION SCHEDULE
FX-602	FIRE SUPPRESSION RISER DIAGRAM
PS-101	PLUMBING SITE PLAN
PD-101	PLUMBING SITE DEMOLITION PLAN
PD-102	FIRST-FLOOR PLUMBING DEMOLITION PLAN
PD-103	SECOND-FLOOR PLUMBING DEMOLITION PLAN
PP-104	FIRST-FLOOR PLUMBING PIPING PLAN
PP-105	SECOND-FLOOR PLUMBING PIPING PLAN
PQ-106	FIRST-FLOOR PLUMBING EQUIPMENT PLAN
PQ-107	SECOND-FLOOR PLUMBING EQUIPMENT PLAN
PL-501	PLUMBING DETAILS
PL-601	PLUMBING FIXTURE SCHEDULE
PL-602	PLUMBING DIAGRAMS
DS-101	PROCESS SITE PLAN
DD-102	FIRST-FLOOR PROCESS DEMOLITION PLAN

DD-102	SECOND-FLOOR PROCESS DEMOLITION PLAN
DL-103	FIRST-FLOOR PROCESS LIQUIDS PLAN
DL-103	SECOND-FLOOR PROCESS LIQUIDS PLAN
DG-104	FIRST-FLOOR PROCESS GASES PLAN
DG-104	SECOND-FLOOR PROCESS GASES PLAN
DP-105	FIRST-FLOOR PROCESS PIPING PLAN
DP-105	SECOND-FLOOR PROCESS PIPING PLAN
DQ-106	FIRST-FLOOR PROCESS EQUIPMENT PLAN
DQ-106	SECOND-FLOOR PROCESS EQUIPMENT PLAN
DQ-201	PROCESS EQUIPMENT ELEVATIONS
DQ-302	PROCESS EQUIPMENT SECTIONS
DQ-401	LARGE-SCALE PROCESS EQUIPMENT PLANS
DQ-501	PROCESS EQUIPMENT DETAILS
DQ-601	PROCESS EQUIPMENT SCHEDULES
DQ-602	PROCESS EQUIPMENT DIAGRAMS
DI-107	FIRST-FLOOR PROCESS INSTRUMENTATION PLAN
DI-107	SECOND-FLOOR PROCESS INSTRUMENTATION PLAN
DI-301	PROCESS BUILDING INSTRUMENTATION SECTIONS
MD-101	FIRST-FLOOR MECHANICAL DEMOLITION PLAN
MD-107	SECOND-FLOOR MECHANICAL DEMOLITION PLAN
MH-102	FIRST-FLOOR MECHANICAL HVAC PLAN
MH-108	SECOND-FLOOR MECHANICAL HVAC PLAN
MH-401	LARGE-SCALE MECHANICAL HVAC PLANS
MH-601	HVAC EQUIPMENT SCHEDULE
MP-103	FIRST-FLOOR CHILLED WATER PIPING PLAN
MP-104	FIRST-FLOOR HEATING WATER PIPING PLAN
MP-105	FIRST-FLOOR STEAM PIPING PLAN
MP-109	SECOND-FLOOR CHILLED WATER PIPING PLAN
MP-110	SECOND-FLOOR HEATING WATER PIPING PLAN
MP-111	SECOND-FLOOR STEAM PIPING PLAN
MP-602	PIPING DIAGRAMS
MI-106	FIRST-FLOOR INSTRUMENTATION PLAN
MI-112	SECOND-FLOOR INSTRUMENTATION PLAN
MI-501	MECHANICAL INSTRUMENTATION DETAILS
ED-101	FIRST-FLOOR ELECTRICAL DEMOLITION PLAN
ED-105	SECOND-FLOOR ELECTRICAL DEMOLITION PLAN
EP-102	FIRST-FLOOR ELECTRICAL POWER PLAN
EP-106	SECOND-FLOOR ELECTRICAL POWER PLAN
EP-401	LARGE-SCALE ELECTRICAL POWER PLAN
EP-501	ELECTRICAL POWER DETAILS
EP-602	ELECTRICAL POWER RISER DIAGRAMS
EL-103	FIRST-FLOOR ELECTRICAL LIGHTING PLAN
EL-107	SECOND-FLOOR ELECTRICAL LIGHTING PLAN
EL-601	ELECTRICAL LIGHTING SCHEDULES
EI-104	FIRST-FLOOR ELECTRICAL INSTRUMENTATION PLAN
EI-108	SECOND-FLOOR ELECTRICAL INSTRUMENTATION PLAN
TD-101	FIRST-FLOOR TELECOMMUNICATION DEMOLITION PLAN
TD-109	SECOND-FLOOR TELECOMMUNICATION DEMOLITION PLAN
TA-102	FIRST-FLOOR AUDIOVISUAL PLAN
TA-110	SECOND-FLOOR AUDIOVISUAL PLAN
TA-401	LARGE-SCALE AUDIOVISUAL PLAN
TC-103	FIRST-FLOOR CLOCK AND PROGRAM PLAN

TC-111	SECOND-FLOOR CLOCK AND PROGRAM PLAN
TC-501	CLOCK AND PROGRAM DETAILS
TI-104	FIRST-FLOOR INTERCOM PLAN
TI-112	SECOND-FLOOR INTERCOM PLAN
TM-105	FIRST-FLOOR MONITORING PLAN
TM-113	SECOND-FLOOR MONITORING PLAN
TM-601	MONITORING SCHEDULES
TN-106	FIRST-FLOOR DATA NETWORKS PLAN
TN-114	SECOND-FLOOR DATA NETWORKS PLAN
TN-602	DATA NETWORKS DIAGRAMS
TT-107	FIRST-FLOOR TELEPHONE PLAN
TT-115	SECOND-FLOOR TELEPHONE PLAN
TY-108	FIRST-FLOOR SECURITY PLAN
TY-116	SECOND-FLOOR SECURITY PLAN
RC-101	EXISTING SITE PLAN

Sheet Keynote Office Master: Example for Architectural Sheets

The following list of sheet keynotes is an example of how a sheet keynote master can be used as a template and then modified as needed for each project. Using this methodology makes it possible to provide a consistent set of sheet keynotes throughout any project, helps prevent typographical errors, and will work with or without keynoting software.

The list is alphabetized, to make the notes easier to locate and the list easier to update. The template can be created as a word processing document and is used by eliminating or modifying any of the sheet keynotes as necessary for the project and then saving it as the project master. When a new sheet keynote is needed for the project, it can be added at the end of the list. The number that appears next to each sheet keynote in this master is the same number that should appear in the sheet keynote symbol in the drawing block. Sheet keynotes with asterisks (*) could be eliminated by using an appropriate reference keynote.

1. ANGLE—SEE STRUCTURAL SHEETS.*
2. BEAM—SEE STRUCTURAL SHEETS.*
3. BEARING ELEVATION—SEE STRUCTURAL SHEETS.*
4. CHANNEL—SEE STRUCTURAL SHEETS.*
5. COLUMN—SEE STRUCTURAL SHEETS.*
6. CAST-IN-PLACE CONCRETE—SEE STRUCTURAL SHEETS.*
7. DASHED LINE INDICATES CABINET BELOW.
8. DASHED LINE INDICATES FINISH FLOOR.
9. DASHED LINE INDICATES FIXTURE/FURNISHING—NOT IN CONTRACT.*
10. DASHED LINE INDICATES FOUNDATION—SEE STRUCTURAL SHEETS.
11. DASHED LINE INDICATES FUTURE CONSTRUCTION—NOT IN CONTRACT.
12. DASHED LINE INDICATES HEADWALL ABOVE.
13. DASHED LINE INDICATES ROOF LINE.
14. DASHED LINE INDICATES ROOF HATCH ABOVE.
15. DASHED LINE INDICATES SKYLIGHT ABOVE.
16. DASHED LINE INDICATES SOFFIT ABOVE.
17. DECK—SEE STRUCTURAL SHEETS.*
18. DRAIN LINE—SEE PLUMBING SHEETS.*
19. DRAIN—SEE CIVIL SHEETS.*
20. DRAIN—SEE PLUMBING SHEETS.*
21. DUCTWORK—SEE MECHANICAL SHEETS.*
22. ELECTRICAL EQUIPMENT—SEE ELECTRICAL SHEETS.*
23. ELECTRICAL GENERATOR—SEE ELECTRICAL SHEETS.*
24. ELECTRICAL LIGHT FIXTURE—SEE ELECTRICAL SHEETS.*
25. ELECTRICAL LIGHT SWITCH—SEE ELECTRICAL SHEETS.*
26. ELECTRICAL OUTLET—SEE ELECTRICAL SHEETS.*
27. ELECTRICAL PANEL—SEE ELECTRICAL SHEETS.*

28. ELECTRICAL SWITCHGEAR—SEE ELECTRICAL SHEETS.*
29. EXHAUST FAN—SEE MECHANICAL SHEETS.*
30. EXPOSED ROOF STRUCTURE.
31. FINISH FLOOR.
32. FINISH FLOOR—SEE CIVIL SHEETS FOR CONTROL DATUM.
33. FINISH GRADE.*
34. FINISH GRADE—SEE CIVIL SHEETS FOR CONTROL DATUM.
35. FRAMING MEMBER(S)—SEE STRUCTURAL SHEETS.
36. GAS PIPING—SEE MECHANICAL SHEETS.*
37. GROUT—SEE STRUCTURAL SHEETS.*
38. GROUT AND REINFORCING STEEL—SEE STRUCTURAL SHEETS.
39. HVAC UNIT—SEE MECHANICAL SHEETS.*
40. HVAC GRILLE—SEE MECHANICAL SHEETS.*
41. JOIST—SEE STRUCTURAL SHEETS.*
42. LADDER—SEE STRUCTURAL SHEETS.*
43. LINTEL—SEE STRUCTURAL SHEETS.*
44. LOUVER—SEE MECHANICAL SHEETS.*
45. MECHANICAL EQUIPMENT CURB—SEE MECHANICAL SHEETS.*
46. MECHANICAL EQUIPMENT—SEE MECHANICAL SHEETS.*
47. OVERFLOW DRAIN—SEE PLUMBING SHEETS.*
48. PAVING—SEE CIVIL SHEETS.*
49. PLATE—SEE STRUCTURAL SHEETS.*
50. PLUMBING CLEANOUT—SEE PLUMBING SHEETS.*
51. PLUMBING DRAIN—SEE PLUMBING SHEETS.
52. PLUMBING FIXTURE—SEE PLUMBING SHEETS.*
53. PLUMBING VENT—SEE PLUMBING SHEETS.*
54. PROCESS COMPONENT(S)—SEE PROCESS SHEETS.*
55. PROCESS EQUIPMENT—SEE PROCESS SHEETS.*
56. PROCESS PIPING—SEE PROCESS SHEETS.*
57. REINFORCING STEEL—SEE STRUCTURAL SHEETS.*
58. SEWER PIPING—SEE PLUMBING SHEETS*
59. SLOPE PAVING AWAY FROM BUILDING—SEE CIVIL SHEETS.*
60. SPRINKLER RISER—SEE FIRE PROTECTION SHEETS.*
61. TOP OF LOUVER.
62. TOP OF MASONRY.
63. TOP OF ROOF.
64. TOP OF ROOF FRAMING.
65. TOP OF WALL FRAMING.
66. TOP OF WINDOW
67. WATER PIPING—SEE PLUMBING SHEETS*

Reference Keynote Office Master: Example for Architectural Sheets

This reference keynote office master is based on a methodology that automatically determines the alphabetic character of the reference keynote suffix by matching it with the first alphabetic character that appears in the first word of the notation. Note, however, that when a term in the notation begins with the letter I or O, the next compliant letter in the word is used. This exception is required because the National CAD Standard does not allow these two letters to be used in the suffix since they can be confused with numerals.

> **FYI:** Most of the reference keynotes that appear in the drawings in this book are taken from the reference keynotes in this office master.

01 10 00	**SUMMARY OF WORK**
01 10 00.T	ITEM REMOVED BY OWNER
01 10 00.T01	ITEM NOT IN CONTRACT
01 10 00.T02	ITEM DISCONNECTED BY OWNER BEFORE RELOCATION BY CONTRACTOR
01 10 00.W	OWNER-FURNISHED, OWNER-INSTALLED ITEM
01 10 00.W01	OWNER-FURNISHED, CONTRACTOR-INSTALLED ITEM
01 23 00	**ALTERNATES**
01 23 00.A01	ALTERNATE NUMBER 1
01 23 00.A02	ALTERNATE NUMBER 2
01 23 00.A03	ALTERNATE NUMBER 3
01 23 00.A04	ALTERNATE NUMBER 4
01 23 00.B01	BID LOT NUMBER 1
01 23 00.B02	BID LOT NUMBER 2
01 23 00.B01	BID LOT NUMBER 3
01 23 00.B02	BID LOT NUMBER 4
01 50 00	**TEMPORARY FACILITIES AND CONTROLS**
01 50 00.C	CONSTRUCTION FENCE
01 50 00.F	FIELD OFFICE
01 50 00.P	PEDESTRIAN GATE
01 50 00.V	VEHICULAR GATE
01 58 00	**PROJECT IDENTIFICATION**
01 58 00.P	PROJECT SIGN
01 70 00	**EXECUTION AND CLOSEOUT REQUIREMENTS**
01 70 00.E	EXISTING TO REMAIN

01 70 00.P	PATCH WALL TO MATCH EXISTING
01 70 00.P01	PATCH CEILING TO MATCH EXISTING
01 70 00.P02	PATCH FLOOR TO MATCH EXISTING
01 70 00.P03	PATCH FINISH TO MATCH EXISTING
01 70 00.P04	PATCH EXISTING ELEMENT(S) TO MATCH EXISTING
01 70 00.R	REMOVE
01 70 00.R01	REMOVE AND RELOCATE
01 70 00.R02	REMOVE AND SALVAGE
01 70 00.R03	RELOCATED ITEM(S)

02 41 00   DEMOLITION

02 41 00.E	EXISTING TO REMAIN
02 41 00.R	REMOVE
02 41 00.R01	REMOVE AND RELOCATE
02 41 00.R02	REMOVE AND SALVAGE
02 41 00.R03	RELOCATED ITEM(S)

03 01 30   MAINTENANCE OF CONCRETE

03 01 30.B	BONDING AGENT
03 01 30.C	CEMENTITIOUS MORTAR
03 01 30.C01	CEMENTITIOUS GROUT
03 01 30.E	EPOXY RESIN ADHESIVE
03 01 30.E01	EPOXY MORTAR

03 20 00   CONCRETE REINFORCING

03 20 00.R	REINFORCING STEEL
03 20 00.S	SMOOTH STEEL DOWEL
03 20 00.S01	SLEEVE
03 20 00.W	WELDED WIRE REINFORCEMENT

03 30 00   CAST-IN-PLACE CONCRETE

03 30 00.B	BONDING AGENT
03 30 00.C	CAST-IN-PLACE CONCRETE
03 30 00.C01	CONSTRUCTION JOINT DEVICE
03 30 00.E	EPOXY BONDING SYSTEM
03 30 00.E01	EPOXY GROUT
03 30 00.E02	EPOXY MORTAR
03 30 00.J	JOINT BACKER
03 30 00.J01	JOINT
03 30 00.N	NONSHRINK GROUT
03 30 00.R	REINFORCING STEEL
03 30 00.S	SAW-CUT JOINT
03 30 00.S01	SCORED JOINT
03 30 00.V	VAPOR RETARDER
03 33 00.W	WATERSTOP

03 35 13   HIGH-TOLERANCE CONCRETE FLOOR FINISHING

03 35 13.A	ACID STAIN AND SEALER

03 35 23   EXPOSED AGGREGATE CONCRETE FINISHING

03 35 23.A	EXPOSED AGGREGATE CONCRETE FINISH

03 41 13	**PRECAST CONCRETE HOLLOW CORE PLANKS**
03 41 13.B	BEARING PAD
03 41 13.C	CONNECTION PLATE
03 41 13.C01	CORE HOLE END PLUG
03 41 13.G	GROUT
03 41 13.H	HANGER TAB
03 41 13.N	NONSHRINK GROUT
03 41 13.P	PRECAST PLANK
03 41 13.R	REINFORCING STEEL
03 41 13.T	TENSIONING STEEL TENDONS
03 45 00	**PRECAST ARCHITECTURAL CONCRETE**
03 45 00.D	DOWEL
03 45 00.P	PRECAST CONCRETE SILL
03 45 00.P01	PRECAST CONCRETE COPING
03 45 00.P02	PRECAST CONCRETE SCUPPER
03 45 00.P03	PRECAST CONCRETE TRASH RECEPTACLE
03 45 00.P04	PRECAST CONCRETE SPLASH BLOCK
03 45 00.P05	PRECAST CONCRETE CAP
03 45 00.P06	PRECAST CONCRETE COLUMN
03 45 00.P07	PRECAST CONCRETE BENCH
03 45 00.P08	PRECAST CONCRETE ACCENT
03 45 00.P09	PRECAST CONCRETE PANEL
03 45 00.P10	PRECAST CONCRETE LINTEL
03 45 00.R	REINFORCING STEEL
03 45 00.W	WELDED WIRE REINFORCEMENT
03 47 13	**TILT-UP CONCRETE**
03 47 13.B	BEARING PAD
03 47 13.C	CONNECTING DEVICE
03 47 13.N	NONSHRINK GROUT
03 47 13.N01	INTEGRAL INSULATION
03 47 13.S	SUPPORTING DEVICE
03 47 13.T	TILT-UP PRECAST CONCRETE UNIT(S)
03 52 16	**LIGHTWEIGHT INSULATING CONCRETE**
03 52 16.L	LIGHTWEIGHT INSULATING CONCRETE
03 52 16.N	INSULATION
04 20 00	**UNIT MASONRY**
04 20 00.B	BUILDING (COMMON) BRICK
04 20 00.B01	BOND BEAM LINTEL
04 20 00.B02	BOND BEAM
04 20 00.C	CONCRETE MASONRY UNIT(S)
04 20 00.C01	COMPRESSIBLE FILLER
04 20 00.C02	CAVITY DRAINAGE MATERIAL
04 20 00.C03	CONCRETE BRICK
04 20 00.C04	CERAMIC GLAZED FACE BRICK
04 20 00.F	FLASHING
04 20 00.F01	FLASHING MASTIC
04 20 00.F02	FLASHING TERMINATION BAR

04 20 00.F03	FLASHING REGLET
04 20 00.F04	FLASHING DRIP EDGE
04 20 00.F05	FACING BRICK
04 20 00.G	GROUT
04 20 00.H	HORIZONTAL JOINT REINFORCEMENT
04 20 00.H01	HORIZONTAL JOINT REINFORCEMENT PREFORMED TEE
04 20 00.H02	HORIZONTAL JOINT REINFORCEMENT PREFORMED CORNER
04 20 00.J	JOINT BACKER
04 20 00.L	LOOSE FILL INSULATION
04 20 00.M	MORTAR
04 20 00.M01	MULTIPLE WYTHE HORIZONTAL JOINT REINFORCEMENT
04 20 00.M02	MASONRY CONTROL JOINT
04 20 00.N	INSULATION INSERT
04 20 00.P	PREFORMED CONTROL JOINT
04 20 00.P01	PRE-FACED MASONRY UNIT(S)
04 20 00.S	SOLID CONCRETE MASONRY UNIT(S)
04 20 00.S01	SINGLE WYTHE HORIZONTAL JOINT REINFORCEMENT
04 20 00.S02	STRAP ANCHOR
04 20 00.S03	SOUND-ABSORBING CONCRETE MASONRY UNIT(S)
04 20 00.T	TWO-PIECE WALL TIE
04 20 00.W	WALL TIE
04 20 00.W01	WEEP

04 23 00	**GLASS UNIT MASONRY**
04 23 00.A	ASPHALT EMULSION
04 23 00.E	EXPANSION STRIP
04 23 00.H	HOLLOW GLASS UNIT(S)
04 23 00.M	MORTAR
04 23 00.P	PANEL REINFORCEMENT
04 23 00.P01	PANEL ANCHOR
04 23 00.P02	PERIMETER CHANNEL
04 23 00.S	SEALANT

05 12 00	**STRUCTURAL STEEL FRAMING**
05 12 00.A	ANCHOR BOLT
05 12 00.B	BASE PLATE
05 12 00.N	NONSHRINK GROUT
05 12 00.S	STEEL BEAM
05 12 00.S01	STEEL COLUMN
05 12 00.S02	STEEL PIPE COLUMN
05 12 00.S03	STEEL ANGLE
05 12 00.S04	STEEL PLATE
05 12 00.S05	STEEL BAR
05 12 00.S06	SHEAR STUD CONNECTOR
05 12 00.S07	SUSPENSION CABLE
05 12 00.S08	SAG ROD
05 12 00.S09	SLIDING BEARING PLATES
05 12 00.S10	STEEL CHANNEL
05 12 00.T	TUBE STEEL COLUMN

05 21 00	**STEEL JOIST FRAMING**
05 21 00.A	ANCHOR BOLT

05 21 00.B	BRIDGING
05 21 00.B01	BEARING PLATE
05 21 00.G	GROUT
05 21 00.J	JOIST CHORD EXTENSION
05 21 00.J01	JOIST SEAT
05 21 00.L	LEDGE ANGLE
05 21 00.P	OPEN-WEB STEEL JOIST
05 21 00.S	SHEAR STUD CONNECTOR

05 31 00   **STEEL DECKING**

05 31 00.A	ACOUSTICAL ROOF DECK
05 31 00.A01	ACOUSTICAL INSULATION
05 31 00.B	BEARING PLATE
05 31 00.B01	BEARING ANGLE
05 31 00.C	CANT STRIP
05 31 00.C01	COMPOSITE FLOOR DECK
05 31 00.C02	CELLULAR FLOOR DECK
05 31 00.C03	COVER PLATE
05 31 00.F	FLOOR DRAIN PAN
05 31 00.F01	FLUTE CLOSURE
05 31 00.M	METAL FORM DECK
05 31 00.M01	METAL CLOSURE STRIP
05 31 00.R	ROOF SUMP PAN
05 31 00.R01	ROOF DECK
05 31 00.S	STEEL DECK
05 31 00.S01	STUD SHEAR CONNECTORS
05 31 00.W	WET CONCRETE STOP

05 40 00   **COLD-FORMED METAL FRAMING**

05 40 00.A	ANCHORAGE DEVICE
05 40 00.B	BRIDGING
05 40 00.B01	BRAKE METAL
05 40 00.C	CLIP
05 40 00.C01	CEILING HANGER
05 40 00.D	DEEP LEG TRACK
05 40 00.F	FURRING CHANNEL
05 40 00.F01	FASTENER
05 40 00.G	GUSSET
05 40 00.G01	GIRT
05 40 00.J	JOIST
05 40 00.P	PURLIN
05 40 00.P01	PLATE
05 40 00.S	STEEL STUD
05 40 00.T	TRACK
05 40 00.T01	TENSION STRAPPING
05 40 00.W	WALL SHEATHING

05 50 00   **METAL FABRICATIONS**

05 50 00.A	ALUMINUM ANGLE
05 50 00.A01	ALUMINUM CHANNEL
05 50 00.A02	ALUMINUM BAR
05 50 00.A03	ALUMINUM TUBE

05 50 00.B	BOLT
05 50 00.B01	BENT STEEL PLATE
05 50 00.B02	BOLLARD
05 50 00.B03	BUMPER POST AND GUARD RAIL
05 50 00.B04	BULB TEE SUBPURLIN
05 50 00.C	CHAIN
05 50 00.C01	CHEMICAL ANCHOR
05 50 00.C02	CANE BOLT
05 50 00.D	DEFORMED ANCHOR
05 50 00.E	EYELET
05 50 00.E01	EXPANSION ANCHOR
05 50 00.E02	EXPANDED METAL SHEET
05 50 00.E03	EXPANDED METAL EDGING
05 50 00.F	FASTENER
05 50 00.G	GATE
05 50 00.G01	GATE HINGE
05 50 00.G02	GUY WIRE
05 50 00.H	HINGED PLATE
05 50 00.H01	HASP
05 50 00.L	LADDER
05 50 00.L01	LADDER SIDE RAIL
05 50 00.L02	LADDER LANDING
05 50 00.L03	LADDER LANDING SUPPORT ANGLE
05 50 00.L04	LADDER RUNG
05 50 00.L05	LADDER WALL BRACKET
05 50 00.L06	LADDER BOTTOM SUPPORT
05 50 00.L07	LADDER SAFETY POST
05 50 00.L08	LADDER SAFETY CAGE
05 50 00.L09	LOCK WASHER
05 50 00.L10	LOCKING NUT
05 50 00.L11	LADDER SECURITY DOOR
05 50 00.M	METAL STRUT FRAMING
05 50 00.M01	METAL STRUT FRAMING CHANNEL
05 50 00.M02	METAL STRUT FRAMING ANGLE
05 50 00.M03	METAL STRUT FRAMING TUBE
05 50 00.M04	METAL STRUT FRAMING CLAMP
05 50 00.M05	METAL STRUT FRAMING THREADED ROD
05 50 00.M06	METAL STRUT FRAMING HANGER
05 50 00.M07	METAL STRUT FRAMING BRACKET
05 50 00.M08	METAL STRUT FRAMING FITTING
05 50 00.M09	METAL STRUT FRAMING COUPLER
05 50 00.M10	METAL STRUT FRAMING NUT
05 50 00.M11	METAL STRUT FRAMING CABLE TRAY
05 50 00.M12	METAL STRUT FRAMING UTILITY SUPPORT
05 50 00.M13	METAL STRUT FRAMING FALL ARREST SYSTEM
05 50 00.N	NOSING
05 50 00.P	PROTECTION PLATE
05 50 00.P01	PLAIN WASHER
05 50 00.P02	PERFORATED METAL SHEET
05 50 00.P03	PERFORATED METAL EDGING
05 50 00.P04	PIANO HINGE
05 50 00.S	STEEL ANGLE

05 50 00.S01	STEEL CHANNEL
05 50 00.S02	STEEL PLATE
05 50 00.S03	STEEL PLATE CLOSURE
05 50 00.S04	STEEL TUBE
05 50 00.S05	STEEL BAR
05 50 00.S06	STEEL PIPE
05 50 00.S07	STUD ANCHOR
05 50 00.S08	SCREW
05 50 00.S09	SHIP LADDER
05 50 00.S10	SAFETY POST
05 50 00.T	THREADED ROD
05 50 00.T01	TOILET PARTITION SUSPENSION MEMBER
05 50 00.T02	TOGGLE BOLT
05 50 00.T03	THREADED INSERT
05 50 00.T04	TAMPER-RESISTANT ANCHOR
05 50 00.T05	TAMPERPROOF ANCHOR
05 50 00.T06	TURNBUCKLE
05 50 00.W	WIRE MESH

05 51 00   **METAL STAIRS**

05 51 00.A	ANCHOR
05 51 00.M	METAL STAIRS
05 51 00.M01	METAL STAIR TREAD
05 51 00.M02	METAL STAIR RISER
05 51 00.M03	METAL STAIR STRINGER
05 51 00.M04	METAL STAIR LANDING
05 51 00.M05	METAL STAIR BALUSTER
05 51 00.M06	METAL STAIR FRAMING
05 51 00.M07	METAL UNIT STAIR TOWER
05 51 00.M08	METAL STAIR RAILING

05 52 13   **PIPE AND TUBE RAILINGS**

05 52 13.A	ALUMINUM RAILING SYSTEM
05 52 13.A01	ANCHOR
05 52 13.C	COVER FLANGE
05 52 13.C01	CHAIN
05 52 13.G	GROUT POCKET
05 52 13.N	NONSHRINK GROUT
05 52 13.R	RAILING
05 52 13.S	STEEL RAILING SYSTEM
05 52 13.S01	STEEL BAR
05 52 13.S02	SLEEVE
05 52 13.S03	STUD ANCHOR
05 52 13.T	TOE BOARD
05 52 13.W	WALL BRACKET
05 52 13.W01	WIRE MESH

05 53 05   **METAL GRATINGS AND FLOOR PLATES**

05 53 05.A	ALUMINUM ANGLE
05 53 05.B	BEARING BAR
05 53 05.C	CROSS BAR
05 53 05.F	FLOOR PLATE

05 53 05.F01	FLANGE BLOCK
05 53 05.G	GRATING
05 53 05.S	SHEET STEEL
05 53 05.S01	STEEL ANGLE
05 53 05.S02	SADDLE CLIP

06 10 00 **ROUGH CARPENTRY**

06 10 00.A	APA-RATED ROOF SHEATHING
06 10 00.A01	APA-RATED WALL SHEATHING
06 10 00.A02	ANCHORAGE DEVICE
06 10 00.A03	ANCHOR BOLT
06 10 00.A04	ADHESIVE
06 10 00.B	BLOCKING
06 10 00.B01	BUILDING PAPER
06 10 00.B02	BRIDGING
06 10 00.D	DIMENSION LUMBER
06 10 00.D01	DIE-STAMPED CONNECTOR
06 10 00.D02	DECK SCREW
06 10 00.F	FURRING
06 10 00.F01	FRAMING ANCHOR
06 10 00.F02	FOAM PLASTIC SHEATHING
06 10 00.F03	FIRE-RETARDANT TREATMENT BLOCKING
06 10 00.F04	FIRE-RETARDANT TREATMENT DIMENSION LUMBER
06 10 00.F05	FIRE-RETARDANT TREATMENT PLYWOOD
06 10 00.G	GYPSUM SHEATHING
06 10 00.J	JOIST HANGER
06 10 00.J01	JOIST FRAMING
06 10 00.L	LAG BOLT
06 10 00.P	PRESSURE-TREATED DIMENSION LUMBER
06 10 00.P01	PRESSURE-TREATED BLOCKING
06 10 00.P02	PRESSURE-TREATED FURRING
06 10 00.P03	PLYWOOD WALL SHEATHING
06 10 00.P04	PLYWOOD
06 10 00.P05	PLYWOOD ROOF SHEATHING
06 10 00.R	RAFTER FRAMING
06 10 00.R01	RIGID INSULATION
06 10 00.S	STUD FRAMING
06 10 00.S01	SHIM
06 10 00.S02	SILL GASKET
06 10 00.S03	SELF-TAPPING SCREW
06 10 00.S04	SHEATHING SCREW

06 15 00 **WOOD DECKING**

| 06 15 00.L | LUMBER DECKING |

06 17 33 **WOOD I-JOISTS**

06 17 33.B	BEARING PLATE
06 17 33.B01	BLOCKING PANEL
06 17 33.J	JOIST BRIDGING
06 17 33.P	PREENGINEERED WOOD I-JOIST
06 17 33.W	WEB STIFFENER

06 17 53	**SHOP-FABRICATED WOOD TRUSSES**
06 17 53.B	BEARING PLATE
06 17 53.P	PLATE-CONNECTED WOOD TRUSS
06 17 53.T	TRUSS BRIDGING
06 18 00	**GLUED-LAMINATED CONSTRUCTION**
06 18 00.A	ANCHOR BOLT
06 18 00.B	BEARING PLATE ANCHOR
06 18 00.G	GLUE-LAMINATED WOOD BEAM
06 18 00.G01	GLUE-LAMINATED WOOD PURLIN
06 18 00.S	STEEL BRACKET
06 20 00	**FINISH CARPENTRY**
06 20 00.A	ALUMINUM DRIP EDGE
06 20 00.E	EXTERIOR HARDBOARD
06 20 00.H	HARDWOOD LUMBER
06 20 00.H01	HARDWOOD PLYWOOD
06 20 00.H02	HARDBOARD
06 20 00.L	LOW-PRESSURE LAMINATE
06 20 00.P	PLASTIC LAMINATE
06 20 00.P01	PARTICLEBOARD
06 20 00.P02	PLASTIC EDGE TRIM
06 20 00.P03	PREFINISHED PANELING
06 20 00.P04	PEGBOARD
06 20 00.R	RAILING
06 20 00.R01	RUNNING TRIM
06 20 00.S	SOFTWOOD LUMBER
06 20 00.S01	SOFTWOOD PLYWOOD
06 20 00.S02	SOLID LAMINATE
06 20 00.S03	SHIM
06 20 00.S04	STANDING TRIM
06 20 00.W	WOOD PANEL SIDING
06 41 00	**ARCHITECTURAL WOOD CASEWORK**
06 41 00.A	APRON
06 41 00.A01	ADJUSTABLE SHELVES
06 41 00.A02	ADJUSTABLE SHELF
06 41 00.A03	ANCHORAGE DEVICE
06 41 00.B	BACKSPLASH
06 41 00.B01	BASE CABINET
06 41 00.B02	BLOCKING
06 41 00.B03	BULLET-RESISTANT PANEL
06 41 00.B04	BUSHING
06 41 00.C	COUNTERTOP
06 41 00.C01	CUSTOM CABINETS
06 41 00.C02	CULTURED MARBLE SURFACING
06 41 00.C03	CATCH
06 41 00.C04	CABINET LOCK
06 41 00.C05	COUNTERTOP SUPPORT BRACKET
06 41 00.C06	COUNTERTOP SUPPORT LEG
06 41 00.C07	COMPUTER KEYBOARD DRAWER

06 41 00.C08	CABLE TRAY
06 41 00.C09	COUNTERTOP SUPPORT ANGLE
06 41 00.D	DRAWER FRONT
06 41 00.D01	DOOR FRONT
06 41 00.D02	DRAWER SLIDE
06 41 00.F	FINISHED END
06 41 00.F01	FILLER PANEL
06 41 00.G	GROMMET
06 41 00.G01	GLAZING FRAMING SYSTEM
06 41 00.H	HARDWOOD LUMBER
06 41 00.H01	HARDWOOD CABINET FRAME
06 41 00.H02	HARDWOOD STILE
06 41 00.H03	HARDWOOD RAIL
06 41 00.H04	HARDBOARD
06 41 00.H05	HARDWOOD PLYWOOD
06 41 00.H06	HINGE
06 41 00.H07	HOOK
06 41 00.L	LOW-PRESSURE LAMINATE
06 41 00.L01	LEDGER
06 41 00.L02	LABEL HOLDER
06 41 00.M	METAL SURFACE COUNTERTOP
06 41 00.P	PLASTIC LAMINATE
06 41 00.P01	PARTICLEBOARD
06 41 00.P02	PULL
06 41 00.P03	PLASTIC EDGE TRIM
06 41 00.P04	PENCIL DRAWER
06 41 00.P05	PIVOT
06 41 00.S	SHELF STANDARD
06 41 00.S01	SHELF BRACKET
06 41 00.S02	SIDE SPLASH
06 41 00.S03	SOFTWOOD LUMBER
06 41 00.S04	SOFTWOOD PLYWOOD
06 41 00.S05	SOFTWOOD RAIL
06 41 00.S06	SOFTWOOD CABINET FRAME
06 41 00.S07	SOFTWOOD STILE
06 41 00.S08	SLIDING-DOOR TRACK ASSEMBLY
06 41 00.S09	SHIM
06 41 00.S10	SHELF
06 41 00.W	WALL CABINET
06 41 00.W	WOOD STORAGE SHELVING PLYWOOD
06 82 00	**GLASS-FIBER-REINFORCED PLASTIC**
06 82 00.F	FIBERGLASS-REINFORCED PLASTIC (FRP) PANEL
06 82 00.M	MOLDING
07 11 13	**BITUMINOUS DAMPPROOFING**
07 11 13.B	BITUMINOUS DAMPPROOFING
07 11 13.D	DRAINAGE PANEL
07 11 13.P	PROTECTION BOARD
07 13 00	**SHEET WATERPROOFING**
07 13 00.C	COUNTERFLASHING
07 13 00.C01	CANT STRIP

07 13 00.D	DRAINAGE PANEL
07 13 00.F	FLEXIBLE FLASHING
07 13 00.P	PROTECTION BOARD
07 13 00.S	SHEET WATERPROOFING
07 13 00.T	TERMINATION BAR

07 21 00　　　**THERMAL INSULATION**

07 21 00.A	AIRWAYS
07 21 00.B	BLANKET INSULATION
07 21 00.B01	BOARD INSULATION
07 21 00.E	EXTRUDED POLYSTYRENE BOARD INSULATION
07 21 00.F	FOIL-FACED INSULATION
07 21 00.F01	FURRED INSULATION
07 21 00.F02	FOAM INSULATION
07 21 00.M	MOLDED POLYSTYRENE BOARD INSULATION
07 21 00.N	INSULATION FASTENER
07 21 00.N01	INSULATION SUPPORT
07 21 00.N02	INSULATION COVER
07 21 00.P02	POLYISOCYANURATE BOARD INSULATION
07 21 00.S	SHEET VAPOR RETARDER
07 21 00.W	WIRE MESH

07 21 19　　　**FOAMED-IN-PLACE INSULATION**

07 21 19.A	ACOUSTICAL INSULATION
07 21 19.A01	ACOUSTICAL INSULATION FASTENER

07 24 00　　　**EXTERIOR INSULATION AND FINISH SYSTEMS**

07 24 00.A	AESTHETIC JOINT
07 24 00.C	CEMENTITIOUS COATING
07 24 00.D	DRIP SCREED
07 24 00.E	EXTERIOR INSULATION AND FINISH SYSTEM
07 24 00.E01	EXPANSION JOINT
07 24 00.F	FINISH COAT
07 24 00.N	INSULATION
07 24 00.R	REINFORCING SYSTEM
07 24 00.S	SYNTHETIC COATING

07 31 13　　　**ASPHALT SHINGLES**

07 31 13.A	ASPHALT SHINGLES
07 31 13.E	EAVE PROTECTION MEMBRANE
07 31 13.F	FLEXIBLE FLASHING
07 31 13.L	LAP CEMENT
07 31 13.M	MINERAL-FACED ROLL ROOFING
07 31 13.M01	METAL FLASHING
07 31 13.P	PLASTIC CEMENT
07 31 13.R	RIDGE VENT
07 31 13.S	SMOOTH-SURFACE ROLL ROOFING
07 31 13.S01	SHEET METAL
07 31 13.U	UNDERLAYMENT

07 32 00　　　**ROOF TILES**

07 32 00.B	BATTEN
07 32 00.C	CONCRETE ROOF TILE

07 32 00.E	ELASTOMERIC MEMBRANE UNDERLAYMENT
07 32 00.E01	ELASTOMERIC MEMBRANE FLASHING
07 32 00.F	FASTENER
07 32 00.H	HIP CAP
07 32 00.M	METAL FLASHING
07 32 00.M01	MORTAR
07 32 00.R	RIDGE CAP
07 32 00.R01	RAKE EDGE
07 32 00.R02	ROOFING MASTIC
07 32 00.S	SMOOTH-SURFACED ROLL ROOFING
07 32 00.S01	SNOW GUARD
07 32 00.T	TERMINATION CAP
07 32 00.U	UNDERLAYMENT
07 32 00.W	WIND LOCK
07 41 13	**METAL ROOF PANELS**
07 41 13.A	ANCHOR
07 41 13.B	BATTEN CAP
07 41 13.B01	BACK-UP PLATE
07 41 13.B02	BEARING PLATE
07 41 13.C	COUNTERFLASHING
07 41 13.C01	COPING
07 41 13.C02	CLEAT
07 41 13.C03	CHANNEL
07 41 13.C04	CLOSURE
07 41 13.C05	CLIP
07 41 13.C06	CRICKET
07 41 13.D	DRIP EDGE
07 41 13.E	EAVE TRIM
07 41 13.E01	EXPANSION JOINT
07 41 13.F	FASTENER
07 41 13.F01	FELTS
07 41 13.F02	FASCIA
07 41 13.F03	OFFSET CLEAT
07 41 13.J	JOINT SEALANT
07 41 13.L	LIGHT PANEL
07 41 13.M	METAL ROOF PANEL(S)
07 41 13.M01	METAL FLASHING
07 41 13.M02	MOISTURE BARRIER
07 41 13.M03	METAL ROOF FRAMING SYSTEM
07 41 13.M04	METAL ROOF FRAMING SYSTEM PURLIN
07 41 13.M05	METAL ROOF FRAMING SYSTEM COLUMN
07 41 13.M06	METAL ROOF FRAMING SYSTEM BASE CHANNEL
07 41 13.M07	METAL ROOF FRAMING SYSTEM BEARING PLATE
07 41 13.M08	METAL ROOF FRAMING SYSTEM OUTRIGGER
07 41 13.M09	METAL ROOF FRAMING SYSTEM CHANNEL
07 41 13.M10	METAL ROOF FRAMING SYSTEM EAVE MEMBER
07 41 13.M11	METAL ROOF FRAMING SYSTEM SOFFIT FRAMING
07 41 13.M12	METAL ROOF FRAMING SYSTEM FASCIA FRAMING
07 41 13.P	PIPE FLASHING
07 41 13.P01	PERFORATED SOFFIT PANEL
07 41 13.R	ROOF PANEL CLIP

07 41 13.R01	RIDGE CAP
07 41 13.R02	ROOF VENT
07 41 13.R03	ROOF CURB
07 41 13.R04	ROOF PANEL END CAP FLASHING
07 41 13.S	SOFFIT PANEL
07 41 13.S01	SOFFIT CLOSURE
07 41 13.S02	SHEET METAL
07 41 13.S03	SNOW GUARD
07 41 13.S04	SOFFIT VENT
07 41 13.S05	SKYLIGHT
07 41 13.S06	SKYLIGHT CURB
07 41 13.S07	SKYLIGHT CURB BASE FLANGE
07 41 13.S08	SKYLIGHT CURB BASE FLANGE CAP STRIP
07 41 13.S09	SKYLIGHT CURB BACK-UP CHANNEL
07 41 13.S10	SKYLIGHT CURB SUBFRAME
07 41 13.T	TRIM
07 41 13.T01	TAPE SEALER
07 41 13.V	VALLEY TRIM
07 41 13.E	WATER DIVERTER

07 42 13   **METAL WALL PANELS**

07 42 13.A	ANCHOR
07 42 13.B	BACK-UP PLATE
07 42 13.C	COUNTERFLASHING
07 42 13.C01	COPING
07 42 13.C02	CLEAT
07 42 13.C03	CHANNEL
07 42 13.C04	CLOSURE
07 42 13.C05	CLIP
07 42 13.E	EXTERNAL CORNER
07 42 13.E01	EXPANSION JOINT
07 42 13.F	FASTENER
07 42 13.F01	FELTS
07 42 13.J	JOINT SEALANT
07 42 13.L	LINER PANEL
07 42 13.M	METAL WALL PANEL(S)
07 42 13.M01	METAL FLASHING
07 42 13.N	INTERNAL CORNER
07 42 13.S	SHEET METAL
07 42 13.S01	SILL SUPPORT
07 42 13.T	TRIM
07 42 13.T01	TAPE SEALER

07 46 33   **PLASTIC SIDING**

07 46 33.V	VINYL SIDING

07 51 00   **BUILT-UP BITUMINOUS ROOFING**

07 51 00.A	AGGREGATE SURFACING
07 51 00.B	BUILT-UP BITUMINOUS ROOFING
07 51 00.B01	BASE SHEET(S)
07 51 00.C	CRICKET
07 51 00.C01	CANT STRIP

07 51 00.C02	COVER BOARD
07 51 00.F	FLEXIBLE FLASHING
07 51 00.F01	FASTENER
07 51 00.L	LEAD FLASHING
07 51 00.P	PIPE BOOT
07 51 00.P01	PAVERS
07 51 00.P02	PREFABRICATED ROOFING EXPANSION JOINT FLASHING
07 51 00.R	ROOF INSULATION
07 51 00.R01	ROOFING FELTS
07 51 00.R02	ROOFING EXPANSION JOINT FLASHING
07 51 00.R03	ROOF CEMENT
07 51 00.R04	ROOF INSULATION VENTS
07 51 00.S	SEALANT
07 51 00.S01	SHEET METAL SEALANT POCKET
07 51 00.T	TAPERED BOARD INSULATION
07 51 00.T01	TERMINATION BAR
07 51 00.W	WALKWAY PADS

07 52 00   **MODIFIED BITUMINOUS MEMBRANE ROOFING**

07 52 00.B	BASE SHEET
07 52 00.B01	BASE FLASHING PLY
07 52 00.C	COVER BOARD
07 52 00.C01	CRICKET
07 52 00.C02	CANT STRIP
07 52 00.C03	CLAMPING RING
07 52 00.D	DRIP EDGE
07 52 00.D01	DECK SHEATHING
07 52 00.F	FASCIA
07 52 00.F01	FLEXIBLE FLASHING MATERIAL
07 52 00.F02	FIRE-RESISTANT VAPOR RETARDER
07 52 00.F03	FOAM INSULATION
07 52 00.F04	FASTENER
07 52 00.G	GRAVEL STOP
07 52 00.L	LEAD FLASHING
07 52 00.M	MODIFIED BITUMINOUS ROOFING
07 52 00.M01	MEMBRANE
07 52 00.N	INSULATION FASTENER
07 52 00.P	PIPE BOOT
07 52 00.P01	PAVERS
07 52 00.P02	PREFABRICATED ROOFING EXPANSION JOINT FLASHING
07 52 00.P03	PREBASE SHEET
07 52 00.R	ROOF INSULATION
07 52 00.R01	ROOFING EXPANSION JOINT FLASHING
07 52 00.R02	ROOF PAVER TERMINATION
07 52 00.R03	ROOF CEMENT
07 52 00.S	SEPARATION SHEET
07 52 00.S01	SHEATHING ADHESIVE
07 52 00.S02	SEALANT
07 52 00.S03	SHEET METAL SEALANT POCKET
07 52 00.T	TAPERED BOARD INSULATION
07 52 00.T01	TERMINATION BAR
07 52 00.V	VAPOR RETARDER FELT

07 52 00.W	WALKWAY PADS
07 52 00.W01	WATER-PERVIOUS FABRIC

07 53 00   **ELASTOMERIC MEMBRANE ROOFING**

07 53 00.B	BALLAST
07 53 00.B01	BONDING ADHESIVE
07 53 00.C	COVER BOARD
07 53 00.C01	CRICKET
07 53 00.C02	CANT STRIP
07 53 00.C03	CLAMPING RING
07 53 00.C04	CUSHION SHEET
07 53 00.D	DRIP EDGE
07 53 00.D01	DECK SHEATHING
07 53 00.D02	DRY SHEATHING PAPER
07 53 00.E	ELASTOMERIC MEMBRANE ROOFING
07 53 00.E01	ELASTOMERIC MEMBRANE ROOFING SEALANT
07 53 00.F	FASCIA
07 53 00.F01	FASTENER
07 53 00.F02	FLEXIBLE FLASHING
07 53 00.F03	FOAM INSULATION
07 53 00.G	GRAVEL STOP
07 53 00.H	HOT AIR WELD
07 53 00.J	JOINT CUSHION
07 53 00.M	MEMBRANE ADHESIVE
07 53 00.M01	MASTIC
07 53 00.N	INSULATION ADHESIVE
07 53 00.P	PIPE BOOT
07 53 00.P01	PAVERS
07 53 00.P02	PREFABRICATED ROOFING EXPANSION JOINT FLASHING
07 53 00.R	ROOF INSULATION
07 53 00.R01	ROOF PAVER TERMINATION
07 53 00.R02	ROOFING EXPANSION JOINT FLASHING
07 53 00.S	SEAM CAULK
07 53 00.S01	SHEATHING ADHESIVE
07 53 00.S02	SEALANT
07 53 00.T	TAPERED BOARD INSULATION
07 53 00.T01	TERMINATION BAR
07 53 00.V	VAPOR RETARDER
07 53 00.W	WALKWAY PADS

07 62 00   **SHEET METAL FLASHING AND TRIM**

07 62 00.A	ANCHOR
07 62 00.A01	ANCHOR PLATE
07 62 00.C	COPING
07 62 00.C01	CLEAT
07 62 00.D	DOWNSPOUT
07 62 00.D01	DOWNSPOUT SUPPORT
07 62 00.D02	DRIP SCREED
07 62 00.D03	DRIVE PIN
07 62 00.F	FASCIA
07 62 00.F01	FLEXIBLE FLASHING RETAINER
07 62 00.F02	FLASHING

07 62 00.F03	FASTENER
07 62 00.G	GUTTER
07 62 00.G01	GUTTER SUPPORT
07 62 00.G02	GRAVELSTOP
07 62 00.L	LEADERHEAD
07 62 00.M	MASONRY TYPE REGLET FLASHING
07 62 00.P	PREFABRICATED ROOFING EXPANSION JOINT FLASHING
07 62 00.R	RIP RAP
07 62 00.S	SHEET METAL
07 62 00.S01	SURFACE-MOUNTED REGLET FLASHING
07 62 00.S02	STUCCO-TYPE REGLET FLASHING
07 62 00.S03	SPLASH PAD
07 62 00.S04	SPLICE PLATE
07 62 00.S05	SPIKE AND FERRULE
07 62 00.T	THROUGH-WALL SCUPPER
07 62 00.V	OVERFLOW SCUPPERS
07 62 00.V01	OVERFLOW CUT0UT

07 71 00   **ROOF SPECIALTIES**

07 71 00.C	CURB
07 71 00.C01	CURB FLANGE
07 71 00.C02	COUNTERFLASHING
07 71 00.F	FASTENER
07 71 00.G	GASKET SEAL
07 71 00.N	NAILER
07 71 00.R	ROOF VENT
07 71 00.S	ISOLATION BASE
07 71 00.T	THIMBLE
07 71 00.T01	THIMBLE WEATHERSHIELD
07 71 00.T02	THIMBLE FLANGE
07 71 00.W	WATER DIVERTER

07 71 23   **MANUFACTURED GUTTERS AND DOWNSPOUTS**

07 71 23.D	DOWNSPOUT
07 71 23.D01	DOWNSPOUT SUPPORT
07 71 23.G	GUTTER
07 71 23.G01	GUTTER SUPPORT
07 71 23.S	SPLASH PAD

07 72 34   **ROOF HATCHES AND SMOKE VENTS**

07 72 34.A	ANCHORAGE DEVICE
07 72 34.F	FASTENER
07 72 34.H	HATCH LADDER EXTENSION
07 72 34.N	INTEGRAL CAP FLASHING
07 72 34.R	ROOF HATCH
07 72 34.R01	ROOF HATCH COVER
07 72 34.R02	ROOF HATCH CURB
07 72 34.R	ROOF HATCH CURB FLANGE

07 81 00   **APPLIED FIREPROOFING**

07 81 00.M	METAL LATH
07 81 00.S	SPRAYED-ON FIREPROOFING

07 84 00	**FIRESTOPPING**
07 84 00.E	ELASTOMERIC FIRESTOPPING
07 84 00.F	FIRESTOPPING
07 84 00.F01	FIBER PACKING MATERIAL
07 84 00.F02	FOAM FIRESTOPPING
07 84 00.F03	FIBERED COMPOUND FIRESTOPPING
07 84 00.F04	FIRESTOP DEVICE
07 84 00.F05	FIRESTOP PILLOW
07 84 00.F06	FIRESTOP MASTIC
07 84 00.N	INTUMESCENT PUTTY

07 92 00	**JOINT SEALANTS**
07 92 00.S	SEALANT TYPE ES-1
07 92 00.S01	SEALANT TYPE ES-2
07 92 00.S02	SEALANT TYPE ES-3
07 92 00.S03	SEALANT TYPE AE-1
07 92 00.S04	SEALANT TYPE SIL-1
07 92 00.S05	SEALANT TYPE SIL-2
07 92 00.S06	SEALANT TYPE AS-1
07 92 00.S07	SEALANT TYPE EP-1
07 92 00.S08	SEALANT TYPE EP-2
07 92 00.J	JOINT BACKING
07 92 00.J01	JOINT BACKING TYPE JB-1
07 92 00.J02	JOINT BACKING TYPE JB-2

07 95 13	**EXPANSION JOINT COVER ASSEMBLIES**
07 95 13.A	ANCHOR
07 95 13.E	EXPANSION JOINT COVER
07 95 13.F	FIRE BARRIER

08 11 13	**HOLLOW METAL DOORS AND FRAMES**
08 11 13.F	FRAME ANCHOR
08 11 13.F01	FASTENER
08 11 13.G	GLAZING STOP
08 11 13.H	HOLLOW METAL DOOR
08 11 13.H01	HOLLOW METAL FRAME
08 11 13.K	KNOCKDOWN FIELD-ASSEMBLED FRAME
08 11 13.L	LOUVER
08 11 13.M	MORTAR GROUT GUARD
08 11 13.N	INSULATING METAL PANEL
08 11 13.R	REMOVABLE MULLION
08 11 13.S	SHIM

08 11 16	**ALUMINUM DOORS AND FRAMES**
08 11 16.A	ALUMINUM DOOR FRAME
08 11 16.A01	ANCHOR
08 11 16.F	FLUSH ALUMINUM DOOR
08 11 16.F01	FASTENER
08 11 16.G	GLAZING GASKET
08 11 16.P	PUSH/PULL SET
08 11 16.R	REMOVABLE MULLION
08 11 16.S	SILL SWEEP

08 11 16.S01	SHIM
08 11 16.T	THRESHOLD
08 11 16.T01	TUBULAR ALUMINUM DOOR
08 11 16.W	WEATHERSTRIPPING

08 12 13	**HOLLOW METAL FRAMES**
08 12 13.C	CASING
08 12 13.F	FIXED-THROAT BORROWED-LIGHT FRAME
08 12 13.F01	FIXED-THROAT SIDELIGHT FRAME
08 12 13.N	INSULATING METAL PANEL
08 12 13.S	SLIP-ON METAL FRAME

08 14 16	**FLUSH WOOD DOORS**
08 14 16.F	FLUSH WOOD DOOR

08 14 33	**STILE AND RAIL WOOD DOORS**
08 14 33.F	FIRE-RATED WOOD FRAME
08 14 33.M	MOLDING
08 14 33.S	STILE AND RAIL WOOD DOOR
08 14 33.W	WOOD FRAME

08 31 00	**ACCESS DOORS AND PANELS**
08 31 00.F	FIRE-RATED ACCESS DOOR AND FRAME UNIT
08 31 00.F01	FIRE-RATED HATCH AND FRAME UNIT
08 31 00.N	NONFIRE-RATED ACCESS DOOR AND FRAME UNIT
08 31 00.N01	NONFIRE RATED HATCH AND FRAME UNIT

08 32 00	**SLIDING GLASS DOORS**
08 32 00.S	SLIDING DOOR

08 33 13	**COILING COUNTER DOORS**
08 33 13.A	ANCHOR
08 33 13.C	COILING COUNTER DOOR
08 33 13.C01	COILING COUNTER DOOR BOTTOM
08 33 13.F	FIRE-RATED COILING COUNTER DOOR
08 33 13.G	GUIDES
08 33 13.H	HOOD ENCLOSURE
08 33 13.M01	MANUAL HAND CHAIN

08 33 23	**OVERHEAD COILING DOORS**
08 33 23.A	ANCHOR
08 33 23.B	BAFFLE
08 33 23.C	CURTAIN BOTTOM
08 33 23.C01	CONTROL STATION
08 33 23.G	GUIDES
08 33 23.H	HOOD ENCLOSURE
08 33 23.M	MANUAL HAND CHAIN
08 33 23.M01	MOTOR ENCLOSURE
08 33 23.M02	MOTOR COVER
08 33 23.V	OVERHEAD COILING DOOR
08 33 23.V01	VISION PANELS
08 33 23.W	WEATHERSTRIPPING

08 33 26	**OVERHEAD COILING GRILLES**
08 33 26.A	ANCHOR
08 33 26.B	BOTTOM BAR
08 33 26.C	CURTAIN
08 33 26.C01	CONTROL STATION
08 33 26.F	FASTENER
08 33 26.G	GUIDES
08 33 26.H	HOOD ENCLOSURE
08 33 26.M	MANUAL HAND CHAIN
08 33 26.M01	MOTOR ENCLOSURE
08 33 26.M02	MOTOR COVER
08 33 26.S	SAFETY EDGE
08 33 26.S01	STEEL TUBE JAMB
08 33 26.V	OVERHEAD COILING GRILLE
08 34 63	**DETENTION DOORS AND FRAMES**
08 34 63 .D	DETENTION ENCLOSURE
08 34 63 .D01	DETENTION GRID SYSTEM
08 34 63 .D02	DETENTION GRID-TYPE DOOR
08 34 63 .D03	DETENTION GRID-TYPE DOOR FRAME
08 34 63 .D04	DETENTION GRID SYSTEM FRAME
08 34 63 .D05	DETENTION GRID SYSTEM ADJUSTMENT CHANNEL
08 34 63 .D06	DETENTION GRATING SYSTEM
08 34 63 .D07	DETENTION GRATING-TYPE DOOR
08 34 63 .D08	DETENTION GRATING-TYPE DOOR FRAME
08 34 63 .D09	DETENTION GRATING SYSTEM FRAME
08 34 63 .D10	DETENTION GRATING SYSTEM ADJUSTMENT CHANNEL
08 34 63 .D11	DETENTION ENCLOSURE SYSTEM EMBED PLATE
08 34 63 .D12	DETENTION ENCLOSURE SYSTEM EMBED CHANNEL
08 34 63 .D13	DETENTION ENCLOSURE SYSTEM LOCK
08 36 13	**SECTIONAL DOORS**
08 36 13.T	TRACK
08 36 13.V	OVERHEAD DOOR
08 43 13	**ALUMINUM-FRAMED STOREFRONTS**
08 43 13.A	ALUMINUM-FRAMED STOREFRONT
08 43 13.A01	ALUMINUM FRAMING MEMBER
08 43 13.A02	ALUMINUM DOOR FRAME
08 43 13.A03	ALUMINUM WINDOW FRAME
08 43 13.A04	ANCHOR
08 43 13.B	BREAK METAL
08 43 13.C	CROSS RAIL
08 43 13.D	DOOR PULL
08 43 13.D01	DOOR PUSH BAR
08 43 13.D02	DOOR STILE
08 43 13.D03	DOOR RAIL
08 43 13.E	EXPOSED FLASHING
08 43 13.E01	EXIT DEVICE
08 43 13.E02	EXTRUDED SILL FLASHING
08 43 13.F	FLUSH ALUMINUM DOOR
08 43 13.F01	FLUSH FRP DOOR

08 43 13.F02	FASTENER
08 43 13.G	GLAZED ALUMINUM DOOR
08 43 13.G01	GLAZED FRP DOOR
08 43 13.G02	GLAZING GASKET
08 43 13.L	LOUVER
08 43 13.M	MULLION
08 43 13.N	INTERMEDIATE HORIZONTAL
08 43 13.N01	INFILL PANEL
08 43 13.N02	INTERMEDIATE RAIL
08 43 13.P	PUSH/PULL SET
08 43 13.S	SHIM
08 43 13.S01	SWEEP
08 43 13.S02	SILL FLASHING END DAM
08 43 13.T	THRESHOLD
08 43 13.W	WEATHERSTRIPPING

08 44 13   **GLAZED ALUMINUM CURTAIN WALLS**

08 44 13.A	ALUMINUM-FRAMED CURTAIN WALL
08 44 13.A01	ALUMINUM FRAMING MEMBERS
08 44 13.B	BEAM COVERS
08 44 13.B01	BREAK METAL
08 44 13.C	COLUMN COVERS
08 44 13.C01	CONCEALED FLASHING
08 44 13.E	EXPOSED FLASHING
08 44 13.E01	EXPANSION JOINT SEAL
08 44 13.F	FASTENER
08 44 13.G	GLAZING GASKETS
08 44 13.L	LOUVERS
08 44 13.L01	LOUVER SCREENING
08 44 13.N	INFILL PANELS
08 44 13.P01	PERIMETER SEALANT
08 44 13.P02	OPERABLE SASH
08 44 13.S01	STRUCTURAL SUPPORTING ANCHORS
08 44 13.S02	STRUCTURAL GLAZING ADHESIVE
08 44 13.S03	SHIM

08 45 00   **TRANSLUCENT WALL AND ROOF ASSEMBLIES**

08 45 00.B	BATTEN
08 45 00.C	CLAMP CHANNEL
08 45 00.C01	CURB CAP EXTRUSION
08 45 00.F	FLASHING
08 45 00.F01	FASTENER
08 45 00.M	MULLION SECTION
08 45 00.R	RIDGE CAP
08 45 00.S	SUB-SILL
08 45 00.S01	SHEET ALUMINUM
08 45 00.T	TRANSLUCENT PANEL
08 45 00.T01	TRANSLUCENT WALL ASSEMBLY
08 45 00.T02	TRANSLUCENT ROOF ASSEMBLY

08 51 13   **ALUMINUM WINDOWS**

08 51 13.A	ALUMINUM WINDOW
08 51 13.A01	ALUMINUM STORM WINDOW

08 51 13.A02	ALUMINUM STOP
08 51 13.C	COMPOSITE METAL PANEL
08 51 13.D	DOUBLE HUNG-TYPE ALUMINUM WINDOW
08 51 13.F	FIXED ALUMINUM WINDOW
08 51 13.F01	FASTENER
08 51 13.H	HORIZONTAL SLIDING-TYPE ALUMINUM WINDOW
08 51 13.H01	HEAD RECEPTOR
08 51 13.J	JAMB RECEPTOR
08 51 13.M	MULLION
08 51 13.M01	MUNTIN
08 51 13.N	INSECT SCREEN
08 51 13.S	SINGLE HUNG-TYPE ALUMINUM WINDOW
08 51 13.S01	SILL
08 51 13.S02	SHIM
08 51 13.S03	SUB-SILL
08 51 13.S04	SILL FLASHING END DAM
08 51 13.U	OUTSWINGING ALUMINUM CASEMENT WINDOW
08 51 13.U01	OUTSWINGING ALUMINUM AWNING WINDOW

08 52 00 **WOOD WINDOWS**

08 52 00.D	DOUBLE HUNG-TYPE WOOD WINDOW
08 52 00.F	FIXED WOOD WINDOW
08 52 00.H	HORIZONTAL SLIDING-TYPE WOOD WINDOW
08 52 00.S	SINGLE HUNG-TYPE WOOD WINDOW
08 52 00.S01	SHIM
08 52 00.U	OUTSWINGING WOOD CASEMENT WINDOW
08 52 00.U01	OUTSWINGING WOOD AWNING WINDOW
08 52 00.W	WOOD WINDOW

08 62 00 **UNIT SKYLIGHTS**

08 62 00.A	ANCHORAGE DEVICE
08 62 00.C	COUNTERFLASHING
08 62 00.S	SEALANT
08 62 00.U	UNIT SKYLIGHT
08 62 00.U01	UNIT SKYLIGHT FRAME
08 62 00.U02	UNIT SKYLIGHT CURB

08 63 00 **METAL-FRAMED SKYLIGHTS**

08 63 00.A	ANCHORAGE DEVICE
08 63 00.F	FASTENER
08 63 00.F01	FLASHING
08 63 00.M	METAL-FRAMED SKYLIGHT
08 63 00.N	INTERNAL REINFORCEMENT
08 63 00.P	PERIMETER SEALANT
08 63 00.S	SKYLIGHT FRAME
08 63 00.S01	SKYLIGHT GLAZING

08 71 00 **DOOR HARDWARE**

08 71 00.A	ANCHOR
08 71 00.C	CYLINDRICAL LOCK
08 71 00.C01	CANE BOLT
08 71 00.D	DRIP WEATHERSTRIP
08 71 00.G	GATE HASP

08 71 00.G01	GATE LATCH
08 71 00.H	HINGE
08 71 00.H01	HIGH-SECURITY KEY BOX
08 71 00.K	KEY CABINET
08 71 00.L	LATCH SET
08 71 00.M	MORTISE LOCK
08 71 00.P	PUSH/PULL
08 71 00.R	REMOVABLE MULLION
08 71 00.S	SWEEP
08 71 00.T	THRESHOLD
08 71 00.W	WEATHERSTRIPPING

08 80 00   **GLAZING**

08 80 00.A	ACOUSTIC INSULATING GLASS
08 80 00.A01	ACRYLIC SHEET
08 80 00.B	BENT GLASS
08 80 00.C	CLEAR FLOAT GLASS
08 80 00.C01	CERAMIC GLASS
08 80 00.F	FIBER-REINFORCED POLYESTER SHEET
08 80 00.G	GLAZING
08 80 00.G01	GLAZING CUTOUT
08 80 00.H	HEAT-ABSORBING GLASS
08 80 00.L	LOW-E GLASS
08 80 00.L01	LEAD GLASS
08 80 00.N	INSULATING GLASS UNIT
08 80 00.N01	ONE-WAY REFLECTIVE MIRROR GLASS
08 80 00.P	PATTERNED GLASS
08 80 00.P01	POLYCARBONATE SHEET
08 80 00.P02	PLASTIC FILM
08 80 00.P03	PASS-THROUGH
08 80 00.R	REFLECTIVE GLASS
08 80 00.S	SAFETY GLASS
08 80 00.S01	SPANDREL GLASS
08 80 00.S02	SEALANT
08 80 00.T	TINTED GLASS
08 80 00.T01	TALK-THROUGH
08 80 00.W	WIRED GLASS

08 83 00   **MIRRORS**

08 83 00.M	MIRROR GLASS
08 83 00.M01	MIRROR GLASS TYPE MR-1
08 83 00.M02	MIRROR GLASS TYPE MR-2
08 83 00.M03	MIRROR ADHESIVE
08 83 00.M04	MIRROR ATTACHMENT ACCESSORY

08 91 00   **LOUVERS**

08 91 00.A	ACOUSTICAL LOUVER
08 91 00.B	BIRD SCREEN
08 91 00.B01	BACK-DRAFT DAMPER
08 91 00.B02	BLANK-OFF PANEL
08 91 00.C	CHANNEL SUBFRAME
08 91 00.F	FRAME

08 91 00.F01	FLASHING
08 91 00.F02	FILTER RACK
08 91 00.F03	FILTER
08 91 00.H	HINGED FRAME
08 91 00.H01	HINGED LOUVER
08 91 00.H02	HINGED SIGHTPROOF LOUVER
08 91 00.M	MOUNTING ANGLE
08 91 00.N	INSECT SCREEN
08 91 00.P	OPERABLE LOUVER
08 91 00.S	STATIONARY LOUVER
08 91 00.S01	STATIONARY SIGHTPROOF LOUVER
08 91 00.S02	SILL
08 91 00.T	TRIM
08 91 00.W	WALL LOUVER

09 21 16	**GYPSUM BOARD ASSEMBLIES**
09 21 16.A	ACOUSTIC FURRING
09 21 16.A01	ACOUSTIC INSULATION
09 21 16.A02	ANCHORAGE DEVICE
09 21 16.C	CEILING HANGER
09 21 16.C01	CONTROL JOINT
09 21 16.C02	CORNER BEAD
09 21 16.C03	CEMENTITIOUS BACKER BOARD
09 21 16.D	DEEP LEG TRACK
09 21 16.E	EXTERIOR GYPSUM SOFFIT BOARD
09 21 16.F	FURRING REINFORCING ANGLE
09 21 16.F01	FIRE-RATED GYPSUM BOARD
09 21 16.F02	FOIL-FACED GYPSUM BOARD
09 21 16.F03	FIRE-RATED IMPACT-RESISTANT GYPSUM BOARD
09 21 16.F04	FASTENER
09 21 16.G	GYPSUM BOARD
09 21 16.G01	GYPSUM BACKING BOARD
09 21 16.G02	GYPSUM SHEATHING BOARD
09 21 16.G03	GYPSUM COREBOARD
09 21 16.G04	GLASS MAT-FACED GYPSUM BOARD
09 21 16.G05	GYPSUM BOARD SUSPENSION SYSTEM
09 21 16.H	HAT-SHAPED FURRING CHANNEL
09 21 16.H01	HANGER WIRE
09 21 16.M	METAL STUD
09 21 16.M01	MOISTURE-RESISTANT GYPSUM BOARD
09 21 16.M02	MAIN CEILING CHANNEL
09 21 16.M03	METAL STUD CROSS BRACING
09 21 16.M04	IMPACT-RESISTANT GYPSUM BOARD
09 21 16.P	PREDECORATED GYPSUM BOARD
09 21 16.R	RESILIENT CHANNEL
09 21 16.S	STANDARD WALL FURRING
09 21 16.S01	SECURITY MESH
09 21 16.S02	SCREW
09 21 16.T	TRACK
09 21 16.T01	TRIM
09 21 16.V	VAPOR RETARDER
09 21 16.Z	Z-FURRING SYSTEM

09 21 16.Z01	Z-FURRING SECTION
09 21 16.Z02	Z-FURRING SYSTEM BOARD INSULATION
09 22 36	**LATH**
09 22 36.B	BASE SCREED
09 22 36.C	CEILING HANGER
09 22 36.C01	CORNER MESH
09 22 36.C02	CORNER BEAD
09 22 36.C03	CONTROL JOINT
09 22 36.C04	CHANNEL SCREED
09 22 36.D	DRIP SCREED
09 22 36.D01	DIAMOND MESH METAL LATH
09 22 36.E	EXPANSION JOINT
09 22 36.F	FURRING CHANNEL
09 22 36.F01	FLAT RIB METAL LATH
09 22 36.H	HANGER
09 22 36.L	LATERAL BRACING
09 22 36.M	METAL LATH
09 22 36.M01	METAL TRIM
09 22 36.M02	MAIN CEILING CHANNEL
09 22 36.P	POLYETHYLENE SHEET
09 22 36.R	RESILIENT CHANNEL
09 22 36.R01	RIBBED METAL LATH
09 22 36.R02	ROD RIBBED METAL LATH
09 22 36.S	STRIP MESH
09 22 36.V	VAPOR RETARDER
09 22 36.W	WELDED WIRE LATH
09 23 00	**GYPSUM PLASTERING**
09 23 00.G	GYPSUM PLASTER
09 24 00	**PORTLAND CEMENT PLASTERING**
09 24 00.P	PORTLAND CEMENT PLASTER
09 30 00	**TILING**
09 30 00.B	BASE
09 30 00.C	CERAMIC MOSAIC TILE
09 30 00.C01	CEMENTITIOUS BACKER BOARD
09 30 00.C02	COATED GLASS MAT BACKER BOARD
09 30 00.G	GLAZED WALL TILE
09 30 00.G01	GLAZED FLOOR TILE
09 30 00.M	MORTAR BED
09 30 00.N	NONCERAMIC TRIM
09 30 00.P	PAVER TILE
09 30 00.Q	QUARRY TILE
09 30 00.R	REINFORCING MESH
09 30 00.R01	REINFORCED MORTAR BED
09 30 00.S	STAIR TREAD
09 30 00.T	TRIM
09 30 00.W	WAINSCOT CAP
09 30 00.W01	WATERPROOFING MEMBRANE

09 30 33	**STONE TILING**
09 30 33.G	GROUT
09 30 33.M	MARBLE THRESHOLD
09 30 33.M01	MORTAR
09 30 33.S	SLATE TILE
09 30 33.S01	SLATE TILE BASE
09 30 33.T	TILE EDGE
09 30 33.U	UNDERLAYMENT

09 51 00	**ACOUSTICAL CEILINGS**
09 51 00.A	ACOUSTICAL PANEL(S)
09 51 00.B	BREAK METAL ACCORDION DOOR RECEIVER
09 51 00.B01	BRAKE METAL DRAPERY TRACK RECEIVER
09 51 00.E	EXPOSED SUSPENSION SYSTEM
09 51 00.F	FIRE-RESISTIVE ACOUSTICAL PANEL(S)
09 51 00.F01	FIRE-RATED EXPOSED SUSPENSION SYSTEM
09 51 00.H	HANGER WIRE
09 51 00.P	PERIMETER MOLDING
09 51 00.S	SUPPORT CHANNEL AND HANGER
09 51 00.S01	SUPPORT CHANNEL
09 51 00.S02	SUPPORT HANGER
09 51 00.S03	SEISMIC BRACING

09 65 00	**RESILIENT FLOORING**
09 65 00.C	COVED BASE
09 65 00.E	EDGE STRIP
09 65 00.F	FEATURE STRIP
09 65 00.R	RESILIENT TILE FLOORING
09 65 00.R01	RESILIENT SHEET FLOORING
09 65 00.R02	RESILIENT STAIR COVERING
09 65 00.R03	RESILIENT BASE
09 65 00.W	WATERJET-CUT GRAPHIC

09 65 66	**RESILIENT ATHLETIC FLOORING**
09 65 66.R	RESILIENT ATHLETIC FLOORING

09 68 00	**CARPETING**
09 68 00.B	BASE CAP
09 68 00.C	CARPET
09 68 00.C01	CARPET BASE
09 68 00.E	EDGE STRIP
09 68 00.S	SUBFLOOR FILLER

09 68 13	**TILE CARPETING**
09 68 13.C	CARPET TILE
09 68 13.C01	CARPET BASE
09 68 13.E	EDGE STRIP

09 69 00	**ACCESS FLOORING**
09 69 00.A	ACCESS FLOORING
09 69 00.A01	AIR GRILLE

09 69 00.C	CABLE CUTOUT PROTECTION
09 69 00.F	FRAME GRID STRINGER
09 69 00.F01	FLOOR PANEL
09 69 00.F02	FASCIA PANEL
09 69 00.P	PEDESTAL
09 69 00.P01	PERFORATED FLOOR PANEL

09 72 00   WALL COVERINGS

09 72 00.W	WALL COVERING
09 72 00.W01	WALL COVERING EDGE STRIP
09 72 00.W02	WALL COVERING MOLDING

09 84 00   ACOUSTIC ROOM COMPONENTS

09 84 00.A	ACOUSTICAL PANEL
09 84 00.S	SUSPENSION WIRE
09 84 00.T	TRIM MOLDING

09 90 00   PAINTING AND COATING

09 90 00.F	FIRE LANE MARKING
09 90 00.N	INTERNATIONAL SYMBOL OF ACCESSIBILITY
09 90 00.P	PAINT
09 90 00.S	SAFETY STRIPE
09 90 00.S01	STRIPING

09 96 00   HIGH-PERFORMANCE COATINGS

09 96 00.A	ACRYLIC COATING
09 96 00.C	COAL-TAR EPOXY COATING
09 96 00.E	EPOXY COATING
09 96 00.E01	EPOXY FLOOR COATING
09 96 00.H	HIGH-BUILD EPOXY COATING
09 96 00.H01	HIGH-BUILD URETHANE COATING
09 96 00.P	POLYURETHANE FLOOR COATING
09 96 00.R	RUBBER COATING
09 96 00.U	URETHANE COATING

10 11 00   VISUAL DISPLAY SURFACES

10 11 00.C	CHALKBOARD
10 11 00.C01	CHALK TRAY
10 11 00.F	FLAG POLE HOLDER
10 11 00.M	MARKERBOARD
10 11 00.M01	MAP RAIL
10 11 00.T	TACKBOARD
10 11 00.W	WALL STANDARD

10 14 19   DIMENSIONAL LETTER SIGNAGE

10 14 19.C	CAST ALUMINUM SIGN
10 14 19.C01	CAST ALUMINUM CHARACTERS
10 14 19.D	DIMENSIONAL LETTER SIGN
10 14 19.P	PLATE ALUMINUM CHARACTERS
10 14 19.T	TAMPER-RESISTANT ANCHOR
10 14 19.T01	TAMPERPROOF ANCHOR

10 14 24	**PLASTIC SIGNAGE**
10 14 24.E	ENGRAVED SIGN
10 14 24.F	FACE COLOR
10 14 24.N	INJECTION-MOLDED SIGN
10 14 24.P	PLASTIC SIGN
10 14 24.R	RAISED-LETTER SIGN
10 14 24.R01	RAISED PICTOGRAM
10 14 24.R02	RAISED COPY
10 14 24.R03	RAISED BRAILLE
10 14 24.S	SAND-BLASTED SIGN
10 14 24.S01	SILK-SCREENED SIGN
10 14 24.S02	SELF-LUMINOUS EXIT SIGN
10 14 26	**POST AND PANEL/PYLON SIGNAGE**
10 14 26.E	ENGRAVED SIGN
10 14 26.F	FACE COLOR
10 14 26.P	PANEL SIGN
10 14 26.P01	POST
10 14 26.R	RAISED-LETTER SIGN
10 14 26.R01	RAISED PICTOGRAM
10 14 26.R02	RAISED COPY
10 14 26.R03	RAISED BRAILLE
10 14 26.S	SILK-SCREENED SIGN
10 21 13	**TOILET COMPARTMENTS**
10 21 13.A	ANCHOR
10 21 13.B	BRACKET
10 21 13.D	DOOR
10 21 13.H	HEAD RAIL
10 21 13.M	METAL TOILET COMPARTMENT
10 21 13.P	PLASTIC TOILET COMPARTMENT
10 21 13.P01	PLASTIC LAMINATE TOILET COMPARTMENT
10 21 13.P02	PANEL
10 21 13.P03	PILASTER
10 21 13.P04	PILASTER SHOE
10 21 13.S	STAINLESS-STEEL POST
10 21 13.S01	STAINLESS-STEEL POST BASE PLATE
10 21 13.S02	STAINLESS-STEEL POST SHOE
10 21 13.S03	SHOE RETAINER
10 21 13.T	TAMPER-RESISTANT FASTENER
10 21 13.U	URINAL SCREEN
10 21 23	**CUBICLES**
10 21 23.C	CURTAIN
10 21 23.C01	CURTAIN CARRIER
10 21 23.T	TRACK
10 22 13	**WIRE MESH PARTITIONS**
10 22 13.A	ANCHORAGE DEVICE
10 22 13.C	CHAIN-LINK FABRIC
10 22 13.C01	CORNER POST

10 22 13.C02	CROSS BRACING
10 22 13.C03	CYLINDER LOCK
10 22 13.C04	CANTILEVER GATE ROLLER
10 22 13.C05	CANTILEVER GATE ROLLER GUARD
10 22 13.D	DOOR
10 22 13.E	EXPANDED SHEET METAL
10 22 13.F	FLOOR BASE
10 22 13.G	GATE
10 22 13.G01	GATE FRAME
10 22 13.H	HINGE
10 22 13.L	LATCH SET
10 22 13.M	MORTISE LOCK
10 22 13.N	INTERMEDIATE POST
10 22 13.N01	INTERMEDIATE HORIZONTAL MEMBER
10 22 13.P	PILASTER SHOE
10 22 13.P01	POST CAP
10 22 13.S	SLIDING-DOOR HARDWARE
10 22 13.T	TOP RAIL HORIZONTAL MEMBER
10 22 13.W	WIRE MESH PARTITION
10 22 13.W01	WOVEN SCREEN WIRE

10 22 26 **OPERABLE PARTITIONS**

10 22 26.A	ACCORDION-FOLDING PARTITION
10 22 26.A01	ANCHOR
10 22 26.C	CARRIER
10 22 26.H	HANGER ROD
10 22 26.P	OPERABLE PANEL PARTITION
10 22 26.P01	PASS DOOR
10 22 26.T	TRACK

10 26 00 **WALL AND DOOR PROTECTION**

10 26 00.B	BUMPER RAIL
10 26 00.C	CORNER GUARD
10 26 00.C01	CORRIDOR HANDRAIL

10 28 00 **TOILET, BATH, AND LAUNDRY ACCESSORIES**

10 28 00.C	COMBINATION TOWEL DISPENSER/WASTE RECEPTACLE
10 28 00.C01	COMBINATION SANITARY NAPKIN/TAMPON DISPENSER
10 28 00.G	GRAB BAR
10 28 00.L	LIQUID DISPENSING UNIT
10 28 00.M	MIRROR
10 28 00.M01	MOP AND BROOM HOLDER
10 28 00.M02	MEDICINE CABINET
10 28 00.P	PAPER TOWEL DISPENSER
10 28 00.R	ROBE HOOK
10 28 00.S	SOAP DISPENSER
10 28 00.S01	SANITARY NAPKIN DISPOSAL UNIT
10 28 00.S02	SHOWER CURTAIN ROD
10 28 00.S03	SHOWER CURTAIN
10 28 00.S04	STORAGE SHELF
10 28 00.S05	SAFETY COVER
10 28 00.S06	SEAT COVER DISPENSER

10 28 00.T	TOILET PAPER DISPENSER
10 28 00.T01	TOWEL BAR
10 28 00.T02	TOWEL PIN
10 28 00.W	WASTE RECEPTACLE

10 44 00   **FIRE PROTECTION SPECIALTIES**

10 44 00.F	FIRE EXTINGUISHER CABINET
10 44 00.F01	FIRE EXTINGUISHER
10 44 00.F02	FIRE BLANKET CABINET
10 44 00.F03	FIRE BLANKET AND EXTINGUISHER CABINET
10 44 00.S	SURFACE-MOUNTED FIRE EXTINGUISHER

10 51 00   **LOCKERS**

10 51 00.A	ANCHOR(S)
10 51 00.B	BENCH TOP
10 51 00.B01	BASE CLOSURE
10 51 00.E	END PANEL
10 51 00.F	FILLER STRIP
10 51 00.F01	FASTENER
10 51 00.H	HANDICAP-ACCESSIBLE LOCKER
10 51 00.L	LOCKER
10 51 00.L01	LOCKER BENCH
10 51 00.P	PEDESTAL
10 51 00.S	SLOPING TOP
10 51 00.S01	SHIM
10 51 00.T	TRIM
10 51 00.T01	TOP FLANGE

10 56 13   **METAL STORAGE SHELVING**

10 56 13.S	STORAGE SHELVING
10 56 13.S01	STORAGE SHELVING ANGLE POST
10 56 13.S02	STORAGE SHELVING TEE POST
10 56 13.S03	STORAGE SHELVING BEAM
10 56 13.S04	STORAGE SHELVING DECKING

10 75 00   **FLAGPOLES**

10 75 00.F	FLAGPOLE
10 75 00.F01	FLASH COLLAR
10 75 00.F02	FOUNDATION TUBE SLEEVE
10 75 00.F03	FINIAL BALL
10 75 00.G	GROUND SPIKE
10 75 00.P	POLE BASE ATTACHMENT
10 75 00.P01	POROUS FILL
10 75 00.S	STEEL WEDGE
10 75 00.W	WOOD WEDGE
10 75 00.W01	WATERPROOF CEMENT

11 13 19   **STATIONARY LOADING DOCK EQUIPMENT**

11 13 19.C	CONTROL STATION
11 13 19.D	DOCK LEVELER
11 13 19.D01	DOCK BUMPER
11 13 19.D02	DOCK BUMPER SUPPORT BRACKET

11 13 19.F	FRONT PIT CURB ANGLE
11 13 19.P	PIT FRAME CURB ANGLE
11 13 19.S	SAFETY SIGN
11 13 19.W	WHEEL CHOCKS

11 16 16 **SAFES**

11 16 16.N	IN-FLOOR SAFE

11 31 00 **RESIDENTIAL APPLIANCES**

11 31 00 .C	CLOTHES WASHER
11 31 00 .C01	CLOTHES DRYER
11 31 00 .C02	COOKTOP
11 31 00 .D	DISHWASHER
11 31 00 .G	GARBAGE DISPOSER
11 31 00 .M	MICROWAVE
11 31 00 .R	REFRIGERATOR
11 31 00 .R01	RANGE
11 31 00 .R02	RANGE HOOD
11 31 00 .T	TRASH COMPACTOR
11 31 00 .W	WALL OVEN

11 40 00 **FOOD SERVICE EQUIPMENT**

11 40 00 .B	BACKSPLASH
11 40 00 .C	CONVECTION OVEN
11 40 00 .D	DISHWASHER
11 40 00 .D01	DISHWASHER BOOSTER HEATER
11 40 00 .F	FRYER
11 40 00 .G	GARBAGE DISPOSER
11 40 00 .M	MICROWAVE
11 40 00 .M01	MIXER
11 40 00 .R	REFRIGERATOR
11 40 00 .R01	RANGE
11 40 00 .R02	RANGE HOOD
11 40 00 .R03	REACH-IN FREEZER
11 40 00 .R04	REACH-IN COOLER
11 40 00 .R05	RAMP
11 40 00 .S	SHELVING
11 40 00 .S01	SODA FOUNTAIN
11 40 00 .T	TABLE
11 40 00 .T	TRASH COMPACTOR
11 31 00 .V	OVEN
11 31 00 .W	WALK-IN FREEZER
11 31 00 .W01	WALK-IN COOLER

11 52 00 **AUDIOVISUAL EQUIPMENT**

11 52 00.B	BOLT(S)
11 52 00.C	CHANNEL STRUT
11 52 00.E	ESCUTCHEON
11 52 00.F	FLANGE
11 52 00.P	PIPE
11 52 00.P01	PROJECTOR
11 52 00.S	STABILIZER KIT

11 52 00.S01	SUSPENDED PROJECTOR SUPPORT
11 52 00.T	TELEVISION MOUNTING BRACKET

11 52 13   PROJECTION SCREENS

11 52 13.F	FRONT PROJECTION SCREEN
11 52 13.F01	FABRIC REAR PROJECTION SCREEN
11 52 13.P	PROJECTION SCREEN CONTROL
11 52 13.R	RIGID REAR PROJECTION SCREEN

11 53 00   LABORATORY EQUIPMENT

11 53 00 .A	AUTOCLAVE
11 53 00 .B	BALANCE TABLE
11 53 00 .B01	BALANCE
11 53 00 .C	CART
11 53 00 .C01	CANOPY HOOD
11 53 00 .C02	CANOPY HOOD SUPPORT RODS
11 53 00 .D	DRAIN RACK
11 53 00 .D01	DESICCATOR
11 53 00 .D02	DRYING OVEN
11 53 00 .E	EXHAUST STACK
11 53 00 .E01	EXHAUST STACK RAIN SKIRT
11 53 00 .E02	EXHAUST STACK ELBOW
11 53 00 .E03	EXHAUST STACK VIBRATION ISOLATOR
11 53 00 .E04	EXHAUST STACK GUY WIRE
11 53 00 .E05	EXHAUST STACK TURNBUCKLE
11 53 00 .E06	EXHAUST STACK GUY BAND
11 53 00 .E07	EXHAUST FAN
11 53 00 .E08	EXHAUST FAN INLET ADAPTER
11 53 00 .F	FUME HOOD
11 53 00 .F01	FUME HOOD AUXILIARY AIR FAN
11 53 00 .G	GLASSWARE WASHER
11 53 00 .L	LABORATORY EQUIPMENT
11 53 00 .M	MUFFLE FURNACE
11 53 00 .N	INCUBATOR
11 53 00 .R	REFRIGERATOR
11 53 00 .V	VACUUM PUMP
11 53 00 .W	WATER PURIFICATION SYSTEM

11 78 00   MORTUARY EQUIPMENT

11 78 00.A	AUTOPSY TABLE
11 78 00.B	BASE CABINET
11 78 00.B01	BACKSPLASH
11 78 00.C	COUNTERTOP
11 78 00.D	DISSECTING SINK
11 78 00.G	GROSS PATHOLOGY SINK
11 78 00.S	SCRUB SINK
11 78 00.W	WALL CABINET

12 21 13   HORIZONTAL LOUVER BLINDS

12 21 13.H	HORIZONTAL LOUVER BLINDS

12 21 16   VERTICAL LOUVER BLINDS

12 21 16.V	VERTICAL LOUVER BLINDS

12 22 13	**DRAPERIES**
12 22 13.D	DRAPERIES
12 22 16	**DRAPERY TRACK AND ACCESSORIES**
12 22 16.D	DRAPERY TRACK
12 22 16.T	TRACK BRACKET
12 31 00	**MANUFACTURED METAL CASEWORK**
12 31 00.A	AIR OUTLET
12 31 00.B	BACKSPLASH
12 31 00.C	COUNTERTOP
12 31 00.C01	CUP SINK
12 31 00.C02	CABINET LOCK
12 31 00.C03	COCK VALVE
12 31 00.D	DRAWER AND DOOR PULL
12 31 00.E	ESCUTCHEON
12 31 00.E01	ELECTRICAL OUTLET COVER
12 31 00.F	FILLER PANEL
12 31 00.F01	FAUCET
12 31 00.F02	FINISHED SIDE
12 31 00.F03	FINISHED BACK
12 31 00.G	GLASS
12 31 00.L	LAVATORY
12 31 00.M	METAL CASEWORK
12 31 00.N	NATURAL GAS OUTLET
12 31 00.R	REAGENT SHELF UPRIGHT
12 31 00.R01	REAGENT SHELF
12 31 00.S	SIDESPLASH
12 31 00.S01	SHELF STANDARDS AND REST
12 31 00.S02	SHELF BRACKET
12 31 00.S03	SERVICE SHELF
12 31 00.S04	SERVICE FITTING
12 31 00.V	VACUUM OUTLET
12 31 00.W	WATER OUTLET
12 35 30	**RESIDENTIAL CASEWORK**
12 35 30.A	APRON
12 35 30.A01	ADJUSTABLE SHELF
12 35 30.A02	ACCESSORY
12 35 30.B	BACKSPLASH
12 35 30.B01	BASE CABINET
12 35 30.B02	BASE CABINET BOTTOM
12 35 30.C	COUNTERTOP
12 35 30.C01	COUNTERTOP SUPPORT BRACKET
12 35 30.C02	COUNTERTOP SUPPORT LEG
12 35 30.C03	COUNTERTOP SUPPORT LEG LEVELER
12 35 30.C04	CABINET FRAME
12 35 30.C05	CABINET BACK
12 35 30.D	DRAWER AND DOOR PULL
12 35 30.D01	DRAWER FRONT
12 35 30.D02	DOOR FRONT
12 35 30.F	FINISHED END

```
12 35 30.F01    FINISHED BACK
12 35 30.F03    FIXED SHELF
12 35 30.F02    FILLER
12 35 30.G      GROMMET
12 35 30.N      INSIDE CORNER MOLDING
12 35 30.U      OUTSIDE CORNER MOLDING
12 35 30.Q      QUARTER ROUND MOLDING
12 35 30.R      RESIDENTIAL CASEWORK
12 35 30.R01    ROLL-OUT TRAY
12 35 30.R02    REMOVABLE PLASTIC LAMINATE PANEL
12 35 30.S      SIDESPLASH
12 35 30.S01    SHOE MOLDING
12 35 30.S02    SCRIBE MOLDING
12 35 30.S03    SUPPORT BRACKET
12 35 30.T      TOEKICK BACKER
12 35 30.T01    TOEKICK COVER
12 35 30.V      VALANCE
12 35 30.W      WALL CABINET
12 35 30.W01    WALL CABINET BOTTOM
12 35 30.W02    WALL CABINET TOP
```

12 48 13   ENTRANCE FLOOR MATS AND FRAMES

```
12 48 13.F      FLOOR MAT
12 48 13.R      RECESSED FRAME
12 48 13.E      EDGE STRIP
12 48 13.H      HORIZONTAL LOUVER BLINDS
```

12 51 00   OFFICE FURNITURE

```
12 51 00.B      BOOKSHELVES
12 51 00.C      CHAIR
12 51 00.D      DESK
13 51 00.T      TABLE
```

12 55 00   DETENTION FURNITURE

```
12 55 00.C      CHAIR
12 55 00.C01    CLOTHES HOOK(S)
12 55 00.C02    CLOTHES HOOKS WITH SHELF
12 55 00.C03    CELL DESK
12 55 00.C04    CORNER MIRROR
12 55 00.D      DOUBLE BUNK
12 55 00.L      LOCKER
12 55 00.M      MIRROR
12 55 00.S      SINGLE BUNK
12 55 00.S01    SHELF
12 55 00.T      TABLE
12 55 00.T01    TABLE WITH SEATS
12 55 00.T02    TOWEL BAR
```

13 34 19   METAL BUILDING SYSTEMS

```
13 34 19.A      ANCHOR BOLT
13 34 19.B      BRACING
13 34 19.B01    BASE PLATE
```

13 34 19.C	CLIP ANGLE
13 34 19.E	ENDWALL BEAM
13 34 19.E01	ENDWALL COLUMN
13 34 19.E02	EAVE STRUT
13 34 19.E03	EAVE PLATE
13 34 19.F	FASTENER
13 34 19.G	GIRT
13 34 19.H	HEADER FRAMING
13 34 19.J	JAMB FRAMING
13 34 19.M	METAL BUILDING
13 34 19.M01	METAL BUILDING FRAME
13 34 19.M02	METAL BUILDING COLUMN
13 34 19.M03	METAL BUILDING BEAM
13 34 19.N	NONSHRINK GROUT
13 34 19.P	PURLIN

13 34 23　　　　**FABRICATED STRUCTURES**

13 34 23.A	ALUMINUM WINDOW
13 34 23.A01	ADA-COMPLIANT SHOWER
13 34 23.A02	ADA-COMPLIANT LAVATORY
13 34 23.A03	ADA-COMPLIANT WATER CLOSET
13 34 23.A04	ADA-COMPLIANT GRAB BAR
13 34 23.A05	ADA-COMPLIANT MIRROR
13 34 23.A06	ADA-COMPLIANT RAMP
13 34 23.A07	ADA-COMPLIANT HANDRAIL
13 34 23.A08	AIR CONDITIONING UNIT
13 34 23.A09	ANCHOR BOLT
13 34 23.C	CASEWORK
13 34 23.C01	COUNTERTOP
13 34 23.C02	CEILING SYSTEM
13 34 23.C03	CLOSURE
13 34 23.C04	COMBINATION HEATER, LIGHT, AND FAN
13 34 23.D	DOWNSPOUT
13 34 23.D01	DOOR
13 34 23.D02	DRAWER
13 34 23.E	EAVE TRIM
13 34 23.E01	ELECTRIC PANEL
13 34 23.F	FASCIA
13 34 23.F01	FAUCET
13 34 23.F02	FLOOR
13 34 23.G	GRAB BAR
13 34 23.H	HOLLOW METAL DOOR AND FRAME
13 34 23.H01	HOLLOW METAL FRAME
13 34 23.H02	HEATER
13 34 23.H03	HORIZONTAL LOUVER BLINDS
13 34 23.L	LAVATORY
13 34 23.L01	LIGHT FIXTURE
13 34 23.M	MIRROR
13 34 23.P	PORTABLE BUILDING
13 34 23.P01	PORTABLE BOOTH
13 34 23.P02	PAPER TOWEL DISPENSER
13 34 23.R	RESILIENT BASE

13 34 23.R01	ROOF INSULATION
13 34 23.R02	ROOF CURB
13 34 23.R03	ROOF PANEL
13 34 23.S	SIDING
13 34 23.S01	SKIRT
13 34 23.S02	STAIRS
13 34 23.T	TOILET TISSUE DISPENSER
13 34 23.T01	TRIM
13 34 23.W	WALL PANEL
13 34 23.W01	WINDOW
13 34 23.W02	WATER CLOSET
13 34 23.W03	WATER HEATER
13 34 23.W04	WALL INSULATION

14 20 10   **PASSENGER ELEVATORS**

14 20 10.B	BUFFERS
14 20 10.C	CAR OPERATING PANEL
14 20 10.D	DOUBLE BOTTOM CYLINDER
14 20 10.E	ELEVATOR CAR
14 20 10.E01	ELEVATOR CAB DOOR FRAME
14 20 10.E02	ELEVATOR CAB DOOR
14 20 10.E03	ELEVATOR CAB DOOR THRESHOLD
14 20 10.E04	ELEVATOR CAB WINDOW
14 20 10.E05	EMERGENCY COMMUNICATION
14 20 10.E06	EMERGENCY CONTROL BUTTON(S)
14 20 10.F	FIREFIGHTER'S OPERATION
14 20 10.F01	FREIGHT ELEVATOR
14 20 10.F02	FLOOR DESIGNATION BUTTON(S)
14 20 10.G	GUIDE RAIL
14 20 10.G01	GUIDE RAIL BRACKET
14 20 10.H	HOISTWAY DOOR
14 20 10.H01	HOISTWAY DOOR FRAME
14 20 10.H02	HOISTWAY DOOR THRESHOLD
14 20 10.H03	HYDRAULIC MOTOR AND PUMP
14 20 10.H04	HYDRAULIC CYLINDER CASING
14 20 10.H05	HANDRAIL
14 20 10.H06	HYDRAULIC PIPING
14 20 10.J	JACK
14 20 10.L	LANDING BUTTON
14 20 10.L01	LADDER
14 20 10.L02	LOBBY PANEL
14 20 10.P	PASSENGER ELEVATOR
14 20 10.P01	PIT CHANNELS
14 20 10.S	SILL SUPPORT
14 20 10.S01	SILL

22 07 19   **PLUMBING PIPING INSULATION**

22 07 19.P	PLUMBING PIPING INSULATION
22 07 19.P01	PLUMBING PIPING INSULATION JACKET

22 10 05   **PLUMBING PIPING**

22 10 05.A	ABS PIPE
22 10 05.A01	ALUMINUM DWV PIPE

22 10 05.B	BALL VALVE
22 10 05.B01	BUTTERFLY VALVE
22 10 05.B02	BRASS PIPE
22 10 05.C	CAST IRON PIPE
22 10 05.C01	CONCRETE PIPE
22 10 05.C02	COPPER PIPE
22 10 05.C03	COPPER TUBE
22 10 05.C04	CHEMICAL-RESISTANT SANITARY SEWER PIPE
22 10 05.C05	CHLORINATED POLYVINYL CHLORIDE (CPVC) PIPE
22 10 05.C06	COUPLING
22 10 05.D	DUCTILE IRON PIPE
22 10 05.D01	DIELECTRIC CONNECTION
22 10 05.F	FLANGE
22 10 05.F01	FLOW CONTROL
22 10 05.F02	FIBERGLASS PIPE
22 10 05.G	GATE VALVE
22 10 05.G01	GLOBE VALVE
22 10 05.G02	GLASS PIPE
22 10 05.N	NATURAL GAS PIPE
22 10 05.P	PIPE HANGER
22 10 05.P01	PROPANE GAS PIPE
22 10 05.P02	POLYVINYL CHLORIDE (PVC) PIPE
22 10 05.P03	POLYPROPYLENE PIPE
22 10 05.P04	POLYBUTYLENE PIPE
22 10 05.P05	PLUG VALVE
22 10 05.R	RELIEF VALVE
22 10 05.S	SANITARY SEWER PIPE
22 10 05.S01	STORMWATER PIPE
22 10 05.S02	STEEL PIPE
22 10 05.S03	SWING CHECK VALVE
22 10 05.S03	SPRING-LOADED CHECK VALVE
22 10 05.S04	STRAINER
22 10 05.U	UNION
22 10 05.V	VALVE
22 10 05.W	WATER PIPING
22 10 05.W01	WATER-PRESSURE-REDUCING VALVE

22 10 06	**PLUMBING PIPING SPECIALTIES**
22 10 06.R	ROOF DRAIN
22 10 06.D	DOWNSPOUT NOZZLE

22 40 00	**PLUMBING FIXTURES**
22 40 00.B	BATHTUB
22 40 00.B01	BIDET
22 40 00.D	DRINKING FOUNTAIN
22 40 00.E	ELECTRIC WATER COOLER
22 40 00.F	FLUSH VALVE WATER CLOSET
22 40 00.E	EYEWASH FOUNTAIN
22 40 00.E01	EMERGENCY SHOWER
22 40 00.L	LAVATORY
22 40 00.S	SHOWER
22 40 00.S01	SERVICE SINK
22 40 00.S02	STALL URINAL
22 40 00.T	TANK-TYPE WATER CLOSET

22 40 00.U   URINAL
22 40 00.W   WATER CLOSET
22 40 00.W01   WALL-HUNG URINAL
22 40 00.W02   WASH FOUNTAIN

22 43 00   HEALTH CARE PLUMBING FIXTURES

22 43 00.A   AUTOMATIC SURGICAL SCRUB STATION
22 43 00.B   BEDPAN RINSE VALVE
22 43 00.D   DOUBLE BOWL LAVATORY
22 43 00.D01   DISTURBED PATIENT LAVATORY
22 43 00.E   EYEWASH FOUNTAIN
22 43 00.E01   EYEWASH/SHOWER FOUNTAIN
22 43 00.E02   EMERGENCY SHOWER
22 43 00.F   FLUSHING RIM DISPOSAL SERVICE SINK, PEDESTAL TYPE
22 43 00.F01   FLUSHING RIM DISPOSAL SERVICE SINK, WALL-MOUNTED TYPE
22 43 00.F02   FLOOR DRAIN ATTACHMENT
22 43 00.H   HANDHELD SHOWER HEAD
22 43 00.L   LARGE PLASTER TRAP
22 43 00.N   NEUROPSYCHIATRIC PATIENT SHOWER
22 43 00.N01   NEUROPSYCHIATRIC PATIENT WATER CLOSET
22 43 00.P   PIPING INSULATION
22 43 00.P01   PIER-TYPE BATHTUB
22 43 00.P02   PLASTER INTERCEPTOR TRAP
22 43 00.S   SINGLE-BOWL LAVATORY
22 43 00.S01   SITZ BATH
22 43 00.S02   SURGEONS' LAVATORY
22 43 00.S03   SURGEONS' SCRUB-UP SINK
22 43 00.S04   SPECIMEN WATER CLOSET
22 43 00.S05   SAFETY DELUGE SHOWER
22 43 00.T   THERMOSTATIC MIXING VALVE
22 43 00.W   WHEELCHAIR LAVATORY
22 43 00.W01   WRIST CONTROL LAVATORY
22 43 00.W02   WHIRLPOOL
22 43 00.W03   WHIRLPOOL CLEANER

26 51 00   INTERIOR LIGHTING

26 51 00.B   BALLAST
26 51 00.E   EXIT SIGN
26 51 00.E01   EMERGENCY LIGHTING UNIT
26 51 00.F   FLUORESCENT LAMP
26 51 00.F01   FLUORESCENT BALLAST
26 51 00.F02   FLUORESCENT DIMMING BALLAST
26 51 00.F03   FLUORESCENT DIMMING CONTROL
26 51 00.F04   FLUORESCENT LAMP EMERGENCY POWER SUPPLY
26 51 00.H   HIGH-INTENSITY DISCHARGE (HID) BALLAST
26 51 00.L   LAMP
26 51 00.N   INTERIOR LUMINAIRE
26 51 00.N01   INCANDESCENT LAMP
26 51 00.R   REFLECTOR LAMP

26 56 00   EXTERIOR LIGHTING

26 56 00.E   EXTERIOR LUMINAIRE
26 56 00.F   FLUORESCENT LAMP
26 56 00.H   HIGH-INTENSITY DISCHARGE (HID) LAMP

26 56 00.R	REFLECTOR LAMP
26 56 00.N	INCANDESCENT LAMP
26 56 00.P	POLE
26 56 00.P01	POLE BASE

31 22 00	**GRADING**
31 22 00.F	FINISH GRADE
31 22 00.T	TOPSOIL

31 23 00	**EXCAVATION AND FILL**
31 23 00.F	FINISH GRADING
31 23 00.B	BACKFILL
31 23 00.C	CONCRETE FOR FILL
31 23 00.G	GENERAL FILL
31 23 00.G01	GEOTEXTILE FABRIC
31 23 00.G02	GRANULAR FILL
31 23 00.P	POROUS FILL
31 23 00.S01	STRUCTURAL FILL
31 23 00.S02	SCARIFIED AND COMPACTED SUBGRADE
31 23 00.T	TOPSOIL
31 23 00.V	VAPOR RETARDER

31 37 00	**RIPRAP**
31 37 00.G	GEOTEXTILE FABRIC
31 37 00.R	RIPRAP

31 63 29	**DRILLED CONCRETE PIERS AND SHAFTS**
31 63 29.D	DRILLED CONCRETE PIER
31 63 29.S	SHAFT LINER

32 12 16	**ASPHALT PAVING**
32 12 16.B	BASE COURSE
32 12 16.B01	BINDER COURSE
32 12 16.B02	BITUMINOUS CONCRETE PAVING
32 12 16.E	EXTRUDED ASPHALT CURB
32 12 16.F	FIRE-LANE MARKING
32 12 16.N	INTERNATIONAL SYMBOL OF ACCESSIBILITY
32 12 16.P	PAVING GEOTEXTILE
32 12 16.P01	PAVING MARKING PAINT
32 12 16.S	STRIPING
32 12 16.W01	WEARING COURSE

32 13 13	**CONCRETE PAVING**
32 13 13.C	CONCRETE PAVING
32 13 13.C01	CONCRETE STAIR
32 13 13.C02	CONCRETE GUTTER
32 13 13.C03	CONCRETE INTEGRAL CURB
32 13 13.C04	CONCRETE RAMP
32 13 13.C05	CONCRETE CURB
32 13 13.C06	CONTROL JOINT
32 13 13.E	EXPANSION JOINT
32 13 13.P	PAVING MARKING PAINT
32 13 13.R	RIGID JOINT FILLER

32 13 13.R01   RADIUSED EDGE
32 13 13.R02   REMOVABLE JOINT CAP
32 13 13.S   SCORED JOINT

32 17 13   PARKING BUMPERS

32 17 13.D   DOWEL
32 17 13.P   PARKING BUMPER
32 17 13.R   REINFORCING STEEL
32 17 13.S   SLEEVE

32 31 13   CHAIN-LINK FENCES AND GATES

32 31 13.A   ANCHOR
32 31 13.B   BARBED WIRE
32 31 13.B01   BARBED TAPE
32 31 13.B02   BRACE BAND
32 31 13.B03   BRACE RAIL
32 31 13.B04   BOTTOM RAIL
32 31 13.B05   BOLT
32 31 13.C   CHAIN-LINK FENCE
32 31 13.C01   CHAIN-LINK GATE
32 31 13.C02   CORNER POST
32 31 13.C03   CAP
32 31 13.C04   CHAIN
32 31 13.C05   CANTILEVER GATE ROLLER
32 31 13.C06   CANTILEVER GATE ROLLER GUARD
32 31 13.C07   CANE BOLT
32 31 13.C08   CANE BOLT BRACKET
32 31 13.C09   CANE BOLT STOP
32 31 13.C10   CANE BOLT GATE KEEPER
32 31 13.D   DROP ROD
32 31 13.E   EXTENSION ARM
32 31 13.F   FABRIC
32 31 13.F01   FORK LATCH
32 31 13.G   GATE POST
32 31 13.G01   GATE FRAME
32 31 13.G02   GATEKEEPER
32 31 13.G03   GATE OPERATOR
32 31 13.G04   GATE OPERATOR ACCESS
32 31 13.G05   GATE OPERATOR ACCESS OVERRIDE
32 31 13.G06   GATE HORIZONTAL BRACE
32 31 13.G07   GATE VERTICAL BRACE
32 31 13.G08   GROUND ROD
32 31 13.G09   GROUND WIRE
32 31 13.H   HORIZONTAL SLIDE GATE
32 31 13.H01   HINGE
32 31 13.L   LINE POST
32 31 13.M   MIDDLE RAIL
32 31 13.P   PRIVACY SLATS
32 31 13.T   TOP RAIL
32 31 13.T01   TENSION WIRE
32 31 13.T02   TENSION BAND
32 31 13.T03   TENSION STRAP
32 31 13.T04   TIE WIRE

32 31 13.T05	TROLLEY I-BEAM
32 31 13.T06	TROLLEY ASSEMBLY
32 31 13.U	U-BRACKET

32 84 23   **UNDERGROUND SPRINKLERS**

32 84 23.B	BACKFLOW PREVENTER
32 84 23.B01	BUBBLER
32 84 23.B02	BALL VALVE
32 84 23.D	DRAIN VALVE
32 84 23.E	EMITTER
32 84 23.G	GATE VALVE
32 84 23.P	PIPE RISER
32 84 23.R	IRRIGATION PIPING
32 84 23.R01	IRRIGATION OUTLET
32 84 23.R02	IRRIGATION CONTROLLER
32 84 23.R03	ROTARY TYPE SPRINKLER HEAD
32 84 23.S	SPRINKLER HEAD
32 84 23.S01	SLEEVE
32 84 23.S02	SPRAY-TYPE SPRINKLER HEAD
32 84 23.V	VALVE BOX
32 84 23.V01	VALVE BOX COVER

32 92 19   **SEEDING**

32 92 19.E	EROSION FABRIC
32 92 19.E01	EDGING
32 92 19.M	MULCHING MATERIAL
32 92 19.S	SEEDING
32 92 19.S01	SEED
32 92 19.S02	STAKE
32 92 19.S03	STRING
32 92 19.T	TOPSOIL

32 92 23   **SODDING**

32 92 23.E	EDGING
32 92 23.S	SOD
32 92 23.T	TOPSOIL
32 92 23.W	WOOD PEGS
32 92 23.W01	WIRE MESH

32 93 00   **PLANTS**

32 93 00.C	CABLE
32 93 00.D	DECORATIVE COVER
32 93 00.G	GROUND COVER
32 93 00.G01	GRATE
32 93 00.M	MULCH
32 93 00.M01	MEMBRANE
32 93 00.P	PLANT
32 93 00.P01	PLANT PROTECTOR
32 93 00.S	SUBSOIL
32 93 00.S01	SHRUB
32 93 00.S02	SOIL AMENDMENT MATERIAL
32 93 00.S03	STAKE

32 93 00.T	TOPSOIL
32 93 00.T01	TREE
32 93 00.T02	TURNBUCKLE
32 93 00.T02	TOPSOIL BEDDING
32 93 00.T03	TREE PROTECTOR
32 93 00.W	WRAPPING MATERIAL
32 93 00.W01	WIRE

Sample CAD Layer Names for Architectural Sheets

ALL SHEETS

A-ANNO-DIMS
A-ANNO-IDEN
A-ANNO-KEYN
A-ANNO-LABL
A-ANNO-LEGN
A-ANNO-NOTE
A-ANNO-SCHD
A-ANNO-SYMB
G-ANNO-TEXT
G-ANNO-TITL
G-ANNO-TTLB

PLANS

A-AREA
A-CLNG
A-COLS
A-CONV
A-DOOR
A-EQPM
A-FLOR
A-FURN
A-GLAZ
A-HVAC
A-LITE
A-ROOF
A-WALL

DETAILS/SECTIONS

A-DETL-DIMS
A-DETL-IDEN
A-DETL-MARK
A-DETL-MBND-CONT
A-DETL-MBND-HIDN
A-DETL-MCUT-HEVY
A-DETL-MCUT-LITE
A-DETL-MCUT-MEDM
A-DETL-MCUT-XHVY
A-DETL-MCUT-XLIT

A-DETL-OTLN
A-DETL-PATT-LITE
A-DETL-PATT-XLIT
A-DETL-TEXT

Supplement to AIA Document G612—2001

Owner's Instructions to the Architect for Construction Drawing Standards Part D

OWNER *(Name and address):*

Date:

Project Title:

Project Number:

ARCHITECT *(Name and address):*

NOTATION TO OWNER: Complete this form, which will provide your instructions regarding requirements for graphic Construction Documents (Drawings) for this Project. Please return the completed form to your Architect. After reviewing your instructions, the Architect will proceed with the preparation of the construction documents.

CONSTRUCTION DRAWING FORMAT

Construction drawings for this project are to be provided in accordance with:

☐ The U.S. National CAD Standard (NCS) version 3.1

☐ The U.S. National CAD Standard (NCS) version _____

☐ Architect's drawing standards

☐ Owner's drawing standards (attach)

☐ _____

1. **Drawing Set Organization**

(a) Subset Organization *(select one):*

☐ CSI Uniform Drawing System: Drawing Set Organization Module; NCS version 3.1

☐ The U.S. National CAD Standard version _____

☐ Architect's subset organization standards

☐ Owner's subset organization standards (attach)

(b) Sheet Identification *(select as appropriate):*

☐ CSI Uniform Drawing System: Drawing Set Organization Module; NCS version 3.1

☐ Standard Sheet Identification

☐ Abbreviated Sheet Identification

☐ Standard or Abbreviated Sheet Identification (any one can be used)

☐ The U.S. National CAD Standard version _____

☐ Standard Sheet Identification

☐ Abbreviated Sheet Identification

☐ Standard or Abbreviated Sheet Identification (only one can be used)

☐ Architect's sheet identification standards

☐ Owner's sheet identification standards (attach)

(c) File Naming *(select one):*

☐ CSI Uniform Drawing System: Drawing Set Organization Module; NCS version 3.1

☐ The U.S. National CAD Standard version _____

☐ Architect's file-naming standards

☐ Owner's file-naming standards (attach)

(d) File Management *(select one):*

☐ CSI Uniform Drawing System: Drawing Set Organization Module; NCS version 3.1

☐ The U.S. National CAD Standard version _____

☐ Architect's file management standards

☐ Owner's file management standards (attach)

2. **Sheet Organization**

(a) Sheet Layout *(select one):*

☐ CSI Uniform Drawing System: Sheet Organization Module; NCS version 3.1

☐ The U.S. National CAD Standard version _____

☐ Architect's sheet layout standards

☐ Owner's sheet layout standards (attach)

(b) Sheet size(s) *(select as appropriate and indicate use):*

ANSI	ISO	Architectural	Uses
☐ **A** (8.5 × 11)	☐ **A4** (8.3 × 11.7)	☐ **A** (9 × 12)	_____
☐ **B** (11 × 17)	☐ **A3** (11.7 × 16.5)	☐ **B** (12 × 18)	_____
☐ **C** (17 × 22)	☐ **A2** (16.5 × 23.4)	☐ **C** (18 × 24)	_____
☐ **D** (22 × 34)	☐ **A1** (23.4 × 33.1)	☐ **D** (24 × 36)	_____

☐ E (34 × 44)   ☐ A0 (33.1 × 46.8)   ☐ E (36 × 48)   _____

☐ F (30 × 42)   _____

☐ Architect's sheet size standard

(c) Production Data Area *(select one):*

☐ CSI Uniform Drawing System: Sheet Organization Module; NCS version 3.1

☐ The U.S. National CAD Standard version _____

☐ Architect's sheet layout standards

☐ Owner's sheet layout standards (attach)

(d) Drawing Area Coordinate System and Drawing Block Identification *(select one):*

☐ CSI Uniform Drawing System: Sheet Organization Module; NCS version 3.1

☐ The U.S. National CAD Standard version _____

☐ Architect's drawing area coordinate system and drawing block identification standards

☐ Owner's drawing area coordinate system and drawing block identification standards (attach)

(e) Title Blocks *(select as appropriate):*

☐ CSI Uniform Drawing System: Sheet Organization Module; NCS version 3.1

☐ Vertical Text Format

☐ Horizontal Text Format

☐ Horizontal or Vertical Text Format (only one type can be used throughout the drawing set)

☐ The U.S. National CAD Standard version _____

☐ Architect's title block standards

☐ Owner's title block standards (attach)

(f) Cover Sheet *(select one):*

☐ CSI Uniform Drawing System: Sheet Organization Module; NCS version 3.1

☐ The U.S. National CAD Standard version _____

☐ Architect's cover sheet standards

☐ Owner's cover sheet standards (attach)

3. Schedules

☐ CSI Uniform Drawing System: Schedules Module; NCS version 3.1

☐ The U.S. National CAD Standard version _____

☐ Architect's schedules standards

☐ Owner's schedules standards (attach)

4. Drafting Conventions

☐ CSI Uniform Drawing System: Drafting Conventions Module; NCS version 3.1

☐ The U.S. National CAD Standard version _____

☐ Architect's drafting conventions standards

☐ Owner's drafting conventions standards (attach)

5. Terms and Abbreviations

☐ CSI Uniform Drawing System: Terms and Abbreviations Module; NCS version 3.1

☐ The U.S. National CAD Standard version _____

☐ Architect's terms and abbreviations standards

☐ Owner's terms and abbreviations standards (attach)

6. Symbols

☐ CSI Uniform Drawing System: Symbols Module; NCS version 3.1

☐ The U.S. National CAD Standard version _____

☐ Architect's drawing symbols standards

☐ Owner's drawing symbols standards (attach)

7. Notations

(a) Notations *(select one):*

☐ CSI Uniform Drawing System: Notations Module; NCS version 3.1

☐ The U.S. National CAD Standard version _____

☐ Architect's notations standards

☐ Owner's notations standards (attach)

(b) Notations in Drawing Block *(select one):*

☐ Reference Keynotes

☐ Description (text)

☐ Reference Keynotes and Description (text)

(c) Reference Keynote Display Format *(select as appropriate):*

☐ MasterFormat 2004

☐ XX XX XX.XX

☐ XX XXXX.XX

☐ XXXXXX.XX

☐ Match appearance in specifications

☐ MasterFormat 1995

8. **Code Conventions**

☐ CSI Uniform Drawing Standard: Code Conventions Module; NCS version 3.1

☐ The U.S. National CAD Standard version _____

☐ Architect's code convention standards

☐ Owner's code convention standards (attach)

9. **CAD Layer Guidelines**

☐ AIA CAD Layer Guidelines: US National CAD Standard version 3; NCS version 3.1

☐ The U.S. National CAD Standard version _____

☐ Architect's CAD layer standards

☐ Owner's CAD layer standards (attach)

10. **Plotting Guidelines**

☐ Tri-Service Plotting Guidelines: NCS version 3.1

☐ Architect's plotting standards

☐ Owner's plotting standards (attach)

Owner's Representative   By   Date

Glossary

The purpose of this Glossary is to provide a comprehensive list of terms to help the user better understand and implement the U.S. National CAD Standard (NCS). Most of the terms are from components of the NCS; those that are indicated with an asterisk (*) are those of the authors. Every effort has been made to provide terminology and definitions that are consistent with the NCS and the publications referenced by it. The index lists the pages on which the terms can be found throughout the text.

The first time one of the terms is used in this book, it appears in bold type to identify it as a term appearing here in the Glossary. Sources for definitions are indicated within parentheses. When different definitions were available, each has been included. Interpretations, definitions, and/or information provided by the authors are contained within square brackets ([ ]).

abbreviated sheet identification
[A two-character, optional sheet identification format consisting of the level 1 discipline designator followed by the sheet sequence number] (UDS Drawing Set Organization Module).

addenda
(1) Written or graphic instruments issued to clarify, revise, add to, or delete information in the procurement documents or in previous addenda. Typically, addenda are issued before the opening of bids/proposals (CSI Project Resource Manual). (2) Written or graphic instruments issued by the architect prior to the execution of the contract, which modify or interpret the bidding documents by additions, deletions, clarifications, or corrections (AIA Document A701-1997 Instructions to Bidders).

ad hoc task team
A task team established by and serving at the discretion of the NCS Project Committee Steering Committee, formed to investigate, explore, or address specific matters pertaining to the NCS (NCS Project Committee Rules of Governance).

American Institute of Architects (AIA)
[(1) Publisher of the CAD Layer Guidelines, which is a constituent document of the U.S. National CAD Standard. (2) One of the original contributing organizations listed on the U.S. National CAD Standard

Memorandum of Understanding. For more information about the AIA, visit www.aia.org.]

American National Standards Institute (ANSI)
[A nonprofit organization that administers and coordinates the U.S. voluntary standardization and conformity assessment system. For more information about ANSI, visit www.ansi.org.]

American Society for Testing and Materials International (ASTM)
[An international voluntary standards development organization for technical standards for materials, products, systems, and services. For more information about ASTM, visit www.astm.org.]

annotation
Text, dimensions, notes, sheet borders, detail references, and other elements on CAD drawings that do not represent physical aspects of a facility (AIA CAD Layer Guidelines).

assembly
A collection of elements and components that relate to each other and combine to form a whole construction object (UDS Introduction).

attribute
Data stored electronically about specific characteristics of a construction element (UDS Schedules Module).

axonometric drawing
A general term used to describe one of three methods of 3D projection: isometric, dimetric, and trimetric; all three methods represent two vertical and one horizontal plane parallel to corresponding established axes at true dimensions (UDS Drafting Conventions Module).

break line
A line used to indicate the cut between two parts or levels (UDS Drafting Conventions Module).

building information model (BIM)
A computable representation of the physical and functional characteristics of a facility and its related project/life-cycle information using open industry standards to inform business decision making for realizing better value. BIM can integrate all the relevant aspects into a coherent organization of data that computer applications can access, modify and/or add to, if authorized to do so (www.nibs.org). See also **building information modeling.**

building information modeling (BIM)
[Computer-aided approach to facility design, which includes integrated information about design, construction, management, schedule, and cost]. See also **building information model.**

building model
An electronic representation of a building (UDS Drawing Set Organization Module). See also **building information model** and **building information modeling.**

Business Management Group. See NCS Business Management Group.

CAD
(1) Computer-aided drafting (UDS Introduction). (2) Acronym for computer-aided design (or drawing) (NCS Administration). [CAD (not CADD) is the preferred term used in the UDS Modules and the CAD Layer Guidelines.]

CADD
Computer-aided design and drafting (UDS Introduction). See also **CAD.**

CADD/GIS Technology Center (CGTC)
[(1) Publisher of the Plotting Guidelines, which is a constituent document of the U.S. National CAD Standard. (2) One of the original contributing organizations listed on the U.S. National CAD Standard Memorandum of Understanding. (3) Organization formed under the authority of the U.S. Army, Navy, and Air Force to coordinate and promote CAD, geographic information systems, and facilities management technology applications. The complete name of the CGTC is the CADD/GIS Technology Center for Facilities, Infrastructure and Environment. Formerly known as the Tri-Service CADD/GIS Technology Center, the CGTC also provided input during the creation of the UDS Drafting Conventions Module. For more information about the CGTC, visit http://tsc.wes.army.mil.]

CAD file
An electronic computer file containing CAD data entities, which can be changed and manipulated by a CAD software program (NCS Administration).

CAD Layer Guidelines (CLG)
(1) Standard created by the AIA that provides formats for the organization and visual display of CAD information and allows the information to be converted to print media (AIA CAD Layer Guidelines). (2) A data classification system for organizing electronic building data, specifically addressing the names of CAD data files and the names of layers within CAD data files (NCS Introduction). [(3) A constituent document of the U.S. National CAD Standard.]

CAD layer-naming office master*
[A list of CAD layer names used to create CAD library files that are used as templates for the initial setup of each sheet type used in the drawing set.]

centerline
A thin line interrupted at intervals by a dot, used to indicate the center of a column, beam, wall, or opening (UDS Drafting Conventions Module).

column identifier
(1) Columns containing subject titles that define specific information required for each line item listed in the schedule (UDS Schedules Module). [(2) The numerical designator that identifies a column within the drawing area coordinate system.]

column subidentifier
Column(s) that give additional titles for more detailed information to be provided under a subject in the column identifier in a schedule (UDS Schedules Module).

compliant
[Meeting the requirements of the U.S. National CAD Standard.]

construction document(s)

(1) The written and graphic documents prepared or assembled by the A/E for communicating the project design for construction and administering the construction contract. (2) Documents that define the rights of, responsibilities of, and relationships among the parties to the contract (CSI Project Resource Manual). (3) Drawings and specifications that establish in detail the quality levels of materials and systems required for the project (AIA Document B141 Standard Form of Agreement Between Owner and Architect).

construction drawing(s)

Contract drawings and resource drawings (CSI Project Resource Manual).

Construction Specifications Canada (CSC)

[A multidisciplinary, nonprofit association dedicated to the improvement of communication, contract documentation, and technical information in the construction industry. For more information, visit www.csc-dcc.ca.]

Construction Specifications Institute (CSI)

[(1) Publisher of the Uniform Drawing System (UDS), which is a constituent document of the U.S. National CAD Standard. (2) One of the original contributing organizations listed on the U.S. National CAD Standard Memorandum of Understanding. For more information about CSI, visit www. csinet.org.]

Consultative Council

[An organization consisting of elected members of the National Institute of Building Sciences (NIBS), the chairs of NIBS councils and committees, and a NIBS board member chair; established by NIBS to oversee various NIBS programs, projects, councils, and committees, including the NCS Project Committee.] (www.nibs.org)

contract document(s)

Drawings that describe the work of a project (UDS Drawing Set Organization Module).

contributing organizations

Those organizations having an ownership interest in the intellectual property embodied in the NCS (NCS Project Committee Rules of Governance).

cover sheet

A sheet located in front of all other sheets in the drawing set. The cover sheet may identify the project, owner, and other project team members involved in preparing the drawings; it may also contain a photograph, rendering of the project, or logo of the owner or preparer (UDS Sheet Organization Module).

cross-referencing

A system for tracking information from the general to the specific within a drawing set. Items on a drawing that require additional clarification are provided with a cross-reference to another drawing or view on another sheet (UDS Drafting Conventions Module).

dash (-)

[(1) The delimiter that separates the discipline designator from the sheet type designator in the Level 1 and Level 2 sheet identification. Also known as a *hyphen*. (2) The delimiter that separates each data field in the CAD layer name. (3) a character of the field preceding it in an NCS layer name that conceptually conforms with ISO 13567. (4) A placeholder for an unused field in a CAD layer name that conforms with ISO 13567. (AIA CAD Layer Guidelines) (5) The delimiter that separates the sheet sequence number from the user-defined designator and supplemental drawing number in sheet identification (UDS Drawing Set Organization Module); See also **hyphen**.

database files

Database files that include tables that define and label fields (columns) of data (UDS Sheet Organization Module).

database table(s)

Database files that include tables. Examples of database tables are schedules used in construction documents, inventory listings for equipment and furnishings, master keynote listings, and numerous other lists or tabulations (UDS Drawing Set Organization Module).

data block(s)

Modules within the title block area that consist of the designer identification block, project identification block, issue block, management block, sheet title block, and the sheet identification block (UDS Sheet Organization Module).

data field

[(1) A component of the CAD layer-naming format; There are a maximum of four types of data fields in a CAD layer name: the discipline designator, major group, (two) minor groups, and the status (or phase) field. (AIA CAD Layer Guidelines) See also **field code.** (2) A component of the issue or management block, as part of the sheet title block. (UDS Sheet Organization Module)]

description cell
Part of a schedule that contains specific information required by the column identifier and column subidentifier related to each item referenced in the row identifier (UDS Schedules Module).

designer identification block
The data block in the title block area that identifies the designer or preparer of the sheet (UDS Sheet Organization Module).

detail
Plans, elevations, or sections that provide more specific information about a portion of a project component or element than smaller-scale drawings (UDS Introduction).

detail file
An electronic file that is a specific type of model file. Detail files form the majority of the individual files in a project (UDS Drawing Set Organization Module).

diagram
(1) Nonscaled views showing arrangements of special system components and connections not possible to show clearly in scaled views (UDS Introduction). (2) Graphic representations that usually are not drawn to scale but can be noted with dimensions (UDS Drafting Conventions Module).

dimension line
Thin line connecting extension lines, defining the beginning and end of the object being dimensioned (UDS Drafting Conventions Module).

dimetric drawing
An axonometric drawing that simulates a true perspective by projecting the three planes at different angles and scales, and with parallel front and back verticals (UDS Drafting Conventions Module).

discipline
[(1) A category of technical design subject matter. (2) One of the subsets of sheets that makes up a drawing set] (UDS Drawing Set Organization Module).

discipline character
[The character used to identify the Level 1 discipline designator.]

discipline designator
(1) The first component of the sheet identification format, based on the traditional system of alphabetical discipline designators (UDS Drawing Set Organization Module). (2) Two-character data field that denotes the category of subject matter contained on the specified CAD layer; or the category of subject matter contained in the file or layer designated (AIA CAD Layer Guidelines).

discipline set
[One of the subsets of sheets that makes up a drawing set. See also **discipline.**] (UDS Drawing Set Organization Module).

distinguishing feature
A column for identifying some notable characteristics in a schedule. A distinguishing feature is one of four mandatory parts schedules must contain (UDS Schedules Module).

division
MasterFormat classification number (Level 1 number) for the broadest collection of related construction products and activities (MasterFormat 2004).

drawing(s)
(1) Graphic and textual information organized on a two-dimensional surface for the purpose of conveying data about a specific portion of a project (UDS Introduction and UDS Notations Module). (2) Graphic and pictorial portions of the documents showing the design, location, and dimensions of the project, and generally including plans, elevations, sections, details, schedules, and diagrams (NCS Introduction). (3) Graphic and pictorial portions of the contract documents showing the design, location, and dimensions of the work and generally including plans, elevations, sections, details, schedules, and diagrams (AIA Document A201-1997 General Conditions of the Contract for Construction).

drawing area
The portion of the sheet containing drawings, keynotes, key plans, schedules, and other graphic and text data necessary to illustrate the work (UDS Sheet Organization Module).

drawing area coordinate system
[A grid consisting of columns, rows, and identifiers that organizes the drawing area into modules] (UDS Drafting Conventions Module).

drawing block(s)
Drawing modules containing graphic or textual information (UDS Sheet Organization Module and UDS Notations Module).

drawing module
[A cell within the sheet's drawing area created by the columns and rows of the drawing area coordinate system] (UDS Drafting Conventions Module).

drawing set
[The set of sheets included in the contract documents.]

drawing sheet
[A sheet in the drawing set. See also **sheet**.]

drawing users
The changing group of individuals and organizations that participate in a project at various points during the facility cycle (UDS Introduction).

elevations
Views of vertical planes, showing components in their vertical relationship, viewed perpendicularly from a selected vertical plane (UDS Introduction).

extension line
Line leading to the start and finish of the dimension (UDS Drafting Conventions Module).

facility
A physical structure or group of structures, including site construction, serving one or more purposes (UDS Introduction).

facility cycle
Stages during the useful life of a facility, beginning with inception, including changes over time, and eventually ending in reuse or demolition (UDS Introduction).

Facility Information Council (FIC)
[A volunteer organization formed by the National Institute of Building Sciences to improve the performance of the life cycle of facilities by fostering a common integrated life-cycle information model for the A/E/C industry, developing standards that allow for the free flow of graphic and nongraphic information through the information model; and coordinating U.S. efforts with related activities taking place internationally. For more information, visit www. nibs.org.] (www.nibs.org)

facility life cycle
See **facility cycle**.

facility model
All information created relating to a particular facility (UDS Introduction).

field code
[A single or multi-character abbreviation or identifier that represents the information included in one of the data fields of the CAD layer-naming format. See also **data field**.] (AIA CAD Layer Guidelines)

fundamental concepts
[One of the two general categories of NCS content subjected to modification during the NCS revision cycle. Fundamental concepts are the broader formats, methodologies, and organizing and classification principles used by each of the NCS components to establish overall requirements.] Also known as *fundamental concepts of data organization and classification*. See also **prescribed data** (NCS Rules of Governance)

general discipline note
A note that applies only to a particular design discipline (UDS Notations Module).

general notations*
[The combined group of general notes, general discipline notes, and general sheet notes.]

general note
A note that applies to the entire work. As such, general notes apply equally to all disciplines and to all sheets within the drawing set (UDS Notations Module).

general sheet note
A note that applies only to the particular sheet on which it appears (UDS Notations Module).

graphic and notation area
Component of the drawing block containing graphics and notes (UDS Drafting Conventions Module).

grid designator
[The symbol used to identify grid lines. Also known as the *grid indicator* or the *grid line indicator* (UDS Drafting Conventions Module)].

grid indicator
See **grid designator**.

grid line
Line used to indicate structural columns, load-bearing walls, shear walls, and other structural elements on the drawings; used as a basis for dimensioning (UDS Drafting Conventions Module).

grid line indicator
See **grid designator.**

grid system
The grid lines and symbols used to indicate structural columns, load-bearing walls, shear walls, and other structural elements on the drawings (UDS Drafting Conventions Module).

hatching
Patterns of repetitive lines, dots, or figures used to indicate specific types of materials or to designate specific areas (UDS Drafting Conventions Module).

heading
Part of a schedule that contains the subject or title of the schedule. Headings are one of four mandatory parts schedules must contain (UDS Schedules Module).

heading bar
[Component of a note block under which notations are located. Each of the five types of notations located in a note block appears under the appropriate heading bar.]

hidden line
Line that represents items obscured from view by another material (UDS Drafting Conventions Module).

horizontal text format
Format where title block text is oriented parallel to the bottom of the sheet (UDS Sheet Organization Module).

hyphen (-)
[(1) The delimiter that separates the discipline designator from the sheet type designator in the Level 1 and Level 2 sheet identification. Also known as a *dash.* (2) The placeholder that separates the discipline designator from the file type characters in the model file name. (3) The placeholder that separates the sheet identification from the detail identification number in the detail file name] (UDS Drawing Set Organization Module). See also **dash.**

identity symbol
Abstract representations of an item, for example, an electrical outlet. Identity symbols are scale-dependent (UDS Symbols Module).

index
See **legend.**

International Building Code (IBC)
[Model code published by the International Code Council. For more information, visit www.iccsafe.org.]

International Organization for Standardization (ISO)
[Nongovernmental network of the national standards institutes of 148 countries, on the basis of one member per country. For more information, visit www.iso.org.]

ISO 128-20
Technical Drawings—General Principles of Presentation—Part 20: Basic Conventions for Lines, published by the International Standards Organization. (www.iso.org)

ISO 13567
Organization and Naming of Layers for CAD, published by the International Standards Organization. (www.iso.org)

isometric drawing
An axonometric drawing with all three axes at 120 degrees relative to each other (UDS Drafting Conventions Module).

issue block
The portion of the title block area that shows the chronological issue of, and revisions to, the sheet (UDS Sheet Organization Module).

item description
A column for the description of an item in a schedule. Item descriptions are one of four mandatory parts schedules must contain (UDS Schedules Module).

key
See **legend.**

key plan
[A simplified small-scale plan used to indicate the relationship among the elements of complex projects, or when the size of the project requires two or more drawings to illustrate the elements.]

key plan block
The lowest module or modules within the note block, where key plans are located (UDS Sheet Organization Module).

large-scale view
A view of a plan, elevation, or section at a larger scale and with more detail than the referenced view (UDS Introduction).

layer
CAD software function that allows design information to be organized in a systematic fashion, facilitates the visual display of the information on a computer screen, and makes it possible to con-

vert the information efficiently to the conventional print media of drawings (AIA CAD Layer Guidelines).

layer name data field
See data field.

leader
Line that connects a note, dimension, or symbol to a point or item in a drawing (UDS Drafting Conventions Module).

legend
A list of paired items. Also known as a *key, list,* or *index.* Legends are not schedules (UDS Schedules Module).

library file
(1) An electronic file that is used as a source of information for more than one project. (2) A drawing category for generic drawings and master sheet or template files, used many times (UDS Drawing Set Organization Module).

limit of construction lines
Lines that define the area of work beyond which the contractor is not allowed to execute any work (UDS Drafting Conventions Module).

line symbol
A symbol that indicates a continuous object with either single or double lines. Examples of line symbols include walls drawn with two lines and ducts drawn with one or two lines based on the scale of the drawing (UDS Symbols Module).

linking
[The process of connecting elements in a document to referenced items.]

list
See **legend**.

magnetic north
Compass point deviating slightly from true north and plan north (UDS Drafting Conventions Module).

major group
Four-character field in a CAD layer name that identifies a major building system (AIA CAD Layer Guidelines).

management block
The portion of the title block area that contains the management information generally used for project filing, record keeping, or other project management information (UDS Sheet Organization Module).

mark
A column identifying an item in a schedule. A mark is one of four mandatory parts schedules must contain (UDS Schedules Module).

MasterFormat
A master list of numbers and titles classified by work results or construction practices used primarily to organize project manuals, detailed cost information, and relate drawing notations to specifications sections (MasterFormat 2004).

match line
Line that delineates the division between two or more areas of a continuous structure that must be shown on separate sheets because of sheet size limitations (UDS Drafting Conventions Module).

material symbol
A symbol that portrays a material graphically in plan, elevation, or section; a graphic representation of concrete is an example. Material symbols are drawn to scale (UDS Symbols Module).

Memorandum of Agreement (MOA)
[Officially referred to as the "Agreement for Publication and Distribution of the U.S. National CAD Standard (NCS)," the MOA was signed on June 12, 2003, by the CSI, NIBS, and AIA. It established the legal parameters for publication and distribution of the NCS. The MOA replaced the 1997 MOU (memorandum of understanding) and clarified intellectual property rights to allow NIBS to enter into licensing agreements with software developers to incorporate the content of the NCS directly into software applications. The MOA also included provisions for an electronic edition accessible to users on their computers via single-user, workgroup, and companywide licenses.]

Memorandum of Understanding (MOU)
[The agreement establishing the U.S. National CAD Standard, signed in 1997 by NIBS, AIA, CSI, Tri-Services CADD/GIS Technology Center, SMACNA, USCG, and GSA. For more information, visit www.nibs.org/ficcommf.html.]

minor group
Optional, four-character field in a CAD layer name used to further define the major groups (AIA CAD Layer Guidelines).

mock-up drawing set
[Manually sketched or CAD-generated drawing set, at a reduced scale, representing all the project sheets required for a set of the construction drawings and used in the planning of the entire drawing

set by assigning graphic and textual information to specific sheets in the construction document set, in accordance with standards established in the Uniform Drawing System]. Also known as the *mock-up set, cartoon set, story book set,* and *mini-set* (UDS Drafting Conventions Module). See also **mock-up sheets.**

mock-up sheets

Small-scale sheets developed prior to production used to determine the set organization and sheet layout. Individual mock-up sheets are developed as a miniature of each proposed sheet in the drawing set (UDS Sheet Organization Module). See also **mock-up drawing set.**

mock-up worksheet

A form used to estimate the total number of drawings and the total amount of production time required to develop a comprehensive drawing set (UDS Drafting Conventions Module).

model code

A written set of regulations that provides the means for exercising reasonable control over construction. A model code is available for adoption by cities, counties, states, or countries, with such changes as may be desirable or legal to meet local needs (UDS Code Conventions Module).

modification drawings

Supplemental drawings (UDS Drawing Set Organization Module).

modifier character

The second character of a two-character discipline designator, used to further subdivide the discipline for a specific use or purpose (UDS Drawing Set Organization Module).

National CAD Standard (NCS)

See **U.S. National CAD Standard.**

National CAD Standard Project Committee (NCSPC)

See **U.S. National CAD Standard Project Committee.**

National Institute of Building Sciences (NIBS)

[A nonprofit, nongovernmental organization authorized by the U.S. Congress in the Housing and Community Development Act of 1974 (Public Law 93-383). NIBS was established to serve as an authoritative source and interface between government and the private sector to improve facility construction regulations, facilitate the introduction of new and existing products and technology into

the facility construction process, and disseminate nationally recognized technical and regulatory information. For more information about NIBS, visit www.nibs.org.]

NCS

See **U.S. National CAD Standard (NCS).**

NCS Business Management Group

[The group that manages the business affairs of the NCS. The Business Management Group consists of one staff member of each of the NCS contributing organizations. Also known as the **Business Management Group.** (NCS Rules of Governance)

NCS Project Committee (NCSPC)

See **U.S. National CAD Standard Project Committee (NCSPC).**

NCS revision cycle

See **revision cycle.**

NCS Rules of Governance (ROG)

See **U.S. National CAD Standard Project Committee Rules of Governance (ROG).**

NIBS consensus process

Procedures used by the NCS Project Committee to oversee the U.S. National CAD Standard for NCS versions 1.0, 2.0, and 3.0. The NIBS consensus process was replaced by the NCS Project Committee Rules of Governance after NCS version 3.0 (NCS Appendix E).

noncompliant

[Failure to meet the requirements of the U.S. National CAD Standard.]

nonpreferred term

[A term or terminology that should be avoided; a noncompliant term.]

nonscaled view

Diagrams, 3D representations, and schedules (UDS Schedules Module).

notation

A drawing note; textual information on drawings (UDS Notations Module).

notations coordinator*

[The person responsible for maintaining the sheet keynote and reference keynote process used in the workplace.]

note block

(1) The module or modules within the drawing area where keynotes, general notes, and key plans are

located. The note block is located in the far right column of the drawing area (UDS Sheet Organization Module). (2) Module or modules where general notations, keynotes, and key plans are located (UDS Notations Module).

notes column
A special type of distinguishing feature column used in schedules to locate special remarks about items that do not necessarily warrant their own separate column identifier. Notes columns are usually located at the far right side of the schedule (UDS Schedules Module).

notes legend
A column in a schedule that uses a key letter or number that cross-references a general note located elsewhere; the note may also cross-reference other drawings or specification items. Notes legends are used to reduce the width of a notes column (UDS Schedules Module).

object symbol
A symbol that resembles the actual item being objectified; for example, items such as furniture and toilet fixtures. These symbols are drawn to scale (UDS Symbols Module).

object linking and embedding (OLE)
[A software technology that allows elements from different applications to be linked within each other. OLE allows objects like tables and spreadsheets to be linked or inserted (format intact) from other software (UDS Drawing Set Organization Module).

oblique drawing
An axonometric drawing that is similar to a diametric drawing, except that one plane is parallel to the drawing plane (UDS Drafting Conventions Module).

PageFormat
A format for an orderly and uniform arrangement of text on the pages of a specifications section contained in a project manual (UDS Introduction).

perspective
Drawings represented by parallel lines that meet at a vanishing point located at the horizon to give a structure a true image; similar to a photograph (UDS Drafting Conventions Module).

plan
A view of a horizontal plane, showing components in their horizontal relationship (UDS Introduction).

plan north
A reference point parallel to the plan grid (UDS Drafting Conventions Module).

plot file
(1) An electronic file that results from CAD software, using a specific plotter or printer device driver (UDS Drawing Set Organization Module). (2) An electronic computer file containing information necessary to print one drawing sheet formatted for output to a printing or plotting device no longer stored in its native CAD file format (NCS Administration).

plotter time and date block
The portion of the production data area where the time and date of the plot are located (UDS Sheet Organization Module).

preferred term
[A term or terminology that is NCS-compliant.]

preparer
Registered and unregistered designers, manufacturers, contractors, material suppliers, and others (UDS Sheet Organization Module).

prescribed data
[One of the two general categories of NCS content subjected to modification during the NCS revision cycle. Prescribed data is a specific, formatted result that has been created in compliance with the broader, organizational and classification concepts of the NCS.] See also **fundamental concepts** (NCS Rules of Governance).

procurement drawings
Drawings issued for bidding or negotiating before signing of an agreement (UDS Drawing Set Organization Module).

production block
The portion of the production data area that contains management information concerning the production of the sheet (UDS Sheet Organization Module).

production data area
(1) The portion of the sheet containing information on the production of the sheet. (2) An optional portion of the sheet that contains information on the production of the sheet (UDS Sheet Organization Module).

project
(1) A set of related activities taking place in, around, and in connection with a facility (UDS

Introduction). (2) The total construction of which the work performed under the contract documents may be the whole or a part, and which may include construction by the owner or by separate contractors (AIA Document A201-1997 General Conditions of the Contract for Construction).

project cycle

Comprises the stages of a project, which include planning and predesign activities, design and construction documents, bidding/negotiation, construction, and postconstruction activities (UDS Introduction).

project file

(1) [An electronic file that is specific to a project.] (2) Drawing category for project-specific drawings and sheets—used once (UDS Drawing Set Organization Module).

project folder

Component of computer operating system where project files are located. Also known as a *directory* (UDS Drawing Set Organization Module).

project identification block

The data block in the title block area that identifies the project (UDS Sheet Organization Module).

project manual

(1) The bound volume of contract documents that may include the procurement requirements, contracting requirements, and specifications (CSI Project Resource Manual). (2) A volume assembled for the work, which may include the bidding requirements, sample forms, conditions of the contract, and specifications (AIA Document A201-1997 General Conditions of the Contract for Construction).

Project Resource Manual (PRM)

A reference document published by CSI that covers a wide range of information for those involved in the design and construction processes. The PRM is intended to supplement and complement reference material prepared by other document producers, such as the AIA, the Design-Build Institute of America, the Associated General Contractors of America, and the Engineers Joint Contract Documents Committee (CSI Project Resource Manual).

property line

Line interrupted by double dots to indicate the boundary of the site (UDS Drafting Conventions Module).

reference grid and dimension area

Component of the drawing block containing reference grids and dimensions (UDS Drafting Conventions Module).

reference keynote

A note that identifies graphic representations of items and directly references them to specific sections in the specifications (UDS Notations Module).

reference keynote modifier

An optional, user-defined descriptive text note located within parentheses beneath the reference keynote symbol in the drawing block. A modifier is used to reduce the amount of unique keynotes required to identify variations in the size, number, spacing, or other feature of an object or material, where that object or material might be shown elsewhere on the drawing in different configurations (UDS Notations Module).

reference keynote office master

A comprehensive standard listing of reference keynotes established by the user (UDS Notations Module).

reference symbol

A symbol that refers to another part of the documentation. Examples of reference symbols include partition type symbol, section cuts, and elevation references (UDS Symbols Module).

resource drawing

A drawing that shows existing conditions, or new construction related to the work, but is not included in the contract (UDS Drawing Set Organization Module).

revision cycle

[The time period of the ballot process established by the NCS Project Committee Rules of Governance to amend the U.S. National CAD Standard] (NCS Rules of Governance). Also known as the **NCS revision cycle**

root

A component of the reference keynote symbol consisting of the specification section number corresponding to the section number location where the object or material is specified (UDS Notations Module).

row identifier

(1) Part of a schedule that contains the mark or other identifier of the item (project, material, or assembly). The mark is used as a reference to locate

the item on the drawings or in the specifications (UDS Schedules Module). [(2) The alphabetic designator that identifies a column within the drawing area coordinate system.]

Rules of Governance (ROG)
See **U.S. National CAD Standard Project Committee Rules of Governance (ROG).**

scale
The ratio of measuring units expressing a proportional relationship between a drawing and the full-size item it represents (UDS Drafting Conventions Module).

scale-dependent
Actual printed size (of a symbol), which depends on the scale of the drawing or view of the model (UDS Symbols Module).

scale-independent
Actual printed size (of a symbol), which is consistent no matter what the drawing scale; (size of the symbol) is related only to clarity and interpretation (UDS Symbols Module).

scaled views
Plans, elevations, sections, large-scale plans, and details (UDS Drafting Conventions Module).

scanning scale block
The portion of the production data area that contains a graphical scale that may be used if the sheet is to be scanned, photographically reduced, or microfilmed (UDS Sheet Organization Module).

schedule
(1) Tables or charts that include data about materials, products, and equipment (UDS Introduction). (2) A grouping of related items with corresponding distinguishing features, with a heading and a minimum of three columns of related information. A schedule formats information into rows and columns in order to more easily present design information (UDS Schedules Module). (3) Schedules provide a consistent format for representing a related group of items that are keyed to the drawings and, in addition to the headings, are divided into at least three main columns (UDS Drafting Conventions Module).

schedule file
A schedule produced by computer software, including CAD, word processing, spreadsheets, and database applications (UDS Schedules Module).

section
Views of vertical cuts through and perpendicular to components, showing their detailed arrangement (UDS Introduction).

SectionFormat
A format that provides a uniform approach to organizing specification text contained in a project manual by establishing a structure consisting of three primary parts (UDS Introduction).

sheet
As a delivery medium, the document sheet is the hard copy representation of information presented on a vellum or mylar "original" or "tracing"; in an electronic media sense, the document sheet is the screen window (UDS Introduction).

sheet file
An electronic CAD file comprised of a border template (a file that contains graphic and text elements common to all sheets of a specific size), text, symbols, and views of files, representing everything that appears on the final sheet (UDS Drawing Set Organization Module).

sheet identification
[The format used to identify sheets consisting of either the standard sheet identification format or the abbreviated sheet identification format] (UDS Drawing Set Organization Module).

sheet identification block
The portion of the title block area that contains the sheet identifier (UDS Sheet Organization Module).

sheet keynote
A note that identifies, informs, and instructs without reference to the specifications (UDS Notations Module).

sheet keynote office master*
[A comprehensive standard listing of sheet keynotes established by the user.]

Sheet Metal and Air Conditioning Contractors' National Association (SMACNA)
[One of the original contributing organizations listed on the U.S. National CAD Standard Memorandum of Understanding. For more information about SMACNA, visit www.smacna.org.]

sheet sequence number
A component of the sheet identification format used to identify each sheet in a series of the same discipline and sheet type. In standard sheet identification

format, the sheet sequence number consists of two numerical characters beginning with 01; in abbreviated sheet format, the sheet sequence number consists of one numerical character beginning with 1 (UDS Drawing Set Organization Module).

sheet title block
The portion of the title block area that indicates the type of information presented on the sheet (UDS Sheet Organization Module).

sheet type designator
[A component of the standard sheet identification format, consisting of a single numerical character that corresponds to a specific type of drawing view appearing on a sheet] (UDS Drawing Set Organization Module).

specifications
(1) The qualitative requirements for products, materials, and workmanship on which the construction contract is based (UDS Notations Module). Specifications define the requirements for products, materials, and workmanship, on which the contract is based, and requirements for administration and performance of the project; they are generally written for each subject as sections and organized by divisions under MasterFormat or by categories under UniFormat (CSI Project Resource Manual). (2) That portion of the contract documents consisting of the written requirements for materials, equipment, systems, standards, and workmanship for the work, and performance of related services (AIA Document A201-1997 General Conditions of the Contract for Construction).

standard
A published technical document that represents an industry consensus as to how a material or assembly is to be designed, manufactured, tested, or installed so that a specific level of performance can be obtained (UDS Code Conventions Module).

standard sheet identification
Format used to identify sheets consisting of the discipline designator, the hyphen, the sheet type designator, and the sheet sequence number (UDS Drawing Set Organization Module).

standing task team
A task team established by and serving at the discretion of the NCS Project Committee Steering Committee to oversee a particular subset of the existing content of the NCS (NCS Project Committee Rules of Governance).

status
(1) One of the four defined CAD layer name data fields. (2) An optional single-character field in the CAD layer name that distinguishes the data contained on the layer according to the status of the work or the construction phase (AIA CAD Layer Guidelines).

Steering Committee
Members of the NCS Project Committee appointed by the chair of the NCS Project Committee, consisting of the Project Committee chair, vice chair, secretary, and no fewer than five and no more than nine additional NCS Project Committee members, who serve at the discretion of the Project Committee chair. The chair of the Project Committee heads the Steering Committee (NCS Project Committee Rules of Governance).

subset
[Group of sheets categorized according to a common discipline.]

suffix
User-defined, mandatory component of the reference keynote symbol, consisting of a capital letter following the decimal point, which allows multiple keynotes to reference the same specification section. The letters I and O are not used, as they may be confused with the numbers 1 and 0 (UDS Notations Module).

suffix modifier
Optional, user-defined numeric characters following the suffix in the reference keynote and used to create numerous unique reference keynotes that would otherwise be limited to the available letters of the alphabet; suffix modifiers should always include two numerical characters. Suffix modifiers can be customized as needed to further differentiate among related or similar items with different attributes (size, color, thickness, etc.) (UDS Notations Module).

supplemental drawing
(1) A drawing prepared during the construction phase to further illustrate portions of the project. (2) A drawing or sketch that supplements the contract documents (CSI Project Resource Manual).

supplemental drawing sheet
See **supplemental drawing.**

symbol
A graphic representation of an item or material by association, resemblance, or convention. A symbol

often represents a material or object not fully illustrated on the drawings (UDS Symbols Module).

task teams
Subcommittees established by and serving at the discretion of the NCS Project Committee Steering Committee. There are two types of task teams: standing task teams and ad hoc task teams (NCS Project Committee Rules of Governance).

terminator
Short, slanted line (slash) that defines the junction between a dimension line and the extension lines leading to the start and finish of the dimension (UDS Drafting Conventions Module).

text file
(1) A computer file that contains general notes, discipline specific notes, sheet type specific notes, and symbol legends. Text files are usually created with a word processor or database software (UDS Drawing Set Organization Module). [(2) An electronic file that holds text, where each byte represents English characters as numbers, according to the American Standard Code for Information Interchange (ASCII); text files are identified with a .txt suffix.]

text symbol
A symbol that graphically indicates a word or words and may be used in notations on drawings (UDS Symbols Module).

three-dimensional (3D) representations
Perspectives, isometric drawings, and electronic CAD models (UDS Introduction). See also **three-dimensional (3D) views.**

three-dimensional (3D) views
Axonometric drawings, oblique drawings, perspectives, and photographs used to assist the viewer in comprehending complex 3D relationships of shapes (UDS Drafting Conventions Module). See also **three-dimensional representations.**

tier
[A row of column subidentifiers used in a schedule.]

title area
[Component of the drawing block that contains the drawing block title, graphic scale, and text scale.]

title block area
The portion of the sheet containing project, client, designer, sheet identification, and sheet management information needed by the user of the sheet (UDS Sheet Organization Module).

trimetric drawing
[An axonometric drawing that simulates a true perspective by projecting the three planes at different angles and scales, and with front and back verticals that are not parallel.]

Tri-Service CADD/GIS Technology Center
See **CADD GIS Technology Center.**

true north
Compass direction that points to the north pole (UDS Drafting Conventions Module).

Underwriters Laboratories, Inc. (UL)
[A not-for-profit corporation that provides testing and certification of industrial and commercial products. For more information about UL, visit www.ul.com.]

UniFormat
A classification system for construction information based on construction elements, including systems and assemblies that perform a given function without regard to the design solution, specified material, or construction method (UDS Introduction).

Uniform Drawing System (UDS)
(1) Interrelated modules consisting of standards, guidelines, and other tools for the organization and presentation of drawing information used for the planning, design, construction, and operation of facilities (UDS Introduction). [(2) A constituent document of the U.S. National CAD Standard published by the Construction Specifications Institute.]

Uniform Drawing System Program Task Team (UDSPTT)
[A volunteer committee established by the Construction Specifications Institute to develop and maintain the Uniform Drawing System.]

U.S. Coast Guard (USCG)
[One of the original contributing organizations listed on the U.S. National CAD Standard Memorandum of Understanding. The USCG developed the Plotting Guidelines, a constituent document of the U.S. National CAD Standard. For more information about the USCG, visit www.uscg.mil.]

user
See **drawing users.**

user-defined
[At the discretion of the originator, or preparer, of the sheet.]

U.S. General Services Administration (GSA)

[One of the original contributing organizations listed on the U.S. National CAD Standard Memorandum of Understanding. For more information about the GSA, visit www.gsa.gov.]

U.S. National CAD Standard (NCS)

(1) A CAD standard established to advance the art and science of design, construction, management, operation, and maintenance of the vertical and horizontal built environment by providing a means of organizing and classifying electronic design data and thereby fostering streamlined communication among owners, designers, material suppliers, constructors, and facility managers (NCS Rules of Governance). (2) Interrelated modules consisting of standards, guidelines, and tools for the organization and presentation of drawing information used for the planning, design, construction, and operation of facilities (UDS Introduction). (3) A CAD standard established to assist in classifying electronic design data consistently, to streamline and simplify the exchange of data within the design and construction industry, and to illustrate the appropriate presentation of two-dimensional graphic standards (NCS Administration). The complete name of the NCS is the U.S. National CAD Standard for Architecture, Engineering, and Construction (A/E/C) (NCS Administration).

U.S. National CAD Standard Project Committee (NCSPC)

[An NIBS committee, consisting of volunteers representing public- and private-interest categories from the construction industry, that oversees the development and maintenance of the U.S. National CAD Standard, operating under the oversight of the NIBS Consultative Council. More commonly known as the National CAD Standard Project Committee (NCSPC).] (U.S. National CAD Standard Project Committee Rules of Governance)

U.S. National CAD Standard Project Committee Rules of Governance (ROG)

[The procedures used by the NCS Project Committee to oversee and maintain the U.S. National CAD Standard. More commonly known as the Rules of Governance (ROG) or the NCSPC Rules of Governance (ROG). The ROG replaced the NIBS consensus process after NCS version 3.0.] (U.S. National CAD Standard Project Committee Rules of Governance)

vertical text format

Title block text is oriented parallel to the right side of the sheet; the sheet identification block, the sheet title block, and the management block are always oriented horizontally (UDS Sheet Organization Module).

zoning ordinance

A system that regulates the use and development of property within a municipality or county (UDS Code Conventions Module).

BIBLIOGRAPHY

American Institute of Architects. *AIA Document A201-1997: General Conditions of the Contract for Construction.* Washington, DC: American Institute of Architects, 1997.

———. *AIA CAD Layer Guidelines: U.S. National CAD Standard Version 3.* Washington, DC: American Institute of Architects, 2005.

Construction Specifications Institute. *The Project Resource Manual.* Alexandria, VA: Construction Specifications Institute, 2004.

———. *MasterFormat 1995.* Alexandria, VA: Construction Specifications Institute, 1995.

———. *MasterFormat 2004.* Alexandria, VA: Construction Specifications Institute, 2004.

———. *SectionFormat.* Alexandria, VA: Construction Specifications Institute.

———. *UniFormat.* Alexandria, VA: Construction Specifications Institute, 1998.

———. *PageFormat.* Alexandria, VA: Construction Specifications Institute, 2001.

———. *Uniform Drawing System.* Alexandria, VA: Construction Specifications Institute, 1999–2004.

Tri-Services CADD/GIS Technology Center. *Plotting Guidelines. U.S. National CAD Standard for Architecture, Engineering, and Construction (A/E/C).* Washington, DC: National Institute of Building Sciences, 1999–2005.

Index

U.S. National CAD Standard Project Committee (NCSPC)
    (*Continued*)
    defined, 236
    membership in, 6, 150
    PDF documents released by, 11
    standing task teams, 7
    task teams, 7
U.S. National CAD Standard Rules of Governance (ROG), 6–8,
    10, 236
U.S. National CAD Standard Steering Committee, 6, 7, 234
USCG, *see* U.S. Coast Guard
Users, *see* Drawing users
User-defined (term), 47, 235
User-defined designators, 15, 17–19
User-defined sheets, 67

V

Vertical text format, 31, 34, 42, 236
Views:
    detail, 67, 69, 119, 226

large-scale, 22–23, 66, 69, 228
nonscaled, 226, 230
scaled, 233
section, 66, 233
three-dimensional, 29, 68, 235

W

Water, abbreviations for, 80
Worksheets, mock-up, 230
W-series sheets, 24

Z

0-series sheets, *see* General sheets
Zoning ordinance, 236

Lightning Source UK Ltd.
Milton Keynes UK
UKHW030743140119
335408UK00002B/2/P

9 780471 703785